Your Pet's Diet
May Be Killing Him

"When the moist foods came out, we figured they must have a very strong preservative because they needed no refrigeration. Many of them do have a very strong preservative—formalin. Formalin is such a good preservative, in fact, that undertakers use quite a lot of it."

Thomas A. Newland, D.V.M.

"Almost all—if not, indeed, all—cases of hypertension can be traced, I believe, to the commercial foods. I virtually never have to use digitalis or digitoxin anymore."

S. Allen Price, D.V.M.

"Every time a pet eats another bowl of high-sugar pet food, he is being brought that much closer to diabetes, hypoglycemia, overweight, nervousness, cataracts, allergy—and death."

R. Geoffrey Broderick, D.V.M.

KEEP YOUR PET HEALTHY THE NATURAL WAY

by **Pat Lazarus**

Foreword by Richard J. Kearns, D.V.M.

Keats Publishing, Inc. ⚓ New Canaan, Connecticut

KEEP YOUR PET HEALTHY THE NATURAL WAY

Macmillan edition published 1983

Keats/Pivot Health Book edition published in 1986. Copyright © 1983 by
Pat Lazarus. This edition is reprinted by arrangement with Macmillan
Publishing Company, a division of Macmillan, Inc.

Excerpts from HOW TO HAVE A HEALTHIER DOG by Wendell O.
Belfield and Martin Zucker. Copyright © 1981 by Wendell O. Belfield and
Martin Zucker. Reprinted by permission of Doubleday & Company, Inc.

ISBN: 0-87983-388-2

Library of Congress Catalog Card Number: 86-7323

Printed in the United States of America

Keats/Pivot Health Books are published by

Keats Publishing, Inc.
27 Pine Street (Box 876)
New Canaan, Connecticut 06840

To Betty Jean Nelson, the medical editor who nurtured me through my early years of writing for technical medical publications, and who was the first person to encourage me to write this book.

To William S. Koester, the editor who encouraged me as I learned to translate technical medical information for the understanding and interest of the public.

Participating Veterinarians

In a sense, the following veterinarians are really my co-authors.

They gave freely of their time and expertise. Some spent hours with me in personal interviews and hours more checking the accuracy not only of my reporting of their work but of my reporting of the work of other nutritionally oriented veterinarians. Others donated their time and knowledge to help me evaluate the therapies used by the doctors I interviewed, knowing that their time would not be "repaid" by any mention of their own work. They made this book possible.

Sheldon Altman of Burbank, CA; Nino Aloro, Virginia Beach, VA; Ihor John Basko, San Jose, CA; Jan Bellows, Pembroke Pines, FL; J. Keith Benedict, Falmouth, MA; Elinor A. Brandt, Sun Valley, CA; George Browne, Jr., Ferndale, CA; Bruce Cauble, Encinitas, CA; John E. Craige, Sherman Oaks, CA; Frank L. Earl, Adelphio, MD; John S. Eden, Cocoa, FL; Marty Goldstein, Yorktown Heights, NY; Robert Goldstein, Yorktown Heights, NY; Richard J. Kearns, Hingham, MA; Michael Kreisberg, Van Nuys, CA; John B. Limehouse, Corvallis, OR; Michael W. Lemmon, Renton, WA; Jack Long, Sebastopol, CA; Thomas A. Newland, Los Angeles, CA; Alfred Jay Plechner, Los Angeles, CA; S. Allen Price, Birmingham, AL; Norman C. Ralston, Dallas, TX; H. H. Robertson, Higginsville, MO; Joseph Stuart, Fairfax, VA; George M. Thue, Seattle, WA; Carvel G. Tiekert, Bel Air, MD; and Robin M. Woodley, Castro Valley, CA. Animal nutritionists Kathy Berman, West Hempstead, NY; and Pat Widmer, New York, NY, also contributed valuable assistance.

Foreword

by RICHARD J. KEARNS, D.V.M.

Keep Your Pet Healthy the Natural Way will be an exciting experience for all who read its pages with an inquiring mind—from lay people to professionals in the field of medicine, especially the field of veterinary medicine. The author has worked closely with many holistic veterinarians across the country, and has consulted other professional and lay sources to compile a basic primer of the most successful natural, nontoxic techniques of prevention and therapy. She has done painstaking research and has also scrupulously checked all data for accuracy. She has presented this information in a manner that enables even the novice to understand and follow it. In my opinion, this book is the most ambitious undertaking to date in its field.

Many of the ideas are "unorthodox" by some of the standards set by the establishment of veterinary medicine. However, the reader will soon see that the establishment has no monopoly on successful medical treatment. The author shows that:

- There are alternative forms of therapy that do work.
- Despite the fact that heretofore the public has been given very little information on these therapies, there are veterinarians across the country who are achieving excellent practical results with the use of these alternative techniques for prevention and cure of diseases.
- These therapies are based on *health*, not signs and symptoms of *disease*. That is, they are all aimed at rebuilding the animal's body to total health, so that the body can heal itself; they are not aimed at attacking an isolated set of symptoms with a toxic, unnatural drug that may cause serious side reactions in the body as a whole.

The underlying theme of the book is a positive one: *Prevention*. The author tells readers how to prevent the diseases that affect our pets in today's unnatural world. While she explains ways of curing and controlling disorders already present in an unnaturally raised pet, she never lets us forget that "an ounce of prevention is worth a pound of cure." For me, the truth of this adage has never failed.

Readers may even be led to a better understanding of the care of their own bodies, since the author has incorporated some little-known natural therapies for human ailments.

I have enjoyed over twenty-eight years of veterinary medical practice so far, and for more than forty years I have searched for ways to relieve pain and suffering in animals with a minimal use of dangerous drugs and surgery. Yet I feel I have only begun to tap the bottomless well of knowledge that was set aside (and thereby wasted) when the allopathic wave of medicine swept into our world. There is so much more I want to know of the more natural forms of medicine, such as nutritional therapy, homeopathy, and herbology. Before this book, veterinarians like me had to work often in isolation. Reading it, I discovered that some of my colleagues have been using successful therapies that I have not yet tried in all my years of practice. The author tells me that other holistic veterinarians have also discovered in this book successful therapies that they had not known.

The book is a breakthrough in veterinary medical literature. I hope it will help spawn a new age in the prevention and treatment of suffering in all animals.

Table of Contents

Keep Your Pet Healthy
The Natural Way

Introduction

This book began in the moment that my friends Brendan Robinson and Nick Cieri stood beside their totally crippled toy poodle, Little Boy, in their veterinarian's office and listened to the words: "This animal is far too advanced with arthritis to help in any way whatsoever. Put him to sleep. I suggest we do it right now; every moment he lives is torture for him."

Luckily for Little Boy—and for all the dogs and cats I believe will be helped by the little-known information in these pages—Bren and Nick chose to bundle up their little dog and take him home.

About a week later, I went over to visit. Little Boy was lying about six feet away from his bowl of food. He started a laborious attempt to crawl to his bowl. I say crawl, because walking—or even standing—had been impossible for the toy poodle for quite a while.

However, it was all too apparent that now crawling, too, was almost impossible. Each little leg crept out slowly, tentatively; and Little Boy squealed with pain at every movement as he tried to drag his small body along the floor.

While Bren and Nick fell over each other in a race to bring the food bowl to their pet, I found myself thinking something I never would have believed would cross my mind: "He *should* be put to sleep."

A week later, Bren phoned. "Do you think the natural therapy for arthritis in human patients might possibly work for dogs, too?" he asked. Natural therapies involve a pure diet, vitamins, and minerals, rather than drugs and surgery. Bren had studied such therapies for human beings extensively; I am a writer in the same field.

I thought a moment. "It might," I said. Then I added, "If it doesn't, what have you and Little Boy got to lose?"

"Right," Bren agreed. "What have we got to lose?"

Bren set to work adapting human therapy to what he could only hope were the correct differing needs of a dog. He had no book to guide him because there was none. And we did not know then that a small but growing number of veterinarians across the country were already using natural therapies for their patients.

Several weeks later, Bren called again. "Come on over," he said; "we have a surprise for you."

I was led out to the yard, where a tiny poodle of seemingly limitless energy—obviously a puppy—was playing a game by himself of leaping constantly to and fro over a low bush. When he saw me, he bounded over, tail wagging, and greeted me as if he knew me.

"Oh," I said, charmed, "you have a new little puppy!" (At the same time, I was thinking sadly that this new puppy's presence in the house meant that the nine-year-old Little Boy had been "disposed of.")

"Everybody says that!" said Nick, delighted.

"That's Little Boy," said Bren.

"That's Little Boy?" I said. "That can't *possibly* be Little Boy."

"I know it can't possibly be," said Bren, "but it is."*

Several months after Little Boy's return from the land of the hopeless, I took my own little black miniature poodle, Shiki, to one of the top orthodox veterinary centers in the country; I wanted the best for my moppet. Shiki had been holding her right hind leg up in the air in a little ball, and hobbling around on three feet, for progressively longer periods of time. Lately, she had not been able to put her leg down at all.

"It's arthritis," said the veterinarian. "You really can't do anything for it. Just give her half a Tylenol when the pain gets too bad."

As you will see later in this book, I deplore the fact that it often takes so long for new medical ideas to supplant old, imbedded ones. Yet in Shiki's case, I myself almost fell prey to the thinking that keeps new ideas from being accepted in medicine. That thinking goes like this: "If a doctor says something, it must be true, because all doctors know everything" (a belief not held by any doctor I know of, by the way). The second fallacious thought (sometimes shared by the medical profession): "If a disorder has always been hopeless, it must forevermore be hopeless. There cannot possibly be a new advance that is presently not generally known."

Shamefully I must admit that it took me a full month to realize that there *was* something I could try for Shiki, despite the doctor's words. One night I was sitting at my typewriter unable to do much work as I sadly watched my courageous little black moppet playing happily by herself. She would throw her ball across the room, chase it, retrieve it, and then growl at it for having tried to get away. Obviously this was real fun, because she was repeating the game over and over. What bothered me, however, was seeing her hobble across the room on three feet; and maybe I was imagining it, but was she starting to have trouble with one of her other legs, too?

"Oh, what's the use?" I said to myself. "I'm a medical writer; I know what is probably going to happen. She's going to get worse and worse, until she's as crippled as Little Boy used to be. She's going to have to be put to sleep, just as Little Boy was supposed to have been."

I wheeled back and ran that thought through my mind again. ". . . as

---

*Little Boy died five years later, at age fourteen, of a fast-acting virus. But he was still leaping effortlessly over that bush a few hours before the virus struck.

crippled as Little Boy *used to be?*" ". . . be put to sleep, just as Little Boy *was supposed to have been?*"

I leaped across the room to the phone, almost tripping over Shiki, who was crossing my path in pursuit of her errant ball.

Bren answered the phone. "What is the diet you made up for Little Boy?" I asked, without taking the time to introduce myself.

"Who is this?" asked Bren.

"Never *mind* who this is," I said impatiently, and inanely. "JUST TELL ME WHAT THE DIET IS. It might possibly help Shiki, too."

"You know," Bren said, "I was thinking that just the other day."

"The other day?" I said. "What took you so long?"

There was a pause. "I don't know," Bren said. "What took *you* so long?"

That night I threw Shiki's "nutritionally complete" supermarket dog foods out with the trash and started Shiki on the more natural diet Bren had painstakingly devised (which, by the way, turned out to be extremely close to the diet used successfully by the nutritional veterinarians whose work is detailed in this book). One day later I reported happily to my husband: "Shiki was able to put her leg down today! For at least ten minutes!"

Two weeks later I was able to report: "Shiki held her leg up once today. For about two minutes."

Today Shiki trots happily in front of me in her beloved walks in Central Park, tail stuck proudly up in the air, all four feet galloping firmly on the ground in the graceful ballet-like prance characteristic of the poodle.

The last moment she found it too painful to put her back leg down on the ground was seven years ago, approximately three weeks after I started her on the simple, inexpensive natural therapy.

As a medical writer whose main goal is to get new medical information out to the public, my first wish after Shiki's improvement was to let people know about the possibility of helping their pets through the use of diet and vitamins and minerals. However, two isolated case histories do not prove anything scientifically; so I set out to see if there were any veterinarians who were using nutritional medicine in their practice.

I define "nutritional" veterinarians as those who attempt to use a minimum of drugs and surgery, who use instead good diet and vitamin and mineral therapy. These doctors are concerned about the dangers of drugs and surgery and find that, with many disorders, they can get as good—often better—results with natural therapy. In everyday usage, two other terms that are treated as synonyms are "orthomolecular" and "holistic."

To my surprise, I was able to locate about 150 nutritional veterinarians.* I knew then that the remarkable recoveries of Shiki and Little Boy were not isolated instances of success. They were merely two among many

---

*The List of Nutritionally Oriented Veterinarians in the back of the book will tell you how you can contact the veterinarians I found.

thousands. That meant I had something valid and extremely important to tell the public.

How This Book Was Researched and Written

Having found the veterinarians, I sent them questionnaires, asking if they were interested in helping with the book; about their special areas of expertise *within* the field of nutritional veterinary medicine, etc. Thirty-five nutritionally oriented veterinarians volunteered to work closely with me, and it is the practical results of their work that make up the content of this book.

After researching what little literature there was on the subject, I interviewed several nutritional veterinarians for each chapter, choosing those who had indicated particular expertise in the disorders being covered in the chapter. I combined the interview information with the literature information and wrote a rough draft, taking pains to translate the more technical information for the understanding of the general public.

I sent these early drafts of each chapter not only to the veterinarians I had interviewed, so they could check for accuracy, but also to ten to twenty other nutritional veterinarians and one or two orthodox veterinarians. I encouraged the veterinarians not interviewed to offer additional comments and information.

I then coordinated all the corrections and the additional information into my original draft and sent out the new drafts for further checking. Therefore, each chapter is the result of input from fifteen to twenty-five veterinarians.

For the most part, I have not interrupted the basically practical thrust of this book to cite all the medical studies on which these veterinarians have based their work; but you should know that the doctors *are* using solid scientific bases. Also, you should know that when I give only one case history, it is only a representative history chosen from many. And when I quote only one veterinarian, I do so only to personalize the information; it does not mean there is only one veterinarian who uses the therapy being quoted.

This book is meant not only for pet owners but also for veterinarians wishing to learn more about this new field of veterinary medicine. Thus, you will sometimes find notes directing veterinarians to see further information at the end of the chapter. (I did not wish to burden the general reader with technical details that would be of no value to anyone other than a medical professional.)

What This Book Is All About

The purpose of this book is to save lives. First, the nutritional veterinarians who worked with me tell you simple ways to *prevent* the disorders generally considered "inevitable"—such as arthritis, cancer, heart problems, diabetes, etc. (Along the way, we will alert you to medical studies in humans that will show you natural ways you can help prevent some of these same disorders in yourself and your loved ones.)

As you read, you will see that pets raised on a natural diet simply do not tend to get many of the diseases considered "inevitable" in pets fed processed foods.

Of course there will be those of you for whom this book's prevention regimen comes too late, those of you with a pet already stricken with a serious disease. You will find details of successful natural therapies—mostly nutritional, but also homeopathic, herbal, and acupuncture—for many disorders.

Has orthodox veterinary medicine despaired of your pet? Have you been told to put him to sleep? PLEASE DO NOT PUT YOUR PET TO SLEEP BEFORE YOU READ THIS BOOK. You will find that nutritional veterinarians often have extraordinary success with the "rejects" of traditional veterinary medicine; indeed, the majority of the case histories in this book detail recoveries of dogs and cats who were given up on by nonnutritional veterinarians. As a matter of fact, time after time as I gathered material for this book, nutritional veterinarians said to me sadly: "So often we get to see only the pet who has been given up on by traditional medicine. That is because many people don't think of natural medicine until everything else has been tried and has failed. While it is true that we often get good results with 'hopeless' cases, we can do even so much more when we can treat a pet in the early or intermediate stages of a disease."

The natural therapies covered in this book differ in three basic respects from drug and surgery treatments:

- As I have said, the natural therapies do not tend to have the negative side effects of drugs and do not carry the dangers of surgery;
- The natural therapies do not attack just the symptoms of the disorder. Instead, they rebuild the total health of the body—*and the body heals itself*. In this way, as you will see, pets being treated by nutritional veterinarians for one disorder tend to recover from other, seemingly unrelated disorders, too.
- Often, the natural therapies are less expensive than drugs or surgery. When the natural therapy is more expensive, it is often because you are keeping your pet alive to be *on* the therapy. (A fatal dose of anesthesia—that is, euthanasia—isn't all that expensive.)

You may wonder: If nutritional medicine is so successful, why doesn't my veterinarian use it? The answer to that can be given in two parts. First, the dissemination of new medical knowledge tends to be much, much slower than most of the public realizes; and it is quite possible that your own veterinarian simply does not yet have the information put forth in this book. As we have said previously, there is a woeful lack of published information on this subject.

Another possible reason lies in the natural conservatism and skepticism of the scientific mind. This skepticism may very well have saved us from a lot of dangerous quackery; but it has also labeled as "quacks" a number of scientists later proved to be geniuses; and, as I detail later in this book, it has sometimes slowed down the use of new therapies and techniques now recognized as being responsible for saving millions of lives.

What This Book Is Not

This book is not a book about miracles. A miracle is a phenomenon due to unexplainable causes. When nutritional doctors heal "hopeless" dogs and cats, they are well aware of the biochemical reasons why their therapy has worked to save the pet.

This book does not tell the secret of everlasting life. Nutritional veterinarians, too, lose some diseased pets. (Remember here, however, that often these pets are not taken to a nutritional veterinarian until all else has failed to help them.) However, in almost all cases when a veterinarian has persuaded his or her client to raise the pet on a natural diet, the cat or dog lives a long, disease-free life and dies a natural, painless "old-age" death.

This book is not an indictment against orthodox care (either for your pet or for yourself). Indeed, as I researched this book, I came across a few disorders for which our veterinarians will use strictly orthodox therapies; in other words, there are still some disorders for which traditional medicine has some success, and for which nutritional therapy itself presently has no answers. Also, in certain emergency cases of some disorders, nutritional veterinarians will start with orthodox therapy for a short time and gradually shift to the less-toxic natural therapy.

The mention that our veterinarians will occasionally use orthodox techniques should not come as a surprise. As a number of nutritional veterinarians stated to me, "The ideal doctor will use the best techniques from both worlds."

Perhaps I can clarify the above by telling you more precisely what a nutritional veterinarian is:

- He or she was trained just as thoroughly in orthodox veterinary medicine as your traditional veterinarian; indeed, nutritional veterinarians and orthodox veterinarians were trained at the same veterinary medical schools, took all the same courses, and got the same medical degree;
- The orthomolecular veterinarian simply has branched out to make nutritional medicine his or her special interest;
- Orthomolecular veterinarians are sincerely involved in trying to save your pet's life; they are not involved in saying that their special field of study has all the answers for all cases of all disorders.

In other words, having your pet tended by a nutritional veterinarian does not mean abandonment of the successful techniques of orthodox veterinary medicine.

I believe this "best of both worlds" balance is valid in medicine for human patients, too. As a writer for the natural health magazine *Let's LIVE*, I have received a number of letters from my readers indicating a blind antiorthodox animosity, a firm belief that nutritional medicine could do everything and orthodox medicine nothing (except perhaps some *harm* with drugs and surgery). If you tend toward that thinking, let me pose a question: If you came upon an accident victim with severed fingers, would you attempt to rush him to a microsurgery unit, or would you offer him a vitamin C tablet?

How to Use This Book

If you have a new puppy or kitten and apply the principles detailed in the prevention chapters, you very probably will never have any use for the chapters on therapy. However, you may want to look over the therapy chapters now, anyway: very possibly either now or someday you may be able to help a friend's pet by alerting your friend to the information in these chapters.

If you are reading this book because you already have a sick animal, please be sure you read the pertinent information carefully, especially if you do not already know a lot about nutritional medicine.

In some cases, treating your pet yourself is possible; and I have tried to indicate clearly when and exactly how you can administer treatment yourself. In treating your own pet, you *must* first have a clear-cut diagnosis from your veterinarian. Treating your pet for one disorder when he really has something quite different that just happens to have similar symptoms can be tantamount to killing him.

For the most part, however, I am against any medical treatment—either with drugs or natural therapies—that is not conducted by, or at least under the supervision of, a trained doctor.* The addresses of a number of nutritional veterinarians are given in the List of Nutritionally Oriented Veterinarians at the end of this book. If you do not live close to a nutritional veterinarian, take your pet to your own veterinarian and urge him or her to read the relevant section of this book and to call one of the listed doctors for consultation.

If you meet with total resistance (some orthodox doctors are as blindly against nutritional medicine as some nutritionally oriented people are

---

*You will see later, for instance, that nutritional veterinarians often use extremely high amounts of vitamins A and E. However, if you were to try giving the same high amounts of these two vitamins without consulting first with a veterinarian, you might cause your pet great harm. When veterinarians use large doses of vitamins A and E, they use the vitamins in a new, water-soluble form. The commonly available fat-soluble form can be highly toxic in large doses.

against orthodox medicine), you might try to find a more open-minded doctor. Call veterinarians until you find one who is willing to consider nutritional therapy for your pet. Be sure to stress on the phone that you have a book that gives guidelines of the therapy, and that you have a list of nutritional veterinarians who have agreed to act as consultants. Without knowing these two facts, even an open-minded doctor would be reluctant to try a new therapy.

According to the disorder, some of our nutritional veterinarians named in the List will consult directly with a pet owner and offer helpful details.*

A Note for Nutritional Veterinarians

This book is a sincere attempt to compile the work of some thirty-five of you who share the same area of interest and expertise.

When I first sent out the basic idea of this book to those of you I could find, I received such positive comments as, "The book you are preparing is a much needed addition to veterinary literature." As my work progressed—and doctors started checking over the manuscript in its working stages—this comment changed to, "The more I see of your work, the more I am convinced this book will be a much needed addition to the literature."

I hope that this book will lead to more communication and exchange of information among you and your colleagues than presently seem to exist. (I found, for instance, that many of you did not even know of the existence of many of the others.) At one point, a highly knowledgeable nutritional veterinarian commented, in reading the manuscript, that he had never heard of another doctor's treatment for a particular problem and could not even think of a rationale for it. I was able to dig into the technical medical literature and find solid bases for the therapy being questioned. I was on occasion also able to put a doctor who told me he had little success with a particular disorder in communication with another doctor who was reporting good success.

I hope this book also will inform the general public—and orthodox veterinarians—about your work. In my experience as a medical writer, when the public is told of the existence of alternative therapies, many patients demand such therapies from orthodox doctors. In turn this sends orthodox doctors delving into the alternative techniques.

Earlier, I told lay readers my basic "protocol" for writing this book. In those cases where I found one or more doctors reporting more success than others, I "hunted down" the reasons and found, of course, that the more successful results could be attributed specifically to a larger dosage, to usage

---

*I know that many readers on human nutrition do not know where to find a nutritional M.D. for themselves. Your best bet may well be local health food stores; there you can often get a personal recommendation of a good nutritional doctor. Health magazines often offer lists of nutritional M.D.'s. Write to them, sending a self-addressed, stamped envelope.

of the substance in conjunction with a helpful adjunct, to usage of a particular *form* of the substance, etc. In such cases, I have printed the more successful therapy.

In this regard, you may notice some emphasis on the work of Richard J. Kearns, D.V.M. Dr. Kearns has been working in this "new" field of nutritional veterinary medicine for almost thirty years.

I admit that many times—as I struggled with comments, counter comments, and counter counter comments—I cursed myself for not writing this book about one doctor's work, as so many books are written. However, I was driven on by my knowledge—derived from years of writing for technical orthodox publications for M.D.'s—that no one doctor knows all there is to know. I wanted the public, and veterinarians, to get the benefit of the most helpful current information I could find.

A Note for Strictly Orthodox Veterinarians

First, I know that many of you have recently become interested in investigating nutritional therapy for incorporation into your practice. I know also that some of you have become frustrated at the minimal amount of literature on the subject. Some of you have begun, on your own, to extrapolate the literature on nutritional medicine for human beings to your patients; some of you have called the Veterinary Nutritional Associates' (VNA) Health Line for help with practical details.

I hope this book will serve as a basic reference volume for you. The List of Nutritionally Oriented Veterinarians at the end names a number of nutritional veterinarians who have agreed to be available to you for consultation.

Now I would like to address myself to the more skeptical orthodox veterinarians.

I do not ask any orthodox veterinarian to abandon years of training, knowledge, experience, and success for an "opposite" field. I ask only that you consider adding to your success, experience, and knowledge with a successful adjunct therapy.

I have pointed out earlier in this Introduction that this book does not want to promote a schism between orthodox and nutritional veterinary medicine. A number of the veterinarians whose work is included consider themselves basically orthodox veterinarians who incorporate nutritional medicine into their practices.

In short, it is the purpose of this book to encourage veterinarians to use both orthodox and nutritional therapy as needed for the best interest of the animal being treated. (Of course, I do not detail orthodox therapy to nearly the degree I do nutritional, since there are so many books already published on the former subject.) All the nutritional veterinarians in this book also use orthodox therapy; I am merely suggesting that the use of nutritional therapy along with the orthodox may increase your success with the animals you treat.

I think John S. Eden, D.V.M., in checking over a chapter of this book in manuscript form, put the above ideas very well. Dr. Eden describes his approach to veterinary medicine as "largely orthodox." Dr. Eden wrote me: "In my mind a combination of the two fields of knowledge seems the best of both worlds, and that is how I try to guide myself. . . . I deeply resent it when one side of this issue tries to debunk or discredit the other. It is a foolish waste of energy and only serves to prevent any exchange of information and to limit the capacity of both sides to solve problems." As Dr. Eden adds, preventing this exchange of information "diminishes the ability to accomplish the common goal of seeking what is best for the animal."

The next time you have a pet in your office for which surgery or drugs offer no hope, won't you please consult this book to see if it contains an approach relevant to that pet, consult with one of the nutritional veterinarians named in the List, and try the suggested therapy before you put the pet to sleep? If the therapy doesn't work, you and your patient will have lost nothing. If it does, an animal will have been saved.

CHAPTER ONE

How Commercial Pet Foods May Be Killing Your Pet— and Why

R. GEOFFREY BRODERICK, D.V.M.:

"Every time a pet trustingly eats another bowl of high-sugar pet food, he is being brought that much closer to diabetes, hypoglycemia, overweight, nervousness, cataracts, allergy—and death."

WENDELL O. BELFIELD, D.V.M.:

"Do you know what is in meat meal, the major constituent of dry dog food? . . . Urine, fecal matter, hair, pus, meat [from animals, afflicted] with cancer and T.B., etc." [1]

THOMAS A. NEWLAND, D.V.M.:

"When the moist foods came out, we figured they must have a very strong preservative, because they need no refrigeration. Many of them do have a very strong preservative— formalin. Formalin is such a good preservative, in fact, that undertakers use quite a lot of it."

If someone suggested you feed your pet rust every day, you wouldn't do it, would you?   Or do you do just that without knowing it?   How about feeding your pet every day four times the amount of lead it takes to cause lead poisoning in children?   Or two substances that scientists use in laboratories to produce brain defects in animals?   If you feed your dog or cat packaged or canned "nutritionally complete" pet foods—as so very many people in this country do—you may be giving him not only all of the above poisons but a number of others.   The above information may surprise you, because commercial food manufacturers—and even many veterinarians— tell us these foods are the "best" way to feed our pets. However, read on and see what researchers and nutritional veterinarians have to say.

WHAT IS IN COMMERCIAL PET FOOD THAT SHOULDN'T BE?

To begin with, let us look at what commercial pet foods are composed of in general. The Pet Food Institute says: "Forty percent of all pet food is meat by-products and offal [wastes]." One would think that the other sixty percent would have to be better than that, but the Pet Food Institute goes on to say that the other sixty percent is grain and soy meal not used for human consumption because of foreign odors, *debris, germs*, etc.[2] You may remember the similar, even stronger statement by Wendell O. Belfield, D.V.M., on the first page of this chapter.

Commercial pet foods contain a number of other "extra" substances, substances not present in natural foods and therefore foreign (toxic) to your pet's body. For instance:*

- **Sodium nitrite.** You have probably heard that sodium nitrite, which occurs in such processed foods as hot dogs and bologna, can cause cancer in human beings. But did you know that as long ago as 1972 the FDA stated that this chemical is also potentially hazardous to pet health?[3] That hasn't stopped commercial manufacturers from using it, however. You see, sodium nitrite is terribly important: it adds an artificial rosy color to some commercial pet foods. Manufacturers know that this makes a good impression on us; and we, after all, are the ones who shell out the money for these products. It is doubtful, however, that this pleasant red color makes much difference to your dog or cat. Neither dogs nor cats can see colors.

*Not all pet foods contain all the following harmful substances. Note also that this list does not comprise all the harmful substances that occur in various commercial pet foods.

- **BHA and BHT.** These chemicals are ingredients of most popular pet foods. Scientists use them on animals in research laboratories—to produce serious brain defects. These additives also produce kidney and liver problems as well as behavior problems in laboratory animals.

- **Lead.** You have probably read and seen on television a lot of publicity on lead poisoning. As with much medical information transmitted to the lay public, however, what you've seen on lead is only a small part of the full story. For instance, you may have the impression that if you're not a child in a tenement who eats paint peelings, you don't have to worry about lead poisoning.

  However, researchers such as those at the Connecticut Agricultural Experiment Station have found that many canned pet foods contain so much lead that an animal eating only six ounces a day of these foods might be taking into his body *four times* the level of lead potentially toxic to children![4]

- **Artificial flavorings.** These are used to make fake food taste the way it would if it were real food. About ten years ago a California physician, Benjamin Feingold, of the Kaiser Permanente Hospital, came out with a radical theory that put his reputation on the line: many children with autism, hyperactivity, and various other personality disorders could be controlled simply by removing artificial colorings and flavorings from their diets. His theory worked so well in practice that it has since been utilized even by some of the most orthodox physicians.

  In the last several years, veterinarians practicing the new field of nutritional veterinary medicine have been calling for the removal of such artificial flavorings from pet foods. Says R. Geoffrey Broderick, D.V.M.: "These same substances that are known to cause children to be unsociable, unable to learn—to choose to spend hours at a time sitting and banging their heads against a wall—these are the substances that cause your dog or cat to be nervous, hostile, and full of anxiety."

- **Salt.** This substance while it does occur in nature, is added in unnatural proportions to many processed foods. Sometimes, Dr. Broderick says, such foods contain "1,000 times" as much salt as occurs in the natural food the processed food is imitating. You probably know the strong role excessive salt plays in causing human hypertension and heart disease. It does the same thing in dogs and cats and is considered one of the main reasons these two diseases, virtually unknown in our pets until forty years ago, are now top killers.

- **Sugar.** In the last decade sugar in an unnatural form has been implicated as a major cause in human beings not only of diabetes but also of hypoglycemia, alcoholism, and schizophrenia, as well as a number of other new disorders of modern civilization. What was used originally in sweet "treats" was sugar *cane*, a natural food quite different biochemically from the sugar that is now packed into so many of our foods. Sugar cane contained a number of vitamins and minerals and enzymes which allowed our body to utilize it as a helpful food.

Dr. Broderick and his veterinary colleagues are as vehemently against the unnatural form of sugar as are nutritional doctors who treat people. Dr. Broderick calls it "the assassin."*

WHAT ISN'T IN COMMERCIAL FOODS
THAT SHOULD BE?

The labels on most commercial pet foods state emphatically that the morsels contained therein have all the nutrients your animal needs. But do they?

Scientists state that enzymes are absolutely essential for every biochemical function of the body. Yet enzymes occur, as Dr. Broderick and other nutritional veterinarians tell us, "in not one single commercial pet food." You see, enzymes occur in raw foods. (That fact is one of the major reasons why nutritionists urge people to eat raw fruits and raw vegetables.)

You probably won't find on your labels any mention of vitamin C. And yet, as we'll cover in following chapters, nutritional veterinarians help prevent and cure a number of "unpreventable" and "incurable" pet problems with this vitamin. Dogs and cats—unlike people—manufacture vitamin C in their bodies, and this fact has traditionally led veterinary medicine to the conclusion that these animals don't need to get the vitamin from outside sources.

However, this conclusion overlooks the fact that dogs and cats always used to get additional vitamin C from outside sources: in the foods they ate before the commercial foods supplanted their natural diet. It also overlooks the fact that some pets produce much less C in their bodies than others. Further, it overlooks the fact that today's new environmental poisons (including those in commercial pet foods) actually rob the body of substantial amounts of vitamin C.

Today, dogs are sometimes driven to stripping wallpaper off the walls and trying to eat the wallpaper paste. What causes this bizarre behavior? According to famed dog trainer Barbara Woodhouse, it may be a desperate attempt to get some of the minerals and trace elements that are lacking in

---

* Robert Goldstein, V.M.D., and Marty Goldstein, D.V.M., state: "Only the semimoist dog foods tend to be loaded with sugar. Most dry and canned foods are not saturated with sugar—but they contain unnatural ingredients that are just as harmful to the pet."

today's pet foods. If your dog eats his own feces, he may not be a "bad dog"; he may, again, simply be trying to obtain some of the vitally important nutrients missing from his "nutritionally complete" commercial dog food.[5]

Even when something that should be in commercial pet foods *is* in the foods, it may not be there in the proper biochemical form. For instance, let us take that long list of minerals some boxed or canned foods contain. This list may look very impressive. Some labels even carry the correct ratio of copper to zinc, a sophisticated balancing not done in many multivitamin pills for human beings.*

Thus, on occasion your pet food's label regarding minerals may look even better than a label on a human multimineral bottle. However, the minerals in your pet's food are very likely to be *unchelated* minerals. Unchelated minerals tend to pass right through the body without ever being used. Feeding your pet (or yourself) unchelated minerals can therefore be tantamount to not feeding him (or yourself) any minerals at all.

Chelated minerals, according to Richard J. Kearns, D.V.M., not only are absolutely essential in and of themselves, but also are necessary to help the body use vitamins. Therefore, unchelated minerals can sometimes seriously impair the function of the vitamins your pet gets. Moreover, unchelated minerals can sometimes store themselves in the body and help cause such modern-day problems as arthritis.

The reason for this lack of minerals in pet foods is simple. As Dr. Broderick points out, the unnatural forms of minerals "are a lot cheaper."

Now, what about the iron listed on your pet food's label? Well, as we have said, nutrients occur in different forms. Under the heading "iron," for instance, medical dictionaries list almost thirty different forms. One type of iron commonly used in pet foods is iron oxide. This form is more commonly known as rust. Then there is magnesium. This mineral is sometimes even announced on the label in the correct proportion to calcium, another subtlety not bothered with in some supplements for human consumption. (Too much calcium in relation to magnesium—and vice versa—can cause bone and joint deteriorations such as arthritis. The doctors Goldstein emphasize that the wrong calcium-magnesium ratio also can be a cause of neuromuscular problems.)

However, as Dr. Broderick points out, the form of magnesium most commonly used in pet foods is the inexpensive magnesium oxide. "Since very little magnesium oxide can be utilized by the body," this veterinarian says, "it is virtually impossible for the animal to *absorb* the correct

---

*If your own mineral supplement has more copper than zinc, you may be letting yourself in for that new American malady, depression. Carl C. Pfeiffer, Ph.D., M.D., one of the top experts on the subject of minerals, has told me he believes that if tests show that a person has more copper than zinc in the body, it is an excellent indication that the person suffers from depression.

magnesium-calcium ratio, even when the proportion in the box or can is correct."

In other words, even the "best" processed foods can be a direct cause of the new animal disease, arthritis.

WHAT EXACTLY IS MEANT BY THE TERM "NATURAL FOODS"?

Simply put, an animal's natural foods are the ones his body organs and structures are best equipped to utilize. Through evolution, the bodies of cats and dogs have superbly adapted to maintain health on the foods that were most easily available to them in the wild. These foods are called the dog's and cat's natural foods.

It goes without saying, of course, that the foods our pets' bodies have evolved to thrive on throughout millions of years are not the processed commercial pet foods that have been manufactured for only the past forty years. Dogs and cats simply did not lug boxes of dry pellets around the wild with them, and they didn't take their prey home in a can. Nor was their prey stuffed with the dyes, preservatives, and other harmful additives we have shown are contained in today's pet foods.

As we have said, these commercial pet foods have been around for only about forty years. Forty years is not nearly enough time for a species to rebuild its body to utilize new foods for health. Three major diseases of today's pets are cancer, heart disease, and arthritis; yet in the millions of years dogs and cats ate their natural diet, cancer, heart disease, and arthritis were virtually unknown.* These three diseases are also, of course, the main killers of human beings; again, these diseases were virtually unknown in human beings until we started tampering with our own food one hundred years ago.

What were dogs and cats evolved to eat? There is no controversy here among scientists: both species are basically carnivores, animals who naturally eat raw flesh.**

Those of you who are interested in nutrition may point out at this juncture that human beings are supposed to have evolved to be meat eaters, too, but that in the last twenty years medical science has discovered that animal fat—and animal protein—can be detrimental to human health.

The last part of that statement is quite correct: a growing number of

---

*Scientists have ascertained this by studying well-preserved skeletons of wild dogs and cats, as well as veterinary records prior to forty years ago.

**Please don't assume that you can't possibly feed your pet his natural diet because it contains meat. As we will show in Chapter 2, it can cost you *less* to feed a healthful, natural diet than you are presently paying for even the less expensive harmful commercial pet foods.

nutritional authorities state that animal food is at least a contributing factor to a number of our serious disorders.*

However, while we human animals may have been eating meat for a few million years, there has not yet been enough time for our systems to have evolved to accept animal protein as a natural substance.

Let's compare a pet's carnivorous body with ours to see how the pet is adapted to be a meat eater, while we are not. Open your pet's mouth and take a look at his teeth (provided, of course, you have a sweet-tempered pet who will let you do that.) You will notice that all your pet's teeth are a lot sharper than ours. You will notice also those two extremely long teeth to each side, top and bottom. (Even in my six-pound tabby cat they look ferocious.)

Now why don't we have teeth like that? Because our teeth haven't evolved to be the teeth of natural meat eaters. They aren't sharp enough to kill another animal and tear it—raw—to pieces.

Take a look at your dog's nails. Unless they've just been cut, they're very long. Your cat hides his so as not to harm friends; but if you've just angered him by poking around his feet too much to look at his nails, you've seen that his are very long, too. Women who try to grow long nails for cosmetic purposes know that human nails will break, no matter how well they're nurtured, long before they get as long as a dog's or cat's.

You see, the nails of your pet have evolved to this length so that he, again, can kill and tear apart his natural food: animal flesh.

But the most important anatomical difference between our natural meat eater pets and ourselves is the length of the intestines. Meat, in the presence of heat, tends to putrefy and send out poisons. Of course, intestines in any animal's body carry a lot of heat. Conclusion: the shorter the intestine— that is, the quicker the meat can pass through the body—the less harm it's going to do to the body.

Our intestines are very long; therefore, it takes a lot of time for animal food to make its way through them. The length of time, then, that such food is exposed to the heat of our bodies is more than ample to allow it to putrefy and send toxins through our systems. A dog or cat, again, does not

---

*For instance, Allan Cott, M.D., a New York City psychiatrist and president of the Academy of Orthomolecular Psychiatry, reported that schizophrenics have a higher protein level in their bodies than nonschizophrenics. He and Yuri Nicolayev, M.D., of the Moscow Psychiatric Institute, have put thousands of schizophrenic patients—*all previously untreatable by other forms of therapy*—on fasts, in order to remove all possibly harmful foods at the same time. The majority have been relieved of all symptoms including hallucinations while on the fast, and while foods were being added gradually back to their diets. Relapses occurred only among those patients who added back animal protein foods. Withdrawing the animal protein resulted again in remission of all symptoms.[6]

have this problem. His intestines are quite short, even considering the fact that his body is smaller than ours.

Thus, our dog and our cat—unlike ourselves—have been carefully designed by nature to thrive healthily on meat. For this reason—and for all the other reasons we have detailed in this chapter—we are doing our pet's body a great disservice when we feed the animal the unnatural new commercial foods.

The story of the nutrient called taurine is an illustration of how natural food can maintain health, while unnatural food does not. Natural foods contain within them a number of helpful nutrients (such as taurine) that were unknown until a comparatively short time ago. Nutritional authorities believe that many others are still unknown. (Only by eating natural foods can you and your pet be certain to get the whole complement of nutrients, known and unknown, that have in the past protected our ancestors from such ailments as cancer and heart disease.)

The search that uncovered taurine began because scientists were puzzled by a new disease that was striking cats with increasing frequency: progressive retinal atrophy. In less technical terms, progressive retinal atrophy is a condition that leads to total blindness.

Dr. Broderick gives us a dramatic medical description of this disease. "You look in a healthy cat's eyes," he says, "and you see the optic disc with blood vessels radiating out from it." (These blood vessels carry blood and all necessary nutrients to the eye, and in this way keep it alive.) "But when you look in the eyes of a cat with this disease, the optic disc looks like a saucer set apart from the rest of the eye, with no blood vessels. In other words, you see this shiny globe looking back at you unseeingly; the cat is stone blind."

When researchers recently discovered taurine, they discovered also that a lack of this substance causes at least some cases of the "new" disease, progressive retinal atrophy.

Taurine occurs naturally in meat. Cats, of course, always ate an abundance of meat when they were left to their own devices in the wild. Now that taurine has been discovered, it has been added to some commercial cat foods. But for many pets the addition came too late.

The question remains: how many other presently unknown nutrients necessary to pet (and human) health are not included in unnatural foods?

The next chapter will tell you how you can prevent the grim diseases considered inevitable in today's processed-food-fed pet by feeding your dog or cat his natural, healthy diet. As I have said, this diet should cost you less every week than the commercial foods you may presently be using. Be advised, however, that, over the years, the natural diet may end up costing you more—because your pet will probably live many more years to enjoy it.

10

REFERENCES

1. Wendell O. Belfield, D.V.M., *Let's LIVE*, April 1980.
2. Frances Sheridan Goulart, *Let's LIVE*, October 1975, p. 44.
3. *Ibid.*, p. 44.
4. Carl C. Pfeiffer, Ph.D., M.D., *Mental and Elemental Nutrients* (New Canaan, CT: Keats Publishing Inc.), 1975, p. 316.
5. Cited by Margaret Farley in the New York *Daily News*, April 25, 1982, MB 15.
6. Allan Cott, M.D., *Fasting as a Way of Life* (New York: Bantam Books), 1977, Chapter 14.

CHAPTER TWO

What Your Pet Should Eat for a Long and Healthy Life —and Why

ROBERT S. GOLDSTEIN, V.M.D.; MARTY GOLD-STEIN, D.V.M.; RICHARD J. KEARNS, D.V.M.; H. H. ROBERTSON, D.V.M.:

"We just seldom see the so-called inevitable diseases in our patients, when we can get the owners to raise the pets on their natural foods."

RICHARD J. KEARNS, D.V.M.:

"Everybody laughs at me; they say I'm a specialist in geriatrics, because all my animals get to be so old. That's simply because I try to have my clients feed their pets right in the first place."

R. GEOFFREY BRODERICK, D.V.M.:

"My greatest goal is to be known not for what I've cured and controlled, but for what I've prevented."

NINO ALORO, D.V.M.:

"Even the so-called 'sickly' pet can get to live a long, healthy life with the proper diet."

Dogs and cats in the wild usually did not—and still usually do not—become crippled or blind or deaf from the disorders that most veterinarians today consider "inevitable." And dogs and cats today who are raised on natural diets prescribed by nutritional (orthomolecular) veterinarians seldom become crippled or blind or deaf from the disorders that have become "normal" since the commercial pet food industry began building its empire.

It is not by some unexplainable "miracle" that a pet (or a person) can be kept healthy by feeding the body the foods it has evolved to thrive on. You probably know that everything you take into your body affects your cells in one way or another: cigarette smoke adversely affects the cells of your lungs, for instance; Valium alters body chemistry so that depression may be alleviated temporarily; high-blood-pressure medication sets up another biochemical reaction in your body that lowers blood pressure for a while.

Now, what one general substance do you take into your body more often, every day of your life, than any other substance? Certainly: food. And the various nutrients in food set up more biochemical reactions in your body, every minute of your life, than any one drug can do. Therefore, when you (and your pet) take in the right foods, these foods will set up healthy biochemical reactions; when you and your pet take in the wrong foods, they will set up destructive biochemical reactions in the body. It's that simple.

Frank L. Earl, D.V.M., expresses the above idea this way: "I compare vitamins and minerals to the spark plugs in cars. These nutrients are the necessary energizers to move from one chemical reaction to another in each and every cell in the body."

So, healthy, natural foods set up and maintain healthy, natural biochemical reactions in your body. These biochemical reactions set up a natural line of defense—a healthy immune system—that fights off bacteria, viruses, and parasites many times a day. Every veterinarian whose work is covered in this book has said to me in one way or another that without a healthy immune system we would all be sick hundreds of times a day.

For instance, let's say you're in a classroom or at a party with a person who has the flu. Ten of the twenty people in that room "catch" that virus; you're one of the unlucky ones. That virus didn't float mysteriously by the other ten in that room just to pick you out maliciously; it entered the body of the other ten persons, too. But the other ten had immune systems that were strong enough to say, "Get out of here; this is *my* territory," and to destroy the offending stranger.

In the same way, we all have cancer cells in our body every day. As long as our overall health is good, our immune system will keep knocking out these cancer cells.

Almost all of the nutritional veterinarians asked me to "please stress to the readers that it is *not* bacteria or viruses that make their pets sick; it is their pet's weakened immune system that allows the disease-causing organism to take hold."

So by restoring your pet to his natural, health-giving diet, you can restore the myriad natural biochemical reactions that give strength to his immune system. This is the "magic" that keeps pets who are fed natural diets free of today's "inevitable" diseases—diseases that were, and are, virtually unknown among animals in the wild.

The chapters following this one are devoted to a compilation of the work of thirty-five veterinarians working in the new field of nutritional (orthomolecular) veterinary medicine. These chapters detail successful therapies for already existing diseases: therapies that use little or no dangerous drugs or surgery; therapies that often have amazing results with disorders currently thought basically "hopeless."

If you are lucky enough to be reading the chapter at hand on prevention because you're just starting to raise a new puppy or kitten, chances are this book will sit on your shelf for many years before you need the information in the chapters following this one, if you ever *do* need it.

Just as every one of these veterinarians expressed to me that his or her greatest satisfaction comes in preventing diseases rather than in curing them, so I hope that the months I have spent compiling information on the successful treatment of these diseases results in some of the least-needed chapters ever written in the field of veterinary medicine.

YOUR PET'S NATURAL, HEALTHY DIET WILL PROBABLY COST YOU LESS THAN THE FAKE FOODS YOU'RE PRESENTLY FEEDING HIM.

Before I give you information on how your pet, too, can remain disease-free and live longer, let me get one stumbling block out of the way. The dog's and cat's natural diet is high in meat, and the word "meat" these days raises some trepidation in anyone on a budget.

First of all, nutritional veterinarians do not ask you to feed your pet exclusively meat. (Indeed, as we mention later, feeding only meat can harm your pet.) Veterinarians such as Dr. Earl recommend that only one-quarter to one-half of the daily ration for dogs be in the form of meat; you might choose a middle-of-the-road position and make it one-third.

Secondly—and very importantly—you will most probably find that your pet eats less of his natural diet than he does fake foods. As a matter of fact, R. Geoffrey Broderick, D.V.M., reports that almost without exception pets eat one-third less of natural foods than unnatural ones. Why should a pet be so obliging? He eats less of the natural foods because these foods contain all the nutrients his body needs for good health; therefore, his body tends to retain these foods, using them to build fresh new cells, healthy blood, and so on. On the other hand, the pet's body doesn't know *what* the heck to do with the newfangled fake foods, and most of these foods pass almost immediately through the body and out again. Therefore, instant hunger. As Dr. Broderick puts it: "A pound of fake food equals almost a pound of waste" [or feces].

As a matter of fact, many kennel owners who deal with numerous animals in close quarters express relief that the natural diet cuts down so drastically on the amount of waste they have to discard every day. Whereas their animals were previously discarding as foreign substances (which, indeed, they are) much of the chemicals and diseased matter contained in processed foods, the same bodies are now retaining the nutrient-rich natural foods for the purposes of building healthy new cells, strong immune systems, and healthy blood.

Robert Goldstein, V.M.D., and Marty Goldstein, D.V.M., add that excessive—and costly—eating may be caused also by addiction to the chemical appetite stimulants and preservatives in fake foods. When you feed your pet natural foods, he will eat only enough to satisfy natural hunger— not to satisfy an addiction.

Another thing: Nowhere will I be asking you to feed your pet expensive steak as the basis of an optimal diet. As a matter of fact, please do *not* feed steak as the basis of your pet's diet, even if you can afford to. As we'll see a bit later when we follow your pet's ancestor through the wild, he first ate the organ meats of his prey (the heart, gizzard, liver, tripe, spleen). Steak is actually less nutritious overall than these innards. Indeed, your pet's great-great-etc. granddaddy didn't deign to eat this inferior type of meat— steak—unless his prey happened not to have been spirited away when he returned to the scene hours after dinner for a midnight snack.

(For those of us who eat meat, many nutritional M.D.'s point out that our own health would be likely to improve if we went back to eating more organ meats, as we used to, and less steak.)

Now let's compare some specific costs using present (spring 1983) prices in New York City supermarkets. I'm asking you to pass up a box of embalmed kibble (99 cents a pound for the least expensive dry variety, to $1.36 a pound for the semimoist kibble, which nutritional veterinarians point out are the most heavily poisoned). I'm asking you instead to buy a pound of chicken hearts at 89 cents a pound. Then I'm reminding you that your pet will probably eat only two-thirds pound of the chicken hearts, whereas he'd eat the full pound of kibble.

The savings on that single purchase is a minimum of 40 cents; and you have just cut out a number of poisons from your pet's next several meals.

Then, of course, you can compare the 99 cents to $1.36 per pound cost of kibble to 69 cents a pound for chicken, 79 cents a pound for chicken livers,

89 cents a dozen for eggs, and 39 cents a pound for carrots and 49 cents a pound for apples. (As we'll detail later, vegetables and fruits are also part of your pet's natural diet.)

You can probably even get your butcher to give you free some of the animal parts he normally discards that would be highly nutritious for your pet.

All this is not even considering the money you probably will not have to spend in veterinarian's bills trying to save your beloved pet's life from an illness caused by unnatural foods. As I write this, I am reminded of my friend Verna on the West Coast, who for years now has been spending a small fortune on twice-a-day insulin shots and frequent visits to the veterinarian to control diabetes in her husky, Nijinski. Not to mention the fact that she has had to greatly curtail her career in theater so as to be around two times a day to give the insulin shots. Obviously Verna loves her pet or she would have had him put to sleep, as many other owners do to "cure" diabetes. It is sad, therefore, to realize that she probably could have prevented this disease in her dog simply by feeding a natural, sugarless diet in the first place. Still, as we'll see when we cover diabetes in a later chapter, even now she could save herself a lot of money and inconvenience if she would consult an orthomolecular veterinarian for a more natural treatment.

In my own case, I spent a small fortune raising (and almost managing to kill) my little black poodle Shiki on the "nutritionally complete" kibble and canned foods my veterinarian—and all the ads—assured me were all she needed. She had the "inevitable" worms three times in that year; she had gastroenteritis twice; then, at the end of that first year of her life, she developed the "hopeless" arthritis that caused her to be half-crippled.

Luckily, it was just at that time that I discovered my first orthomolecular veterinarian, Dr. Broderick, in the course of my other researches as a medical writer. Not only have I been able to control Shiki's "hopeless" arthritis for seven years now (without expensive, harmful drugs), but I have been able to raise my other black moppet, Little Lady, and my six-pound tabby cat, Ms. Puddy Tat, on their natural diet from the word "go."

Puddy and Little Lady have never been sick a day in their lives. This despite the fact that they are both now seven and eight years old—the equivalent of forty-nine and fifty-six for a human animal. I personally don't know any forty-nine-year-old human beings who have never even had a cold, or a tummyache, or a bad tooth, do you? But then, I don't know of any forty-nine-year-olds who have been raised on their natural diet, either.

By the way, the never-been-sick Little Lady is Shiki's daughter, so you can't attribute her indomitable health to particularly hearty, healthy parentage.

I would say that Shiki's one year on fake foods cost me about $800 in veterinary and drug bills. Total cost of therapy in seven years more for Shiki plus seven years for Little Lady plus eight years for Puddy: $000.

One more word about how a natural diet can save you money. As you probably know, a number of dog and cat diseases can be passed to their owners. If you have a healthy pet, you may never know how much this may have saved you in medical bills—or even in the possible loss of a loved one.*

WHAT YOUR PET'S ANCESTOR ATE

Let's start with the average day in the life of your pet's ancestor in the wild, a day in which he had no loving owner around to provide him with things his body had not been built to deal with. I want to go through this day with your pet's great-many-times-over grandfather so you can more readily visualize the reasons for the specific suggestions we will cover later.

Ruff wakes early in the forest. There is no bowl of kibble in front of his nose for breakfast, but that doesn't surprise him. There never has been a bowl of kibble there. What does surprise him is that the half-eaten prey he had been guarding overnight has disappeared from between his front paws, spirited away in the middle of the night by some darned animal. Well, that happens. Up and at 'em. Walk, search, climb, stalk, run—in other words, exercise.

Now, when great-great-etc. granddaddy killed his prey, he ate the intestines, liver, heart, stomach and spleen first. He didn't know it, of course, but these are what we call organ meats, and they store up certain nutrients that are not stored in the bones and muscles. The organs of the prey also contained partially digested vegetables, fruits, and grains. These nonmeat foods provide certain other nutrients, such as unsaturated fats and carbohydrates, which are necessary for the dog and cat, who are not totally carnivores. Many nutritional veterinarians have told me horror stories of desperately sick pets raised by well-meaning owners who were determined to raise their pets on "natural," nonsupermarket foods. However, these owners mistakenly thought their pets were total carnivores and thus needed only meat for their natural diets.

Next the dog or cat went on to eat his prey's bones, fat, and muscles, to round out a full complement of vitamins, minerals, enzymes, carbohydrates, proteins and fats.

As he later lazed in the sun, digesting his feast, he might occasionally catch himself an insect for a bit of dessert. An insect? Yes, insects contain

---

*Wendell O. Belfield, D.V.M., for instance, reports that human beings may contract cats' upper respiratory diseases. The veterinarian also points to the fact that heartworms—previously thought confined to dogs—are starting to be reported in human patients. Also, Dr. Belfield points out that a pregnant woman can contract a serious disease—if her cat *has* the disease, of course—while cleaning feces from the litter box. The disease, called *Toxoplasma gondii*, can destroy the brain of a fetus.[1] (To be safe, if you become pregnant, you might want to prevail upon another family member to clean up after the cat until the baby is born.)

protein and B₁₂, both of which are necessary parts of a dog's and cat's diet. I hope this paragraph cuts down the number of distraught letters I see in veterinarians' magazine columns from owners who are sure their pets are going to die because they catch and eat flies.

After his feast, our great-etc. granddaddy dog or cat rested awhile or otherwise amused himself before he decided he would go to the nearest watering hole for a drink. He didn't know, you see, that many years hence, many fake food labels would be saying it was best to set out a bowl of water with each feeding, or even to mix water directly with the "food" to make a nice fake gravy. Of course, neither did he have nutritionally oriented veterinarians such as Dr. Broderick around to tell him, "Drinking water at the same time as eating will make minerals pass through the body without being used and will upset the acid-akaline balance of the system." He didn't need such specialists; it's only modern pet owners who do.

As H. H. Robertson, D.V.M., expresses it, "All you have to do is watch a pet today who is not confined in a small apartment with his food bowl and his water bowl filled up under his nose at the same time. A free pet today will still eat first, and then later he'll go looking for a drink of water. But he'll never eat and drink at the same time."

THE OPTIMAL PREVENTIVE DIET
FOR YOUR ADULT DOG

While this section is geared basically to the nutritional needs of dogs, cat owners also should read it, because much of the information applies to cats as well. Specific differences for cats begin on page 33.

THE OPTIMAL DIET

The following is meant merely to sum up what we say elsewhere in this section. *Please read the text for important details.* See page 19 for tips on how to feed this diet to your pet quickly and easily.

Remember always that variety is important.

Meat:
One-third to one-half the daily ration should be meat, preferably raw. Approximately one-sixth of the weekly meat ration should be organ meats—heart, kidney, gizzard, spleen, tripe. Provide fish perhaps twice a week and chicken and turkey often.

Vegetables, fruits, grains:
The rest of the daily ration should be grated raw carrot or other grated raw fruits and vegetables; cooked brown rice or whole grain breads or cereals, or chopped nuts.

Milk products:
Yogurt or raw (unpasteurized) milk should be given several times a week.

Fats:
Polyunsaturated fat daily (in the form of soybean oil, sesame oil, etc.)

Eggs:
One or two raw egg yolks (no whites), or soft-cooked whole eggs a week. (Dogs in the wild are not above swiping an egg from a bird's nest.)

Dry dog food (optional):
Supplement your dog's ration with one of the purer dry foods from a health food store.

Pure water

Vitamin and mineral supplements (some nutritional veterinarians consider these optional for the healthy pet):
Vitamin C (in the form of sodium ascorbate)
Vitamin E
Multivitamin and mineral supplement formulated for dogs

Optional: Veterinarians such as John E. Craige, V.M.D., grind up apricot pits (1 teaspoon daily for a fifty-pound dog). Apricot pits are high in vitamin B_{17} (laetrile), which many M.D.'s and D.V.M.'s consider a preventive for cancer. WARNING: Scale down the teaspoon dosage according to the size of your pet (one-half teaspoon for a twenty-five-pounder, etc.). Never increase the dosage without the express recommendation of a veterinarian experienced in the use of laetrile. The pits should not be soaked in water for any length of time, and they should not be soaked at all after they are ground. After the pits are ground, they must be refrigerated. Failure to heed these warnings may lead to the unlocking of the poison cyanide within the body.

QUICK AND EASY TIPS FOR FEEDING YOUR PET HIS NEW, NATURAL DIET

- You might want to start simply by using, for a few weeks, a high-quality noncommercial pet food in place of the supermarket pet food you and your pet have been using. This will give your pet's body a chance to become free of addiction to the impurities in the commercial pet foods. Meanwhile, you can continue your habit of simply filling your pet's bowl with prepared food a few times a day.

- Then start adding a bit of chicken, turkey, or meat from your family's own dinner—perhaps a bit of leftover that might otherwise be thrown away—to your pet's bowl.
- Next, as you chop up raw vegetables for your family's salad, chop up a few extra pieces for your pet and put them into his bowl.
- Gradually start adding grains and fruits.
- Build a routine for your pet's diet, based closely around the one you follow for your own meals. This routine will mean you do not have to make new choices every day for your pet's menus, and it will also mean you don't have to make a separate work process out of feeding your pet.

  Chances are, for instance, that you tend to eat grains for breakfast. Make breakfast the meal you give your pet his grains. Chances are also that you eat salad and meat, fish or fowl at dinner; give your pet his meat and raw vegetables at dinner.
- The gradual change of your pet's diet, as recommended above, will give you a chance leisurely to reread this chapter so that the information can become "second nature" to you. After all, you don't want to have to go skimming through the chapter every day for weeks just before your pet's meal to check out something you don't remember clearly.
- When for any reason you cannot fulfill the recommendations for your pet's natural diet, it's important that you don't feel guilty. Your pet's health will not deteriorate because of an occasional deviation from the recommended diet; remember, we have termed this diet the *optimal* diet. Keep on hand a noncommercial preformulated pet food (see Appendix) and dump that into your pet's bowl when you will be away for an extended period of time. If you oversleep and don't have even a split second to pour this food out for your pet before rushing off to work, consider his day without food a partial fast; fasts are recommended by many nutritional veterinarians, as we state later in this chapter, if your pet is not chronically ill.
- The bottom line is that you should read this chapter carefully and adhere to every suggestion as closely as possible, as often as possible. If, for any valid reason, one or two recommendations are impossible for you to fulfill, then they are just that: impossible for you to fulfill. Realize that every step you take to remove your pet from a total diet of supermarket foods is bringing him that much closer to a long, disease-free life.

Meat

As we have discussed earlier in this chapter and in Chapter 1, the dog is basically a carnivore, or flesh eater. Through a long process of evolution his teeth have been shaped to be able to rip raw flesh apart. His nails can also rip flesh. His jawbones are powerful enough to chew raw flesh, and his intestines are short so that—unlike the case of our long intestines—there is little time for meat foods to become affected by body heat and thus to spoil so as to send toxins throughout his body.

However, as we followed our pet's ancestor through his average day in the ancient forests, we saw that he also consumed partially digested fruits, vegetables, and grains from his prey's stomach. If you see a contradiction between a dog's being a carnivore and his needing foods besides meat, a quick glance at a medical dictionary will show that members of the Carnivora family are basically—but not exclusively—flesh eaters.

Nutritional veterinarians such as Michael Kreisberg, D.V.M., point out that dogs in nature consumed about one-third of their daily rations in the form of flesh; Dr. Earl adds that they seldom ate more than fifty percent of their daily ration in the form of flesh.

Raw Meat Versus Cooked Meat. There is some difference of opinion among nutritional veterinarians as to whether meat ideally should be given raw or cooked. I will tell you what each side has to say so that you can make an educated choice of your own, and I'll give you some suggestions as to how you can pretty much satisfy both sides of the question.

First of all, how could nutritional veterinarians be in disagreement? Certainly no dog in the wild ever cooked his own meat. Obviously none of the veterinarians disagree about that. None of these doctors disagree, either, that once you begin cooking meat, you begin destroying healthful vitamins, minerals, and enzymes.

What some veterinarians are worried about, however, is compensating for the sick, parasitic-ridden beef and pork we find in the supermarket meat cases today. As you know, cooking can kill harmful parasites (as well as healthy nutrients).

Other nutritional veterinarians, among them Dr. Robertson, feel that the problem of parasites is "probably not so big a problem as we're led to believe. If the strength of the digestive juices is good, very few parasites will get past the stomach. They will be digested, or destroyed, in the stomach. This is, of course, if the dog's mineral levels are high enough to produce strong digestive juices." However, he strikes a note of caution: "When your dog has weak digestive juices," states Dr. Robertson, "you'd better look out for parasites, because your pet has lost his line of defense." (See later pages for more on this subject.)

Now, how can we reach a resolution for this debate as to whether you should feed raw or cooked meat? This is not nearly so impossible a task as it may sound to you at the moment.

First, be advised that all the veterinarians asked agree that you should never feed your dog raw pork or raw rabbit. We all learned in elementary school that pork had to be very well cooked or we could be infected by trichinosis. Your dog or cat is no more immune than we are to infestation with the larvae that cause trichinosis. (In this regard, you might be interested to know that the public has recently been warned that pork should not be cooked in microwave ovens, because such ovens sometimes fail to destroy the larvae that cause trichinosis.)

Rabbits, as Dr. Kreisberg tells me, are intermediate hosts for two different types of tapeworm to which dogs are susceptible and one type of tapeworm that can infect cats. In fact, if you happen to have a rabbit as a pet, as well as a dog or cat, Dr. Kreisberg warns that you should not allow your dog or cat near the rabbit or his feed, bedding, or anything else with which he comes in contact, for that matter, because the rabbit may transmit tapeworm eggs in its feces.

In short, we must not feed raw or partially cooked rabbit or pork to our pets or eat it ourselves.

Remember, nutritional veterinarians say that if a dog or cat has strong digestive juices, these juices will destroy other types of parasites before they can do any harm. If. How can you tell about your pet's digestive juices? Well, if you've been raising him awhile on the "nutritionally complete" fake food diet everyone has been telling you to raise him on, chances are your pet doesn't have the healthy digestive juices he would normally have been able to call upon in the wild to help him out. (You see, your pet needs a steady diet of raw meats in the first place to help him produce the strong digestive juices that can destroy parasites.) So, you had better start him off on cooked—preferably steamed—meat while you begin to build up his health by following the suggestions given in this chapter. Gradually you should cook the meat less and less, until you are feeding your pet the nutrient-rich raw meat his body needs.

You should also take the suggestion of Nino Aloro, D.V.M.: When buying liver, choose only pieces that are reddish brown in color, because liver this color is not apt to be "sick." Dr. Aloro particularly warns against the possibility of sick beef livers and chicken livers. The liver of any animal filters out the poisons from the animal's system; and, as Dr. Aloro points out, today an animal's liver is asked to filter out an almost intolerable amount of poisons, more than it was ever evolved to be able to do.

Dr. Aloro adds: "My warnings against sick liver go for both animal and human consumption, of course."

There is a simpler, albeit more expensive solution to the problem of easing your pet into safely eating raw meat. If you can afford to buy your pet's daily meat ration from a health food store you can trust—that is, meat in the form of "prey" that has been raised without hormones, DDT, and arsenic, much the way your pet's natural prey was raised—you will be feeding him meat of about the same purity as his body has been evolved to thrive on. In other words, you can then probably safely feed your pet the raw meat (except pork and rabbit) that all our consulting veterinarians agree is best for him.

Another possible solution that will allow you to achieve the same result, according to Richard J. Kearns, D.V.M., is to feed your pet proteolytic pancreatic enzymes. As Dr. Kearns says: "Proteolytic enzymes break down harmful products into innocuous ones and eliminate them from the body. Using enough of these enzymes will actually 'sterilize' the intestines and get rid of all harmful products." Proteolytic enzymes can be bought at health food stores and in some lay pharmaceutical houses that advertise in health magazines such as *Prevention*.

Don't Cut Up Your Dog's Meat for Him. You may remember my friends Bren and Nick from the Introduction; it was their advanced thinking about trying natural methods to treat their dog Little Boy's "incurable" arthritis that started the ball rolling for this book. Since Little Boy's return from the land of the totally "crippled," Bren and Nick have slavishly followed every piece of advice they could find about feeding natural diets to their eight poodles. It wasn't easy, of course, because, as I've indicated earlier, there has been very little literature available that doesn't insist everything will be "a-okay" with an unnatural, embalmed diet.

When I visited them recently, Bren was standing at the kitchen counter painstakingly cutting up meat into hundreds of tiny chunks for the eight dogs. "What are you doing?" I asked.

"I'm chopping up our dogs' meat into hundreds of tiny chunks," he said. "We do ourselves the courtesy of cutting up our own meat. Don't my dogs deserve the same courtesy? How are they going to digest big hunks?"

I realize that this does seem logical to many people, so I take time here to point out that it is *not* logical. Again, the dog's body is that of a carnivore; therefore it is substantially different from ours. While we could not digest a large hunk of meat—indeed, we would probably choke on it before we could even get a chance to digest it—a dog or cat *can* handle fairly large chunks, and should be allowed to do so.

Remember that your dog's or cat's teeth are perfectly shaped for chewing flesh; these teeth can do the fine cutting up that we have to rely on our knives to do. Also, if your pet has to chew fairly large chunks of meat, he will be exercising those strong jawbones we talked about. The time he takes to chew will allow saliva to form, which will, in turn, activate certain essential enzymes present in the mouth—enzymes that are found in the dog's and cat's saliva, but not in the saliva of human beings. These enzymes help in digestion.

So you see, contrary to what seems like common sense, if you cut up your pet's food into little pieces for him, you are preventing him from digesting it well.

Dr. Robertson sounds a note of caution here, though. Like people, dogs and cats may have a few bad habits. "Some pets have the habit of just gulping down large hunks, whole." If you see that your particular pet is not using his teeth to chew up the meat, follow Dr. Robertson's suggestion to cut the meat into smaller pieces. After all, if your pet swallows large pieces whole, he won't be digesting them well; he might even choke to death.

Or, if you enjoy training your pet, you might try Dr. Kearns's suggestion of giving him a piece of meat so large he can't possibly attempt to swallow it whole. He'll have to start forming the new habit of chewing—or forego eating. I think we can safely count on his choosing the former. However, Dr. Kearns points out that at the beginning you must keep an eye on your pet as he eats. Make sure the foxy fellow doesn't just take the huge slab of meat you offer him and chew it up into a smaller chunk that is still large enough to choke on.

Vegetables, Grains, Fruits

As we've mentioned, twenty-five to fifty percent of the dog's daily food should be meat. The rest should be fruits, vegetables, and grains. The latter foods give your cat or dog a number of nutrients that don't occur at all in meat but are still necessary for your animal's health, including carbohydrates and essential fatty acids (or polyunsaturated fats).

Now, while the dog's or cat's body has evolved to thrive best on raw, uncut-up meat, it has also evolved to thrive best on partially ground up vegetables, fruits, and grains. Remember that the bulk of these latter foods are obtained in nature partially digested from the intestines of the dog's or cat's animal prey.

An animal who has evolved to thrive mainly on raw fruits, vegetables, and grains has a set of intestines long for its body. Such animals are called herbivores, not carnivores. (May I take a moment to remind you that our intestines are quite long for our bodies?) As I've mentioned, the dog's and cat's intestines are quite short. If you feed your dog or cat uncut-up fruits, vegetables, and grains, the high amount of fiber and bulk in these foods will make it difficult for his short intestinal tract to digest them. In other words, your pet's body won't be able to utilize the necessary nutrients from these foods. Therefore, you should feed your pet his daily ration of fruits and vegetables raw; because, again, cooking destroys enzymes, vitamins, and minerals. However, cut up these foods for your pet.

Polyunsaturated Fats (or Essential Fatty Acids)

All orthomolecular veterinarians agree on the importance of these fats in the diet of your dog and cat. Dr. Robertson believes: "These are the most critical nutrients that we have to deal with today; it is absolutely essential that dogs and cats get adequate amounts of these nutrients."

As we'll see in later chapters, nutritional veterinarians use these unsaturated fats to help in the treatment of a number of disorders, from skin problems to cancer. As always, its easier, cheaper, kinder, and more foolproof to prevent than to cure.

"If the animal is getting the proper proportion of fresh whole grains," says Dr. Robertson, "he's probably getting adequate essential fatty acids. If he's not getting enough whole grains, then the owner had better supplement. The lack of unsaturated fats is the major cause of skin problems and the major reason why dogs and cats don't absorb calcium." (The malabsorption of calcium can lead to a number of bone and joint problems.)

Research in essential fatty acid deficiency has shown that such a deficiency can also lead to stunted growth, reproductive problems, and degeneration of lungs, liver, and kidneys. Too little essential fatty acid intake is also implicated in rheumatoid arthritis and multiple sclerosis.[2]

If you want to offer your pet an optimal preventive diet, you might add one teaspoon to one tablespoon (depending on your pet's size) of essential fatty acids a day to his diet—even if you're fairly sure he's getting enough whole grains. A bit more than necessary won't be harmful. A supplement of essential fatty acids is quite easy to obtain. Just buy a bottle of soybean oil, corn oil, sunflower seed oil, or safflower oil—the cooking and salad oils you can buy in the supermarket. The highest quality oils you can buy are cold pressed. These are available in health food stores and some supermarkets. If the oil is cold pressed, it will say so in bold letters on the label.

Dr. Robertson states that the best source of the most potent fatty acid (gamma linoleic) is oil of evening primrose. You may have trouble getting this particular oil outside of health food stores. Dr. Kearns has a preference for cold pressed sesame oil. "This oil does everything other unsaturated fats do," he tells me, "but it also stimulates the thymus to produce T-cells, which help fight infection and cancer." Dr. Robertson and Drs. Marty and Robert Goldstein also agree that cold pressed sesame oil is a top choice.

As for other oils, wheat germ oil is high in vitamin E and octacosanol, and safflower oil is very high in vitamin F. Joseph Stuart, D.V.M., believes safflower oil is the best oil for cats.

Vitamin and Mineral Supplements

For those of you whose budgets are very, very tight, I can say that a few of the veterinarians surveyed believe you'll be able to have a healthy, long-lived pet without supplements, as long as you feed him the natural diet as detailed in this chapter and give him the supplements mentioned in Chapter 3 for special times in his life. For those of you who can afford a few more pennies a day (and that's all it will cost), you're on much safer ground if you give your pet supplements in the manner explained a bit later.

Readers who have been following this book closely may now be thinking they have discovered an inconsistency: "Dogs and cats," you may say, "never had vitamin and mineral supplements in the wild." You're quite right, of course; they didn't. However, they also did not eat foods grown in nutrient-depleted earth (which both you and your pet are doing, unless you buy all your foods from well-chosen health food stores or grow all your own foods organically). And they didn't have to use much of the nutrients in their bodies for the extra job of fighting off stress from all the new poisons in the environment.

When choosing supplements, I hope you will not "build your own" vitamin and mineral supplement, for either yourself or your pet. I hope you will buy a good multivitamin-mineral supplement, preferably from the health food store, where the nutrients are likely to be from natural sources. (Health food stores carry vitamins especially formulated for dogs and cats.) Often, the vitamins and minerals available in drugstores are chemical copies of the real thing.

First of all, if you build your own from different sources, it will probably cost you several times more than getting all the same nutrients in one pill. But my main concern is that by prescribing your own balance of vitamins and minerals, you may very well do your pet—or yourself—more harm than good.

For instance, you may read something somewhere that convinces you that your pet needs vitamin B_6. If you give him isolated B_6 without the direction of a veterinarian, you can increase his need for the other B-vitamins. In other words, you can, by giving him B_6, make him *deficient* in the other B-vitamins. This can cause severe central nervous system damage, as well as other problems.

In another instance you may read rather simplistic statements that pregnant and lactating dogs and cats, as well as growing puppies and kittens, need extra calcium. This is true; but what these other sources may not tell you is that you can't give a pill containing only calcium. Calcium has to be combined in a delicate balance with phosphorus, as nutritional veterinarian Dr. Kreisberg stresses. It also has to be given in a certain ratio to magnesium or you stand the chance of causing the very health problems you're trying to prevent. In addition, vitamin D is needed or the calcium can't even be used by the body.

I have deliberately tried to make the balancing of vitamins and minerals sound complicated—because it is. I hope you will not attempt to do it on your own. For preventive purposes I hope you will follow the recommendation given here by veterinarians who have devoted their careers to the specific problem of nutrition for pets: Select an already balanced multivitamin and mineral supplement, and add vitamins C and E.

Wendell O. Belfield, D.V.M., one of the true pioneers in the field of orthomolecular veterinary medicine, recommends the following additions of vitamin C for your adult dog: 500 mg for a small, sedentary dog to 1,500 mg for a small, extremely active dog; 1,500 to 3,000 mg for a medium dog; 3,000 to 6,000 mg for a large dog; and 6,000 to 7,500 mg for a giant dog. There will be some vitamin E in the multipill, but there probably won't be any vitamin C, because "everybody knows" dogs and cats produce enough C in their own bodies. The total vitamin E you should give your pet daily is 100 IU for the small dog; 200 IU for the medium; 200 IU for the large; and

400 IU for the giant.[3] If it is impossible to end up with just those amounts by combining your multipill with a separate E supplement, Dr. Belfield advises that it is better to go above the recommended amount than to go below.[4] Saturated fat is necessary for vitamins E, A, D, and K to be used by the body. Feed the vitamins to your pet at the same time you give him meat.

Ideally, you should buy a powdered supplement. If that's not possible, mash up the multivitamin-mineral tablet into your dog's food. Why? If your dog's digestive processes are not tip-top (and if he has been raised awhile on processed foods, chances are his digestive juices are *not* tip-top), the pill may pass through his system and out again without being used at all. As S. Allen Price, D.V.M., puts it: "Sometimes we give a vitamin-mineral tablet to a dog or a cat, and it comes out again later, still a whole tablet." You can see that those vitamins and minerals have not been used by the body.

Of course, if you can monitor your pet's feces and ascertain that the pill is not coming out whole or in small hunks, there's no need to buy a powdered supplement or to mash the tablet. In my own case, my two dogs and my cat have been raised long enough on their natural diets so that nothing passes out of their system undigested.

One more important point: Never give whole tablets to a puppy, a toy-sized dog, or a cat. There is always the possibility that a tablet might get stuck in the throat of a small animal.

How Not to Poison Your Pet with Water

Every time you fill your pet's bowl with cool, fresh water from your faucet, you may very well be bringing him that much closer to death from cadmium poisoning, copper poisoning, and/or lead poisoning. Yes, the same lead poisoning that the public is generally led to believe is caused only by eating paint peelings.

These dangerous heavy metals, of course, find it just as easy to get from your water pipes into your glass as they do to get into your pet's bowl. Many plumbing pipes are made partially from cadmium, copper, or lead; and as these metals start to erode, the water carries particles of the metal out with it.

An overload of heavy metals in your pet's body, and/or your own, can cause kidney damage, emphysema (there's a lot of the heavy metal cadmium in cigarette smoke, by the way), high blood pressure, heart disease, mental retardation, anemia, abortions, epilepsy, depression, and arthritis. That's only a partial list; I didn't want to bore you.

Just consider this one statistic: The U.S. Public Health Service has set a standard for the amount of copper that can safely exist in our water. Some cities have been found to have over five and one-half times that amount in their water supply.[5]

There is another substance that is being added *on purpose* to our drinking water. In many cities fluoride is added as a form of mass medication to help us prevent tooth decay—which might be more safely prevented by cutting out sugar, of course. Medical studies on everything from the fruit fly to mice to human beings have shown increased incidences of cancer caused by fluoride.[6]

Dean Burk, Ph.D., makes a strong statement: "Our data in the United States indicate in my view that one-tenth of all cancer deaths in this country can be shown to be linked to fluoridation of public drinking water. That comes to about 40,000 extra cancer deaths a year. . . . [That] exceeds deaths from breast cancer." Dr. Burk was for thirty-five years a high-level researcher at the U.S. Public Health Service's National Cancer Institute in the Washington, D.C., area.[7]

That's a brief overview of the dangerous substances we drink in our tap water every day. Of course there are other contaminants, too. As I write this, a TV reporter is announcing with some amazement that "thousands of towns" across the country have recently suffered increased incidences of various diseases . . . and that these diseases have been traced to human waste in the water. I'm afraid you did indeed read that right.

Of course you can't cut out water, either for yourself or for your pet. Water is needed to carry wastes out of the system, not only digestive wastes but also dead body cells. However, as Dr. Robertson points out, impure water does not have the "carrying power" of pure water, and many toxins and dead cells are left to float around in our circulatory system a lot longer than they should.

By now you're wishing I would stop telling you horror stories about tap water and give you a clue as to what you can do to get all those poisons out of your pet's bowl* and out of your drinking glass. One simple and inexpensive thing you can do is to let your water run for five minutes before you use it. This will allow time for particles of eroded heavy metals from your pipes to be carried off harmlessly down the drain, although it won't do anything for the more than three hundred contaminants that can be found actually in the water itself.

You can help your and your pet's health even more by investing a small sum in a water filter that you can put permanently over your faucet. Investigate before you buy, however; some filters screen out more contaminants than others.

Probably you have heard of both spring water and distilled water as alternatives for the chemical-laden water that comes from our faucets. Nutri-

---

*Dr. Stuart points out that your pet's bowl, by the way, should not be the common plastic one many owners use. Dr. Kearns agrees, adding that there is a chemical reaction that can cause many pets to lose pigment from their noses. Dr. Kearns also advises that aluminum dishes can cause aluminum toxicity and ceramic dishes can cause lead toxicity. Dr. Kearns recommends stainless steel or glass dishes as the safest.

tional M.D.'s and D.V.M.'s alike argue among themselves as to whether spring or distilled water is the better alternative. I asked a number of nutritional veterinarians to tell me their preference and their reasons for it.

From their responses it seems that your safest bet may be distilled water. Even those veterinarians who prefer spring water, such as Dr. Kearns and Dr. Earl, warn that very often such water is contaminated. If you elect to use spring water, do a bit of research to make sure it comes from pure sources. Just reading the label won't do. After all, no distributor is going to state on the label: "Bottled exclusively from contaminated springs."

I asked a few nutritional vets if the phrase "from U.S. certified springs" I found on some spring water labels might put readers of this book at ease. The answers that came back ranged from "This is a nebulous statement," to "U.S. does not certify springs," to *"No,"* to *"Definitely not."*

So, all in all, distilled water is the best alternative, if you cannot check up on the purity of the spring water available to you.

Still, some nutritional writers have maintained that distilled water can be dangerous because it not only lacks desirable minerals but can also leach minerals out of the body. As for the argument that distilled water contains no desirable minerals, Dr. Robertson states: "The inorganic minerals that are in water are practically useless to the body." Addressing themselves to the argument that distilled water robs the body of minerals, Drs. Robert and Marty Goldstein tell me that the minerals leached out by distilled water are undesirable, inorganic minerals. "Distilled water also leaches out other morbid wastes," the latter two doctors state. Indeed, as we will see later, nutritional veterinarians use distilled water as therapy for conditions such as arthritis, just because it *does* leach out undesirable minerals from the body.

Bones for Your Pet?

I know that most of my friends with pets "have heard" that bones are indispensable for their dog or cat. I personally, however, had doubts about bones because of the possibility of choking, so I asked nine of the veterinarians participating in this book to give their recommendations about letting pets gnaw bones. Seven of the nine vote "no," one votes "yes" with reservations as to the type of bone, and one doctor votes wholeheartedly for bones, citing the fact that carnivores in the wild always chewed on bones—and still do—as a way of cleaning their teeth. The latter doctor states that in thirty years of practice, he has never found a pet that choked or otherwise had problems caused by a splintered bone.

Most strongly against giving pets bones is Dr. Aloro, who believes that bones, far from keeping the teeth healthy, can harm them quite drastically. "When my clients don't listen to me and give their pets bones, I find the teeth get chipped; they break; they get otherwise ruined because the roots get weakened." As if that weren't enough, sometimes the teeth even get "filed down to the gum line." Dr. Aloro does, however, recommend soup bones—which don't tend to splinter—for teething pets, whose baby teeth are meant by nature to come out soon, anyway. Such bones help loosen the baby teeth.

Other veterinarians are against bones because of the possibility of choking or of splinters getting into the intestines. Dr. Craige, for instance, says: "I remember a pitiable little Boston terrier who died with a string of lamb bones blocking his intestines. I have also seen countless dogs who couldn't pass their feces without pain from bone splinters."

Drs. Robert and Marty Goldstein tell me that most of today's pets who are raised on processed pet food "do not have strong enough teeth or digestive juices to handle bones as safely as their ancestors did." In contrast, dogs who have been on natural diets for long periods of time tend to have strong digestive juices that can dissolve bits of bone, preventing these bone fragments from getting imbedded in the intestines.

The doctors Goldstein recommend giving your dog raw carrots (preferably organic), which are almost as much a challenge to chew up as are bones. Carrots will accomplish some of the jaw-exercising and teeth-cleaning results provided by a bone. As for your cat, you could probably wait until doomsday before he would munch on a carrot, so the doctors Goldstein recommend you give him a firm biscuit made of whole grains. Other doctors point out that bone meal tablets (obtainable from health food stores) will give your pet the same minerals he used to get in the wild by chewing bones.

If you have heard from numerous friends that pets must have bones, it is possible that the above has not convinced you. Please at least don't let your pet have bones small enough to swallow or fragile enough to splinter as he gnaws on them. And please take Dr. Craige's advice *not* to cook any bones you give your pet. Dr. Craige explains that cooking denatures the collagen (a protein) of the bone, making it harder to digest.

I have been talking until now about real animal or bird bones. What about the plastic bones, the rawhide bones, and the milk bones touted in ads? When you buy these you are using the fake products we warned against so strongly in Chapter 1. As Thomas A. Newland, D.V.M., states, these artificial products must be excluded from the diet of *all* pets. And Dr. Newland is our veterinarian most strongly in favor of bones (*real* bones) for pets.

ADDITIONAL TIPS

Food Combining

How you combine food groups can be crucial to your pet's health. Why? The digestive organs secrete enzymes to break down food so it can be properly used by the body. When carbohydrates and protein are eaten at the same time, the protein enzymes go to work first, and the digestion of carbohydrates must wait. While the carbohydrates are waiting around to be digested, they ferment and release toxins in the body. Kathy Berman, an animal nutritionist, recommends: "The only harmonious foods to be used with meats or even dairy proteins are vegetables (raw and grated or cut up)."

For more details on proper food combining, see page 129.

Don't Spring This New Diet on Your Pet All at Once

For one thing, any sudden major change in a diet can prove upsetting to the body and cause digestive disturbances. For another thing, a pet addicted to sugar (present in high amounts in some fake foods) or other unnatural additives is not unlike a person addicted to alcohol. If you take away all his additives abruptly, he may literally be beside himself.

Start slowly. Add just a bit of his new diet at a time for about a week; then gradually add a bit more. In this way, not only his digestive system but his taste buds can get a chance to become adjusted to the new (though ancient) diet.

How Much to Feed Your Pet and How Often

You may be surprised to know that most nutritional veterinarians are loath to recommend how many calories you should feed your pet. And rightly so. As Dr. Aloro puts it: "Of course I have in my office all those nice charts about calories and fat, etc., per pound of animal weight. But for practical purposes they are fairly useless. The charts deal with the average animal. In reality, most animals are not average; each pet is an individual."

What Dr. Aloro says is true. Feeding the same number of calories to a twelve-pound dog who spends his days running around the yard and to a twelve-pounder who spends half his time cuddled in your lap and the other half snoozing on the floor could result in one half-starved dog and one bloated butterball.

Even feeding an equal number of calories to two dogs of the same weight, same age, and same exercise habits won't work for certain to maintain perfect weight. These two animals might have quite dissimilar metabolic rates; one dog might burn up only half as many calories a day as the other. As Dr. Newland points out, the same disparity is true of people. "We all know people who eat everything and stay thin, and we all know people who eat little and get fat."

Nutritional veterinarians such as Dr. Craige recommend this sublimely commonsense rule of thumb: If your dog starts gaining weight, cut down a bit on his calories and encourage him to exercise more. If he starts losing weight, indulge him in a bit more food.

However, I'll give you a base to start from, because I know your pet's new natural diet won't be coming out of a box or can that provides you with simplistic instructions. Try 50 calories a day for each pound your pet weighs. But no matter how many calories you include in your pet's new diet, watch his weight carefully for a while.

The following example will show you why Dr. Aloro and other nutritional veterinarians are reluctant to deal with "average" calories for "individual" pets: The above average recommendation works out to 500 calories a day for my ten-pound poodle and 600 calories for my twelve-pounder. Yet both of them have maintained their weight to the dot for seven years on 800 calories a day.

If you read most books now out on the feeding of pets, you'll see a lot of disagreement about whether to feed once a day or twice a day. The arguments go basically like this: Feed a dog or cat only once a day or he will overeat and become fat; feed a dog or cat twice a day or he will overeat and become fat because he will come to his daily meal overhungry.

The truth of the matter is that once you start feeding your pet the diet his body was built to thrive on, you will probably have very little problem with overweight, no matter how often you feed him. Since fake foods have so many empty calories (that is, calories that have little or no nutrients in them), a pet is driven to eat much more of the fake foods than he needs, in a vain attempt to get enough nutrients into his body.

As I've said, my own dogs haven't gained a smidgen of an ounce in seven years of natural dining. And yet I have always kept something nonspoilable (such as apple or carrot) in their bowl for them to knosh on at will. This frees me from always having to be around at their mealtimes and allows them what I assume is the wonderful luxury of being able to eat when they are hungry, not when *I* think they should be hungry.

You don't hear about "free feeding" in other books; and indeed, it probably would prove a disaster to "free-feed" pets with the poisonous, addictive foods recommended by most of these books. However, there is another plus to snacking, as opposed to eating one or two heavier meals a day—and this is a principle that applies to people, too. It has to do with the difference between causing sudden jolts to your metabolism and maintaining a fairly even body chemistry.

When you eat a heavy meal, your metabolism suddenly goes into full gear as the meal is digested and utilized. After all this heavy work, the metabolism tends to slow down and rest. If you eat two meals a day, it has a long time to rest and become sluggish before the second meal happens along, at which time there is another sudden burst of activity. You might compare this to your having to exercise strenuously twice a day, each time just after having been awakened from a heavy sleep. In short, many authorities believe it is best to keep the metabolism on a fairly even, rhythmic keel throughout the day, and the snacking system I use for my dogs allows this even rhythm.

However, as always your dogs and my dogs are individuals; and if you find that your pet starts gaining weight with his new-found freedom on the "snack diet," by all means cut down on the calories and/or the allotted feedings.

Fasting

If you already believe in occasional fasting for yourself because you feel that the digestive system should have a rest now and then to let the body rid itself of toxins, you'll be glad to know that there's a rationale for fasting your dog or cat occasionally, too. The dog and cat in the wild didn't get "lucky" enough every single day to make a catch and therefore were forced occasionally to fast.

Some animal nutritional experts, such as Juliette de Bairacli Levy, recommend that you fast an adult dog two years of age and over one day weekly. Of course you must give him water during the fast. If your pet is between four months and two years of age, Levy recommends a half-day fast every week, and a full-day fast every month.[8]

Warning: Do *not* fast your chronically sick pet without the guidance of a veterinarian who thoroughly understands fasting. The poisons that concentrate in the body before they are expelled can kill a degenerated pet.

Other experts, such as Dr. Robertson, take a more *laissez-faire* attitude toward periodic fasting. As Dr. Robertson states, "Your pet is the one who knows when he should fast. Whenever a dog or cat doesn't feel in top form, the first thing he'll do is stop eating. Leave it to him. He has a better idea of when he should fast than we do."

Dog owners will find more useful diet tips by skimming through the following section on cats.

THE OPTIMAL PREVENTIVE DIET
FOR YOUR ADULT CAT

Since both cats and dogs are basically carnivores, almost all that I have just covered for dogs applies to your cat, too. However, although dogs and cats come from the same animal family (Carnivora), dogs are decidedly not cats, and cats are decidedly not dogs. The differences between your cat's natural diet and what we have covered for dogs will be detailed here.

You might be surprised to learn that your sweet placid kitty is more exclusively a natural eater of animal flesh than is your neighbor's ferocious 150-pound German shepherd. You might also be surprised to know that, pound for pound, your tiny cat needs more calories than that Great Dane down the block. Since the cat is more truly a carnivore than the dog, he requires more protein and more saturated fat (which are found in meat) and requires fewer carbohydrates and less roughage (which are found in vegetables and grains). Since he requires so much saturated fat, you're not doing your cat a favor if you buy the more expensive lean meats or if you take the time to trim off fat from around the edges.

THE OPTIMAL DIET

The following is meant merely to sum up what we say elsewhere in this chapter. *Please read the text for both dogs and cats for important details*. Also, see page 19 for tips on how to feed this diet to your pet quickly and easily.

Remember always that variety is important.

Meat:
About 75% of the daily food ration should be meat, raw preferably. Approximately one-sixth of the weekly meat ration should be organ meats—heart, kidney, gizzard, spleen, tripe. Provide fish perhaps twice a week and chicken and turkey often. Do not give any type of bones.

Vegetables, fruits, grains:
Most of the rest of the daily ration should be cooked brown rice or cereal, cut-up raw fruits and vegetables, and occasionally chopped nuts.

Milk products:
Yogurt or raw (unpasteurized) milk should be given several times weekly.

Fats:
Polyunsaturated fat daily (in the form of safflower oil, sesame oil, etc.)

Eggs:
One or two eggs a week. (Cats in the wild are not above swiping an egg from a bird's nest.)

Dry cat food (optional): Supplement with one of the purer dry foods for cats from the health food store.

Pure water

Vitamin and mineral supplements (some nutritional veterinarians consider these optional for the healthy pet):
Vitamin C (in the form of
    sodium ascorbate)
Vitamin E
Cat multivitamin and mineral pill

Optional: Veterinarians such as Dr. Craige grind up apricot pits (¼ teaspoon for a twelve-pound cat). Apricot pits are high in vitamin B_{17} (or laetrile), which many M.D.'s and D.V.M.'s consider a preventive for cancer. WARNING: *Do not use any source of laetrile without reading the warning in the optimal diet for dogs (see page 19).*

Meat

Wild cats ate basically rodents, small rabbits, and birds. I doubt that many of you will choose to spend your days catching mice or rats to offer to your cat. However, if you do have a mouse running around, chances are your kitty won't need a mousetrap to help him catch it. If you do choose to feed rabbit to your cat occasionally, remember our admonitions against feeding rabbit raw.

Most nutritional veterinarians recommend chicken and turkey whole-heartedly, not only because the cat evolved to thrive on birds, but because fowl today tends to be—along with veal and lamb—one of the least polluted sources of animal protein available outside of health food stores. As Dr. Aloro points out, chickens are usually killed young and therefore have had less time to be polluted with hormones, pesticide-contaminated feed, etc.

So you would do well to make fowl a central part of your cat's diet and add veal and lamb when possible. Chicken and turkey have the added blessing of being less expensive than other meats. As we've discussed for dogs, one-sixth of your cat's meat allotment should be in the form of organ meats—thymus, spleen, kidney, heart, liver—not only because cats ate that proportion of organ meats in the wild, but because these meats contain many nutrients that are less abundant in other parts of the animal.

Don't Make the Mistake of Feeding Only Meat to Your Cat. When the cat is referred to as a carnivore, some members of the public can be misled. For that reason, many nutritional veterinarians are careful to refer to the cat as "almost a true carnivore," or "more truly a carnivore than the dog." Also, as I've pointed out, medical dictionaries define the family Carnivora as eating basically—but not exclusively—flesh.

Dr. Aloro tells me a chilling story of a lady who breeds cats. She latched onto a "carnivore" label years ago and has tenaciously refused to believe that a carnivore should eat anything except meat. Not only that, but she has decided that beef is *the* food, and feeds her cats nothing but beef. As I keep pointing out, variety is important, since no one food contains all necessary nutrients for any one body. Also, an allergy to any food is always possible, and to keep bombarding a body with an allergen may be tantamount to murder.

But, as Dr. Aloro tells me, "I have never been able to convince that breeder that there is no such thing as a good all-meat diet for dogs or cats. She has one cat that was bred to be a champion. And that poor cat has bad kidneys; he has chronic conjunctivitis; his coat is terrible-looking, because his body is so sick. She keeps looking for drugs to take care of these health problems and to make his skin look good, because, after all, he was supposed to be a champion for her. And I tell her: 'You can look from here to eternity, but unless you change the diet, that cat will not look good.' "

Another client purchased a young cat from this same breeder and brought it to Dr. Aloro only a month after buying it. Dr. Aloro tells me sadly, "That poor thing was so weak, I couldn't do anything at all. He died."

Just one of the things wrong with an all-meat diet is that it's low in minerals. Your pet needs minerals (although as a result of the cat's having evolved as basically a meat eater, he does need less in the way of minerals than we do, or even than dogs do.) Not only does your cat need minerals for all the good they can do for the body, but minerals are necessary before vitamins can be put to use by the body. Depriving your cat of minerals is tantamount to depriving him of vitamins, too.

Another problem with an all-meat diet is that carbohydrates, which are present in grains, fruits, and vegetables but not in meats, are needed to help your cat's body use proteins. Without carbohydrates, your cat can't efficiently use the proteins in meat that his body needs so much.

For these reasons, our nutritional veterinarians emphasize that besides feeding your cat the recommended variety of meats, you should add a small amount of grains and mashed raw vegetables and fruits. Remember, if you were to set your cat loose today without his food bowl, he would eat not only his natural prey (meat), but also the nonmeat contents of his prey's stomach.

Many nutritional veterinarians recommend cooked brown rice as a common supplement to your cat's meat diet. Why *brown* rice? Because it has more nutrients in it than white rice, including more B-vitamins that are necessary for the health of the brain and the spine.*

While we're on the subject of brown grains versus white grains, let me digress to the subject of bread. Even if you've never previously made it a point to read about nutrition, you've probably heard that white bread has many of the vitamins processed out of it. True, the labels on white breads state proudly that certain vitamins have been added to the bread. What you're not supposed to know is that these "added" vitamins are a partial replacement for the vitamins the manufacturers have robbed from the natural grain in the manufacturing process.

Fish

Some books written by veterinarians who don't have a special interest in nutrition will tell you that fish is not a natural food for the cat. However, Dr. Newland points out, "Cats in the wild are natural fishermen."

Fish can be a good addition to your cat's diet. Fish contains polyunsaturated fats, for instance, which meat does not. We covered how crucial polyunsaturated fats are in the previous section on dogs.

---

*Our veterinarians have asked me to stress that rice must be cooked very, very well or your pet may not be able to digest it. On the face of it, this may seem inconsistent with our previous warnings that cooking destroys many nutrients. However, rice and other grains grow naturally in very hot, sunny climates. As a result, the nutrients in these foods are unusually stable when exposed to heat.

Here again, however, I must emphasize that you should not concentrate on fish for the mainstay of your cat's diet. Like any other single class of food, fish does not contain all the nutrients necessary for health. For instance, fish is low in Vitamin E, and cats happen to require very high amounts of E. One of the terrible things that can happen to your cat if he eats too much fish (particularly tuna) is a disorder known as steatitis, caused by a deficiency of vitamin E. First your cat will become extremely nervous; then every time something or someone touches his skin, he will meow and cringe in extreme pain, because the disorder will have caused his nerve endings to become excruciatingly sensitive. Veterinarians can often cure this disorder with massive amounts of the missing vitamin E; but why cause it in the first place? By the way, many commercial cat foods are high in tuna because tuna has such a strong taste that cats often will become addicted to it. The idea is that you're supposed to notice that your cat will "only eat" X brand, so you buy it for him all the time. You're not supposed to know about vitamin E deficiency and steatitis. Fish is also low in Vitamin B_1 and, as Dr. Kreisberg points out, "A B_1 deficiency can cause vomiting, weight loss—and brain damage."

Raw Versus Cooked Foods for Cats
One of medical history's most dramatic scientific studies of the effect of raw versus cooked foods for cats was begun, oddly, because an M.D. was trying to do research on something quite different. The doctor, Francis M. Pottenger, Jr., was trying to standardize adrenal cortical material, and he was using cats for this research. However, he was in a quandary. So many cats were dying that he was having difficulty carrying on his study, and he did not know why the cats were dying.

It occurred to Dr. Pottenger that animals in zoos contracted the same diseases as man and died earlier than animals in the wild. It also occurred to him that animals in the wild ate raw foods, and animals in zoos often did not. And it did not escape him that he had been feeding his laboratory cats cooked meats.

Thus, Dr. Pottenger embarked on a ten-year study of three generations of cats. He fed half the cats the customary cooked meats and pasteurized (or cooked) milk; the other half he fed raw meats and unpasteurized (raw) milk. It didn't take even the first generation of cats fed cooked foods long to develop some of the new "inevitable" disorders of both animals and man: teeth loss, paralysis, irritable behavior. As time went on, heart lesions became common; so did arthritis, nephritis, hepatitis, cystitis, etc.

Abortions in the first generation were about twenty-five percent—that is, one in four should-have-been-born kittens never made it into the world. By the second generation, seventy percent didn't make it. Of those kittens who did see the light of day, many died soon after. Many mother cats died in labor.

Lice and internal parasites were common among the "cooked-food cats"—that is, among those who lived long enough to suffer these things in the first place; so were skin lesions and allergies.

Meanwhile, the cats being "pampered" with raw foods rarely suffered abortions, lice, parasites, or infections. They also had calmer, more even-tempered personalities.

If you remember, Dr. Pottenger began those experiments because not enough cats were surviving the operations he was performing in his research on adrenal cortical material. Once he started giving raw foods to some of his cats, he found he could perform these operations on them with little or no problem.

By the way, my summation of these experiments is not meant to give you a sense of hopelessness if you happen to have raised a cat on an unnatural diet and he now shows some of the signs of Dr. Pottenger's "cooked-food cats." You should know that in the fourth generation, Dr. Pottenger fed his "cooked-food cats" raw foods. In many cases, he was able to restore them to health.*

Milk Products

I know that many people consider cats and milk practically synonymous with each other. This *is* true of kittens; after all, all mammals start life living exclusively off the milk their mothers so graciously provide. However, let's investigate this for a moment. If you're feeding your grown cat milk, you're feeding him cow's milk or goat's milk, aren't you? As a kitten he got, naturally, from his mama—yes, cat's milk.

Also, let's go back to our average day in the life of our pet's great-great-etc. granddaddy, to check out how natural milk is for our grown cat. Great-etc. granddaddy is now weaned; he is a big, ferocious cat of, let's say, six months and weighs eight pounds. He wakes up and starts his day looking for prey. He strikes it rich with a bird. No milk there. He waits awhile before going to the spring to drink. No milk there. Assuming he would still have a longing from his babyhood for the milk his mother can no longer give him, where would he find milk in the wild? There is no dairy he can loot, and I doubt he has taken the trouble to learn to milk cows. The answer, then, is inescapable. Contrary to a lot of popular opinion, milk is not a natural food for your grown cat.

Dr. Kearns states the above ideas this way: "I feel that milk is an unnatural food unless it goes from nipple to host by suction." The doctors Goldstein add that cow's milk contains growth hormones that serve to take a 40-pound cow and build him to a 700- to 1,000-pound cow. "This is great for the cow," the doctors say, "but not for the cat."

---

*Reprints available from Pottenger Foundation, P.O. Box 2614, La Mesa, CA 92041.

Having said all these negatives against milk, let me add that nutritional veterinarians believe that milk (especially raw, unpasteurized milk and, most especially, raw goat's milk) can be a good addition to your cat's basic diet—*if your cat shows no signs of being allergic to milk.* On the plus side, milk contains calcium. In the wild, dogs and cats got calcium from chomping on the bones of their prey; this book asks you please not to give bones to your pet. Therefore, you must find other means to give your pet the calcium his body evolved to thrive on. Milk is a good way.

Yogurt may be an even better way to provide your pet with calcium. Yogurt tends to cause fewer animals (and fewer persons) allergy problems. It also contains a type of "friendly" bacteria that is extremely important to the digestive health—and therefore the total health—of your pet (and yourself).

As we have indicated, many cats, and many dogs, are allergic to milk. It is a common misconception that allergies cause stomach problems and skin problems only. However, Alfred Jay Plechner, D.V.M., who has studied allergies extensively, states: "Nearly any disease in the body may be primarily or secondarily related to a food allergy."

Many M.D.'s in recent years have been making a similar statement about human beings. And, by the way, a large number of *us*, too, are allergic to milk and milk products (such as cheese), and many of us aren't aware that this allergy is causing our problems.*

But let's get back to cats. If your cat has bouts of diarrhea, there's a good chance that simply cutting out milk will "miraculously" cure the diarrhea. However, as we've said, diarrhea is not the only sign of an allergy to milk. If your pet has *any* symptoms that your veterinarian has not been able to explain or treat successfully, I hope you'll ask the doctor to consider the possibility of allergies to milk and other foods.

ADDITIONAL TIPS

Temperature of Your Cat's Food

Your cat will have a better appetite and better digestion if you serve his food at a tepid temperature—neither cold right out of the refrigerator, nor hot right off the stove. Many people who are owned by cats have noticed this revulsion to hot and cold foods and have passed it off as a profound "finickiness" on the part of their pampered one. It's not finickiness: it's a desire on

---

*The reason dogs, cats, and people start out life thriving greatly on milk and then many suddenly become allergic to it is that most baby mammals have an enzyme in their stomach (lactase) which breaks down a sugar in milk (lactose) and helps their bodies to thrive on milk. However, as many babies reach adulthood, their stomachs lose this helpful enzyme. Their bodies can no longer break down the lactose in milk, and milk suddenly becomes a harmful substance.

your cat's part that his food be served at its "natural" temperature. The temperature of the body of your cat's newly killed prey was always tepid.

How Much to Feed Your Cat

Again, with a few exceptions, what I have said in the section for dogs goes for cats, too. However, as we've said, cats need more calories per pound of body weight than do dogs. Therefore, you might start your cat with approximately 75 calories per pound of body weight rather than the 50 calories recommended as a possible starting point for dogs.

HOW TO SUPPLEMENT YOUR PET'S DIET WITH INEXPENSIVE PACKAGED FOODS

This statement is going to surprise you. Your pet's optimal diet might very well include a regular serving of prepared pet foods bought at the store. Right now you're getting ready to throw back at me all the grisly facts we covered in Chapter 1 about packaged pet foods from the supermarket shelves. What I am recommending here are packaged pet foods available primarily at health food stores. Some enlightened pet shops also carry them, as do a few grooming shops. These pet foods bear little resemblance to those you pick up at the supermarket. The prepared foods I'm recommending here are really tailored to your pet's needs; they tend to come from more natural sources; and they do not contain the poisons that plump out the commercial pet foods.

These pure, prepared pet foods can serve as a nice source of balanced nutrition now and then, in case you're not sure you're able to balance things our perfectly in nonprepared foods. They can also serve as healthful nibbles when you're not home to serve a meal. And they can be just about invaluable when you have to travel and leave your pet in the care of someone else. Your friend or kennel owner may say he's going to provide your pet with raw meat and balance it with vegetables and grains, but you can more safely trust him or her to shake out some kibble from the bag you leave on hand.

Surprisingly, these more natural prepared foods are no more expensive than the lethal packaged foods in supermarkets. Are these distributors, then, philanthropists? No. For one thing, as we have covered previously, the more nutritious a food is, the less a pet will eat of it—because he will need less to fulfill his body's requirements. For another thing, you don't have to pay these distributors for nationwide TV ads. As Dr. Newland points out to me: "A few-seconds' TV commercial costs $60,000 to $150,000. I ask you, is there any nutritional value in this hot air? If you buy the product, you are paying for this advertising, right through the nose."

Now, if there are fairly perfect prepared foods available, why have I bothered you with everything I've told you in the earlier part of this chapter? These more nutritional prepackaged foods are still not raw, and you're missing out on the vitamins, minerals, and enzymes available only from raw foods—more accurately, your pet is missing out on them.

Another argument against serving even the purest packaged foods as the mainstay of your pet's diet is that the longer foods sit around in packages or cans, the more nutrients they lose. And once you open the package or can, exposing the food to air, the nutrients start disappearing even faster, through the oxidation process.

Now, while there are some superb pet foods in health food stores (as superb as packaged foods can be), not every product available for pets in these stores is all that much better than foods on the supermarket shelves. At the same time, not everything available to human beings in health food stores is all that much better for us—contrary, I'm afraid, to popular belief. Whether you're shopping in these stores for yourself or for your pet, it is important that you become an educated label reader.

Here's a very quick rundown on what you should look for on labels, once you think you may have found a pure, nonsupermarket food in either a health food store, a pet shop, or a grooming shop. First of all, the label should state that there are no artificial preservatives, flavorings, or color. Some labels state only "no artificial preservatives." This isn't good enough. The label should say also that the product contains no refined sugar. In those two statements alone, you can feel secure that you're making great strides toward saving your pet from the serious health problems these substances can cause.

In addition, your label should *not* contain the word "by-products" after the beef, liver, and other meat ingredients. Those by-products, if you remember, can contain parts of extremely diseased animals.

Somewhere along the line, the label should read that the product has one or more preservatives. Haven't I said that preservatives are practically going to kill your pet on the spot? I've warned against *artificial* preservatives. If you don't have any preservatives at all in prepackaged food, there's nothing to prevent that food from spoiling while it sits on the shelf. The label you're investigating should specify *natural* preservatives, ingredients such as vitamins C and E.

Avoid using too often a product that lists fish as one of the major ingredients. (Proportions of ingredients on any label can be ascertained by how early in the list they are mentioned; the first ingredient on the label is the main ingredient, etc.) Also be suspicious of cans and packages that claim you can use the product equally well for both dogs and cats, since—as we have explained—dogs and cats have substantially different needs.

If you remember, there is a danger that the lead content of the cans themselves will permeate the food inside the cans. As Dr. Aloro says, "Cans in health food stores should be coated inside with a tin that is inert and doesn't cause any problems." They *should* be, but that doesn't mean they always are. Check with the manufacturer.

Before ending this label-reading discussion, let us examine an idea you may have read elsewhere. There's a popular catchphrase that much of the general public has unfortunately latched onto: "Don't eat anything you can't pronounce." This phrase may have originated with some well-meaning person who wanted to warn the public against the use of unnatural chemicals.

Now, I'm going to list a few ingredients on the labels of the pet foods I happen to use as a supplement for my pets. If you're new to the field of nutrition, I'd be surprised if these ingredients don't sound suspiciously like unnatural chemicals to you, and if you aren't a little unsure of how to pronounce them. How about riboflavin, choline chloride, thiamine hydrochloride, pyridoxine hydrochloride? They're B-vitamins. Ferrous gluconate? That's an excellent form of the necessary mineral iron. So, not every substance with a multisyllabic name is a hazard.

You will find on page 177 a list of some of the new, purer prepared foods that our orthomolecular veterinarians themselves recommend to their clients and use for their own pets. Also included is information on how you can order these products if stores near you don't stock them.

A VEGETARIAN DIET FOR YOUR PET

If you are a vegetarian because you do not believe meat is healthy for human beings, I hope you will carefully read Chapters 1 and 2 to evaluate how your pet's natural needs differ from yours.

If you are loath to feed meat to your pet because you do not believe in contributing to the slaughter of other animals, I can offer no argument. For you, I am including in this book some recommendations for an optimal vegetarian diet for your pet, although one of our veterinarians chastised me for this, calling the inclusion "contradictory." However, a well-devised vegetarian diet—although not your pet's natural diet—is preferable to fake supermarket foods.

In order to give you the benefit of the best possible advice, I have chosen these recommendations from the authority I found who believes most strongly in vegetarian diets for dogs and cats. She is animal nutritionist Kathy Berman, who has been formulating vegetarian diets extensively for her clients' pets for a number of years.

In a long correspondence, Ms. Berman writes me: "Vegetarian diets are not only feasible but extremely practicable in terms of simplicity, economics, and disease prevention for both your dogs and your cats. By vegetarian diets I do not mean sending Rover or Morris out to the backyard to graze randomly on the lush vegetation, replete with chemical fertilizers, insecticides, etc. . . . Even the organically cultivated backyard does not contain enough nutritional variety for your vegetarian animal to thrive on. . . .

"With vegetarianism, we must remember that variety is the key to success. We must be sure to offer healthful proteins to our cats and dogs. Therefore, I strongly feel that the diet must be lacto-ovo vegetarian and not purely vegan or fruitarian. . . .

"Choices of main protein for the vegetarian dog and cat will include eggs, yogurt, tofu, cottage cheese, farmer cheese, ricotta, feta cheese, lappi, mild cheddar, muenster, edam, gouda, swiss, or any other natural, unprocessed cheese; nut and seed butters including peanut, sunflower, sesame, and almond. Just about any seed or nut that you can pulverize or process as a butter will serve as a good source of the main protein for that meal. Avocado is a fruit that can serve on occasion as the main protein, also. It is high in fats and very useful for puppies and kittens, along with mashed bananas, in a weaning ration.

"The main heavy proteins mentioned should not be mixed together three or four at a time. The body's digestive enzymes do their most efficient work on a simple diet of one or two main heavy proteins, complemented by vegetable fare.

"For your vegetable foods, there is really a great variety to choose from. The key is to serve these vegetables raw and grated up, initially. This is partly so that the dog or cat can't pick the vegetable out of his or her food, and partly for increased digestibility. . . . Some of the vegetables that I have found to be most successful are: raw carrots, beets, cucumbers, broccoli, zucchini, peppers, cauliflower, turnips, celery (tops, stems, and roots), parsley (leaves and roots), parsnip (roots), romaine lettuce, dandelion, bok choy, chicory, fennel, sweet potatoes, spinach, tomatoes, and corn fresh off the cob.

"From the mustard oil family, we have onions, garlic, watercress, radishes (black, red, white), mustard greens, scallions, horseradish root. These pungent vegetables are most optimally used in small daily amounts during the summer months to clean out the intestinal environment. A filthy and stagnant intestinal environment provides the ideal breeding ground for parasites such as roundworm, whipworm, hookworm, and tapeworm. . . .

"Animals need unsaturated fats in their diets, as well as the saturated fats of animal products (yogurt, cheese, eggs, etc.). Good daily dietary supplemental unsaturated oils are safflower, corn, olive, sesame, avocado, and sunflower. Use an expeller processed oil from a health food store, such as Erewhon, Arrowhead Mills, or Hain. The supermarket brands are very inferior in nutritive value. . . . Anywhere from a half-teaspoon to a tablespoon can be used as a daily addition for your cats and dogs.

"The herbs that I use most frequently in the daily regime of dogs and cats include alfalfa, kelp, comfrey, red raspberry, dandelion, couch grass, corn silk, rosemary, sage and thyme. . . . The application of herbology to existing diseases, however, is very complex and must be studied extensively in order to be used as a viable specific against disease."

The animal nutritionist adds that some dogs and cats take a long time to accept the new, vegetarian diet. These are mainly, she says, "the junk food junkies, with very perverted taste buds." However, "most owners are shocked at how enthusiastic their animals are over their new diet. Many dogs and cats I have counseled into this diet," she says, "turned out to have been closet vegetarians all the time."

The nutritional veterinarians I surveyed agreed with Ms. Berman's recommendations for a vegetarian diet. Drs. Robert and Marty Goldstein added the observation that some pets, when placed on a vegetarian diet, will tend to gain or to lose weight. Therefore, owners should keep an eye on the pet's weight for a while, and add or subtract calories as needed.

The doctors Goldstein also add: "Each animal is an individual. We have found some animals who are put on a vegetarian diet do poorly, and we have had to put some meat back into their diet." The occasionally poor adaptation to a vegetarian diet is especially true of cats, the two veterinarians tell me. This is not surprising in view of the fact—as previously mentioned—that cats are more truly carnivores (meat eaters) than are dogs.

The veterinarians who worked with me on this chapter have given you detailed information to use to give your cat or dog a supremely healthy and long life. Now let us investigate ways to keep your pet in prime health during critical times, such as pregnancy and old age.

REFERENCES

1. Wendell O. Belfield, D.V.M., *Let's LIVE*, July 1980, p. 139.
2. Jonathan Rothschild, *Let's LIVE*, January 1982.
3. Wendell O. Belfield, D.V.M. and Martin Zucker, *How to Have a Healthier Dog* (Garden City, New York: Doubleday and Co., Inc., 1981), p. 157.
4. Belfield and Zucker, *op. cit.*, p. 154.
5. Carl C. Pfeiffer, Ph.D., M.D., *Mental and Elemental Nutrients* (New Canaan, Connecticut: Keats Publishing), 1975, p. 331.
6. See, for instance, the following studies cited by John A. Yiamouyiannis, Ph.D., in *Let's LIVE*, June 1975, pp. 58, 59: *Nippon Sakumotsu Gakkai Kiju*, 32(2):132–8 (1963); *Genetics*, 48:307–10 (1963); and *Proc. Soc. Exptl. Biol. Med.*, 119:252–5 (1965).
7. Jim Sibbison, *Bestways*, April 1982, p. 42.
8. *Natural Animal Care*, NR Products Ltd., Star Rte., Box 348, Placitas, NM 87043.

CHAPTER THREE

Special Diets for Special Times in Your Pet's Life

JOHN E. CRAIGE, V.M.D.;
H. H. ROBERTSON,
D.V.M.; and RICHARD J.
KEARNS, D.V.M.:
*"Dead mothers and dead babies:
We seldom see them anymore if
the mother is fed a natural diet
with supplements."*

ROBERT GOLDSTEIN,
V.M.D., AND MARTY
GOLDSTEIN, D.V.M.:
*"Many people come to us with
old, degenerated pets for whom
other vets have told them there
is 'no hope.' When the owners
see how their pets become
young again—and recover from
the 'hopeless' disorders—they
start taking themselves and
their families to nutritionally
oriented physicians. They
realize that 'If nutritional
medicine can work wonders for
my pet, it can work wonders
for us, too.'"*

HOW TO PREVENT PROBLEMS OF
PREGNANCY AND BIRTH

It may surprise you to know that nutritional veterinarians have found that many of the "nonpreventable" pregnancy problems and deaths just suddenly stop occurring when simple vitamin and mineral supplementation is given once a day. It may interest you to know, too, that forward-thinking doctors have for decades been reporting the same sudden disappearance of pregnancy problems and deaths in human mothers, not only in clinical results but in scientifically conducted studies.

Even if you're quite positive you have had your dog or cat on the optimal preventive diet (Chapter 2) for quite a while, all the nutritional veterinarians I talked with agree that her pregnancy is a time you *must* add supplements. This is a time of extreme stress to the mother's body, which no reader who has borne a child needs to be told. And it's not such an easy time for the unborn babies, either.

It doesn't take too much imagination, really, to realize that one body that is now suddenly trying to provide for up to a dozen more bodies needs some help. Nutrients that have been sufficient to keep one body running smoothly aren't going to become, magically, enough to keep several more going nicely. Someone's body is going to have to be robbed—probably both the mother's body and the tiny developing bodies—and everybody is going to suffer.

Orthodox veterinarians, of course, recognize this fact. As a result, many books you read today will tell you that the prospective or nursing mother should increase her food, sometimes to three or more times her normal amount. However, nutritional veterinarians believe it is not a greater quantity the mother is desperately seeking when she starts wolfing down triple the amount of food, but more nutrients. Indeed, most of the nutritional veterinarians I asked told me they find that the mothers-to-be in their practices generally choose to eat only a little more than they normally do, when they are given a supplement.

Whether or not your individual pet chooses to eat more during her confinement, it would be of optimal benefit to your pet if you divide her food up into four or five smaller meals a day, rather than feeding her one or two larger meals. Large meals can overload a mother's stomach, already being crowded by her growing babies, and can cause serious digestive problems. Also, be sure to offer the mother-to-be more water. It will help to flush out her kidneys. You must realize that her kidneys are at this time not only flushing out her own wastes, but also those of her fast-forming babies.

Returning to the subject of preventing birth problems with supplementation: for those of you who like experimental rather than clinical proof of medical statements, let me point out just a few of the many studies proving that vitamin deficiencies can cause birth problems and that supplementation can help prevent them. One experiment deliberately fed too little vitamin A to a number of pigs. One sow thereupon presented to the world eleven baby pigs—all without eyeballs. Other pigs in the experiment produced piglets with such birth defects as cleft palates and too many ears. When experimenters put enough vitamin A back into their diets, the same pigs produced healthy offspring.[1] This nutritional experiment was run more than a half-century ago.

A number of studies have been run concerning birth problems and wheat germ oil, which has a high vitamin E content and contains another natural substance, octacosanol. I have on my desk scientific studies going back to 1926 on cattle, branching off to studies with human beings in 1937, and continuing on to present-day studies. Some of the results of the human studies show premature births reduced to half their previous level when wheat germ oil was given, babies' deaths in emergency resuscitation entirely eliminated, miscarriages almost halved, and only twenty percent of the "usual" number of babies born dead.[2]

However, it is not the basic goal of this book to prevent laboratory studies, but rather to concentrate on the daily *practical* results being obtained by nutritional veterinarians who have built the large number of laboratory studies into the daily saving of lives. Only from time to time will I refer to laboratory studies as a reminder that the veterinarians specializing in this new field of medicine have not built their practice out of thin air.

Your pet may be happily nursing her little ones and suddenly develop muscle spasms, a high temperature, and convulsions—symptoms of eclampsia. She may die. The least that can happen is that your new mother's milk production stops and she rejects her babies. Veterinarians estimate that every time your dog has puppies, she has one chance out of twenty of developing this condition. Yet nutritional veterinarians such as Richard J. Kearns, D.V.M.; H. H. Robertson, D.V.M.; Nino Aloro, D.V.M.; Robert Goldstein, V.M.D.; and Marty Goldstein, D.V.M., report that they have yet to see *one case* of eclampsia in an animal on a proper supplementation program.

Also, nutritional veterinarians such as Dr. Kearns rarely find litter runts. Whelping time is cut in half; pets who could never breed suddenly breed, even with the same mate; and uterine atony has virtually disappeared. (Atony is a weakening of the uterus during the birth process that traps the tiny puppy in the uterus without oxygen. Obviously the puppy dies, or at best survives with severe brain damage.)

Furthermore, orthomolecular veterinarians and nutritionally minded breeders report the virtual disappearance of many birth defects: cleft palates, "swimmers" (puppies who are huge and, as Wendell O. Belfield, D.V.M., puts it, just "lie around in the litter box, feet sprawled out and helpless,")[3] and puppies born with only a thin covering of skin over the brain (usually these puppies die when the tiniest pressure touches this part of the brain.)[4] Dr. Kearns adds that when the mother cat has been properly fed and given the right supplements, there is a virtual disappearance of kittens born with malformed legs and tails, spinal curvatures, and other birth defects.

Cesarean operations are often done in a last-ditch attempt to save the mother's life and/or the lives of her little ones when birth complications result, just as such operations are performed on human mothers. Dr. Belfield offers his clients with newly pregnant animals a choice: "You can pay a few dollars for some vitamins now or pay $250 or more for a cesarean operation later on." With the simple vitamin and mineral supplementation, Dr. Belfield reports he has cut the number of cesarean operations he has had to perform by at least ninety-five percent.[5] Joseph Stuart, D.V.M., tells me he has found similar results in his practice.

Now what can you do to save your pet and the little ones still sheltered in her body from the horrors we've been describing? While such "miracle-working" might seem like hard work, it isn't. Simply purchase a bottle of dog or cat multivitamin and multimineral pills from a health food store, your own veterinarian, or even a pet store. Give the pills as directed. Please do not double or triple the recommended amounts at your own discretion. Contrary to popular simplistic thinking, it *is* possible to overdose your pet—and yourself—with vitamins and minerals.

However, as we discuss elsewhere, the pet multivitamin and mineral pill you purchase will most probably contain no vitamin C at all and will probably contain too little E for your pregnant pet and her unborn offspring. (As I touched on briefly, vitamin E has been shown to be especially helpful for preventing problems connected with pregnancy and birth.) Dr. Belfield recommends adding the following amount of C for the pregnant dog: for the small dog, 1,500 mg; medium, 3,000 mg; large, 6,000 mg; giant, 7,500 mg. The doctor recommends adding the following amounts of vitamin E: for the small dog, 100 IU; medium, 200 IU; large, 400 IU; giant, 600 IU.[6]

FOODS AND SUPPLEMENTS FOR LACTATING DOGS

The same recommendations regarding vitamins and number of feedings are given as for the pregnant pet.

Oats should be a high proportion of the "working mother's" cereal allotment, because this food helps produce breast milk. So do goat's milk and grated raw carrots. For those of you interested in herbs, let me say that the marshmallow plant and fennel will also help mothers produce milk. A bit of garlic in mama's food will pass itself along in her milk to help prevent worms in her babies.

THE OPTIMAL PREVENTIVE DIET FOR PUPPIES

Until you begin weaning the pups, relax and leave all feeding worries to the mother. After all, she'll be feeding her little ones with the same natural food she would be feeding them in the wild. Of course, I'm assuming you're feeding mama her natural diet so that the milk she produces will have a minimum of poisons and a maximum of nutrients and antibodies.

If you're dealing with orphaned babies, DON'T FEED THEM WITH PLAIN OLD COW'S MILK. The milk they would be getting from their mother is, not surprisingly, not cow's milk; it's dog's milk. Dog's milk is richer in protein and fat and has less of the offending milk sugar lactose in it. A number of nutritional veterinarians recommend goat's milk as being the closest thing to dog's milk.

If you can't get goat's milk (available in health food stores), you can get special formulas approximating your pet's mother's milk from your veterinarian or even some grocery stores. Dr. Aloro recommends preparing the following old baby formula, which has more of the desirable protein and fat than cow's milk: Blend 4 ounces evaporated milk, 4 ounces water, 1 egg yolk (*no egg white,* which can make two of the B-vitamins unusable by the body), and 1 tablespoon raw honey. Keep refrigerated, and don't heat before using.

Orphaned puppies have a unique peril to face: the fact that they are not receiving the protective antibodies they should be receiving in their mother's milk. Dr. Kearns recommends that you add thymus extract to their formula, to help build the immune system (10–15 mg daily for each pound of body weight). GIVE ALL SUPPLEMENTS IN DROP (LIQUID) FORM FOR PREWEANED PUPPIES.

A puppy under a week old should be fed every two hours night and day. After the first week, start cutting down very gradually on the number of feedings until you are feeding your four-month-old puppy three times a day. After six months, you should shift to two feedings a day or the "free feeding" method we discussed in Chapter 2.

Michael Kreisberg, D.V.M., adds the following helpful tips on feeding your orphans. "Wake the pups before mealtime and let them eliminate.* Place them on their stomachs when you feed them. Don't let them nurse too rapidly from the bottle, because puppies can get colic just as easily as babies can. Give enough food so that the abdomen is enlarged but not overly distended."

---

*Dr. Aloro adds: "Sometimes, to help elimination, it is necessary to massage lightly the area around the anus with a soft cloth wet with warm water."

As Dr. Kearns has stressed to me, it is vitally important to check with your veterinarian regarding the proper temperature climate for your pups. I'll never forget the grief of a neighbor of mine when she came home to find all seven of her new puppies dead, simply because she had left them near a radiator on a cold day.

Even those few nutritional veterinarians who believe supplements aren't really necessary for an adult pet if he's receiving his natural diet recommended a multivitamin and mineral supplement during the first year of life. When your puppy is older, the nutrients he eats will be used to keep his cells, bones, and organs as they are, but in this first year he needs a lot of extra help so that those bones and organs can grow at almost breakneck speed.

Dr. Belfield recommends adding vitamin C for small breeds: 1 to 6 months—250 mg; 6 months to 1 year—250, eventually to 500 mg. For medium breeds: 1 to 6 months—500, eventually to 1,500 mg. For large breeds: 1 to 4 months—500, eventually to 1,000 mg; 4 to 18 months—1,000, eventually to 3,000 mg. For giant breeds: 1 to 4 months—750, eventually to 2,000 mg; 4 to 18 months—2,000, eventually to 6,000 mg.[7]

DO NOT GIVE TABLETS WHOLE TO A YOUNG PUPPY; ONE MAY CHOKE HIM. Crush the tablets and sprinkle them over his food.

How much should you feed your puppies? Again, there is no such thing as *the* right amount to feed your puppy, because every little body is unique. However, puppies may need as much as three times the adult caloric requirement per pound of body weight. One chart lists the puppy's need as approximately 105 calories per pound at age six weeks, declining to 35 calories at the forty-second week.

This particular chart, you may notice, indicates 35 calories per pound of body weight of adult dog, as opposed to the 50 calories we've previously indicated from another chart. This 35-calorie chart goes to great pains to adjust recommended calorie amounts to specific ages, breeds, and activities. However, this chart, like our nutritional veterinarians, ends up admitting that everything really depends on the individual dog itself.

Of course, our previously recommended rule of thumb—simply to cut down on calories if your pet starts to gain weight—won't hold true for your puppy. After all, if he *doesn't* gain weight, something is pretty drastically wrong.

Simply ask your veterinarian to give you a healthy weight range for your particular puppy's breed at each stage of growth—and step up or cut down on calories if he slips out of that range.

THE PROPER DIET FOR THE OLDER DOG

It's just about axiomatic that you should cut down on your pet's calories when he gets to be about seven years old. One basic reason is that today's processed-food pet starts to slow down at that age; he hasn't the energy or the strength to exercise the way he did when he was a youngster. The reduced exercise, of course, leads to reduced calorie expenditure; and reduced calorie expenditure without reduced calorie intake equals overweight. Which, in turn, can lead to heart disease and other life-threatening disorders, the same as it can in people.

However, if you have been raising your pet for several years on the natural diet proposed in this book, I would urge you *not* to cut down arbitrarily your pet's calorie intake on his seventh birthday. Chances are he will still have the physical energy and the psychological outlook of a puppy, and a curtailment of his calories might result in an emaciated dog.

I know that I myself own a seven-year-old puppy, an eight-year-old puppy, and an eight-year-old kitten—and they go racing around the house and the yard all day (and half the night) like mad. The usual whirrrrrr of energy starts with two black blobs of poodles racing past, pell-mell, in hot pursuit of one gray cat. When they reach the end of the yard, the cat is finally cornered against the fence, "captured." Whereupon the racing whirrrr promptly reverses itself and becomes two black blobs of poodles racing madly away, with one gray cat in hot pursuit.

If you have not before followed the plan suggested in Chapter 2 of offering several smaller meals rather than one or two large ones, you really should consider it now. Chances are, unless your pet was raised from "scratch" on the optimal diet, his stomach muscles are not so strong as they once were, nor are his digestive juices so plentiful. Large meals, therefore, can overwhelm the weaker stomach muscles and digestive juices, and this can result in stomach upsets and poor utilization of nutrients.

You can—and should—help your aging dog, if he has lost many of his teeth, by cutting up his meat for him, as you did when he was a puppy. Half-chewed food will be half-digested food, which means his body won't be utilizing many of the nutrients he takes in.

If you have not had your dog on a multivitamin, multimineral supplement before now, you should start him on one as he enters his later years. Chances are, as he grows older, his body will be able to utilize a smaller proportion of the nutrients he takes in. As is true for dogs of all ages, a multivitamin, multimineral pill made especially for dogs is recommended, preferably obtained from a health food store. Dr. Belfield recommends a higher amount of E for older dogs, however, than he does for dogs of other ages: 200 IU daily for the small dog, 400 IU for the medium and large, and 800 for the giant.[8] Why more vitamin E? For a number of reasons, really, but the basic biochemical effect E has on the body that can help your aging dog is that it slows down oxidation. The process of oxidation is what is mainly responsible for aging; even that yellowed (aging) picture you have in your photo album got that way through oxidation.

Drs. Robert and Marty Goldstein suggest that you add more vitamin C to the supplement than is recommended in Chapter 2 for the adult dog. Your older pet's ability to produce vitamin C in his own body may be diminishing. These two doctors also use superoxide dismutase to prevent the effects of oxidation.

Other nutritional veterinarians such as Dr. Kearns add the natural substance lecithin to the diet of older dogs. This substance helps prevent heart problems and can help dissolve blood clots.

As I said in the Introduction to this book, it is my greatest hope that you will not destroy your pet—no matter what is wrong with him—until you have given nutritional veterinary medicine a chance. This holds true not only for pets dying of the disorders we'll cover in later chapters, but also for pets falling apart in general from the "normal" problems of old age suffered by pets fed poison-laden processed pet food.

Here is the case history of a dying dog who was "born again" through nutritional therapy. (A similar case history can be found in the section on the older cat.) Dr. Belfield tells of Clyde, a ten-year-old collie cross. Clyde could no longer control his bladder. He couldn't control his bowels. He had no energy and he couldn't eat. As if to add a final indignity to the dying Clyde, flies, attracted by his sickness, swarmed constantly around the poor animal's head and body.

Clyde's owner loved him and couldn't stand to see him suffer so. Not knowing that vitamins and minerals have the biochemical potential to rebuild the body, Clyde's owner brought him in to Dr. Belfield and tearfully requested that his beloved pet be put to sleep.

Dr. Belfield asked if the owner would like to try vitamin and mineral supplementation.

It was only a few weeks later that the owner returned to Dr. Belfield's office and reported that Clyde could now control his urine. He could control his bowels. He was running and leaping about.

Clyde's owner had one question, though. Could vitamins and minerals do something like this for human beings, too?

As Dr. Belfield summarized this case history, it had been over a year since Clyde's owner had wanted him put to sleep. Clyde was still doing fine.

And Clyde's owner and the rest of his human family were taking vitamin and mineral supplements.[9]

SUPPLEMENTS TO PROTECT YOUR PREGNANT CAT AND HER UNBORN KITTENS

Again, what has been said in the section about the pregnant dog is relevant for the pregnant cat. Many of today's "nonpreventable" birth defects and complications *are* preventable in the new field of orthomolecular veterinary medicine.

You will, of course, use a multivitamin, multimineral supplement made for cats, though not for dogs; and unless you have a super-giant cat, you'll add the amount of vitamin C recommended for small dogs. However, you should give more vitamin E than is recommended for the small pregnant dog, because cats have a higher need for E than dogs do. The nutritional veterinarians I surveyed recommended 200 to 400 IU a day for the average pregnant cat.

FEEDING ORPHANED KITTENS

As with puppies, cow's milk is *not* an acceptable substitute for the milk of the mother cat, who does not produce cow's milk any more than a mother dog (or a human mother) does. As is true for orphaned puppies, goat's milk is the top recommendation of many of our veterinarians, since goat's milk is much closer to the milk of both dog and cat mothers than is cow's milk. The goat's milk should *not* be diluted. For optimal health of your orphaned kittens, fortify the milk with the following, recommended by the doctors Goldstein: To 2 ounces of goat's milk, add ¼ teaspoon cold pressed sesame oil, ¼ teaspoon unfiltered raw honey, and 1 raw egg yolk (*not* egg white). Dr. Kearns recommends adding *crushed* thymus tablets to help build the all-important immune system.

If it is impossible for you to get goat's milk (which, by the way, is preferable raw), you might substitute Dr. Aloro's condensed milk formula (given in the section on orphaned puppies), which he also recommends for orphaned kittens.

Food should be given every two hours during the first four days of the kittens' lives; every three hours up to two weeks; and every three hours during the day but only once at night between the ages of fourteen and twenty-four days.

The doctors Goldstein make the following point: "Feed the kitten until the abdomen is slightly larger than the chest. DON'T OVERFEED! ! !" You can see by the capital letters and exclamation points how important the doctors feel this point is.

Finally, the weaning of the kittens can start gradually at three or four weeks.

Further tips on feeding orphaned pets can be found under the section, *The Optimal Preventive Diet for Puppies*.

THE OPTIMAL PREVENTIVE DIET FOR KITTENS

Once the kitten is weaned, you should be giving him five small meals a day, including at least two meat or fish meals (remember as always to vary the foods, and especially don't give fish more than twice a week). Goat's milk, raw cow's milk, or yogurt, as we've discussed, is preferable to pasteurized milk. But remember, if the kitty suffers from diarrhea, try eliminating milk products from his diet.

We've recommended for the adult dog and cat that the meat not be cut up. However, your newly weaned kitten still has his baby teeth; it's not until he's an ancient seven months old that he'll get all his strong adult teeth. Therefore, please don't ask your baby cat to struggle with a whole slab of meat; mince it up for him.

As for the amount of food given at each meal, two teaspoonsful of food should be about right. Increase the amount gradually as your kitten grows bigger. (Keep in mind the recommendation of Drs. Robert and Marty Goldstein: "Feed the kitten until the abdomen is slightly larger than the chest. DON'T OVERFEED.") If the kitten still seems greedy for more food, picture the size of its stomach before you're tempted to throw a few more teaspoonsful of food onto his plate: At ten weeks, your little one's stomach is only the size of a walnut! You can see, then, that even an additional "treat" of one extra teaspoonful could extend that walnut-sized tummy almost to the point of bursting.

By the end of three months, you may feed your kitten only four times a day. By now the intensive demand of his body for protein will be reduced somewhat. Now is the time to start adding a small proportion of cut-up vegetables and cooked grains to the diet. Also, by now you don't have to mince the meat into tiny pieces; just chop it into small chunks.

When your kitten gets to be four to six months old, reduce the number of meals to three, cutting down on the amount of milk rather than on the quantity of meat and grains.

By the time your kitten is six months old, you might try two meals a day, and you might begin letting him eat as much as he wants at each meal. As always, though, keep an eye out to see that he is not starting to look fat. Ask your veterinarian for a good weight range for your pet's age and breed and see that he keeps within that range.

As with puppies, nutritional veterinarians recommend a multivitamin-multimineral supplement to help the kitten through all the physical stresses of growing. As mentioned previously, this supplement should *not* be one made for human beings, nor should it be one made for dogs. Cats are neither human nor dogs; they require different proportions of nutrients to keep their bodies in top shape.

Veterinarians suggest you add to the supplement the amount of vitamin C recommended for puppies of the small breed, and 100 to 200 IU of vitamin E, depending on the age and size of your kitten.

SUPPLEMENTS FOR THE OLDER CAT

What is said in the section for the older dog holds true for the older cat, except that you should use a multivitamin and mineral supplement formulated for cats rather than dogs. Increase the amount of vitamin C, and give your mature cat 400 IU of vitamin E, since the cat has a higher requirement for E than does the dog.

And *please* do not assume that your pet has "had it" and is ready for the graveyard before you give the new field of orthomolecular veterinary medicine a chance to work its natural wonders.

Dr. Kearns tells me about Chloe, a fourteen-year-old cat who was saved from a battery of problems generally considered normal in an aged pet (and in their aging owners). These problems began to disappear within two weeks after a fairly simple, natural regimen of diet and supplements was begun.

When Dr. Kearns first saw Chloe (who had been fed all her life on the commercial packaged foods we are urged to feed our cats), she was weak. She wobbled when she walked. She was having trouble going up and down stairs. She had a form of anemia which Dr. Kearns described as "non-regenerative and usually incurable using orthodox therapy." She was fat. Her coat was scruffy. She had above-average blood sugar, partial kidney failure, and uremia. She was having trouble hearing and seeing.

In short, there was very little that *wasn't* wrong with poor Chloe.

Dr. Kearns put Chloe on a diet of brown rice, turkey, liver, and vegetables. He supplemented this with sesame seed oil, vitamins A, C, E, and B-complex, and bioplasma tablets (Schuessler's tissue salts).

In two weeks, Chloe's old-age problems had begun to disappear. Sight, hearing, and walking had improved. Blood sugar was normal, and kidney function tests were in the normal-to-low range. The "usually incurable" anemia was improved. She was acting sprightly and had regained a long-lost interest in her world. Dr. Kearns describes her overall behavior—not as that of a healthy cat—but as that of a "healthy kitten." In another five months she was also the proud new owner of a beautiful coat of hair and a svelte figure.

A miracle of rebirth? No. Dr. Kearns says: "I feel that the treatment just flushed her system of all the built-up poisons, and that there was enough basic healthy tissue left to generate a healthy body environment."

FEEDING A HALF-STARVED STRAY DOG OR CAT

The animal you find wandering about the street may appear to be half-animal, half-skeleton. If you absolutely cannot take the starving being home with you, any food you may be carrying with you—or can get your hands on quickly—may help keep the animal alive long enough so that he can find an adoptive parent. If you can take the animal home, Dr. Kearns recommends that raw honey and fluids are of prime importance. Maybe a little brandy, raw egg yolks (not whites), and yogurt. "Solid food can always wait."

Probably the easiest, least expensive, and healthiest solid diet you can start your starving stray on a bit later is a diet of cooked chicken or turkey and brown rice. These foods are easily digestible—and we can assume the unlucky fellow is likely to have problems digesting things for a while to come. Also, as we discussed earlier, fowl and brown rice are high in nutrients. Kathy Berman, an animal nutritionist, recommends that you do not feed the chicken or turkey in the same meal with the rice.

Raw foods are not recommended for your half-starved pet, partly because raw foods would probably be a sudden drastic change of diet for him. Chances are his previous owners didn't feed him the delicacies of a natural diet.

Do give a multivitamin, multimineral supplement daily to your new pet. I call him your new pet, even though you may be quite sure you are just keeping the abandoned animal a few days until you can find some way to get rid of him. If you're like many of us, he *will* become your new pet.

Please don't succumb to the "commonsense" idea of letting your half-starved foundling eat unrestrainedly. Give small feedings, four to eight times a day at first. And gradually add just a little bit more food at a time. Dr. Aloro says, "It may take as long as ten days before a half-starved dog or cat can be trusted not to harm himself by overeating."

This deserves repeating: Do *not* let the half-starved animal eat unrestrainedly, no matter how pathetic he may look. You could be leading him, as Dr. Kearns points out, to protein poisoning, inhalation pneumonia, convulsions, and other problems.

REFERENCES

1. Fred Hale, "Pigs Born Without Eyeballs," *J. of Heredity*, March 1933, p. 105.
2. Carlson Wade, *The Rejuvenation Vitamin* (New York: Award Books), 1970, p. 122.
3. Wendell O. Belfield, D.V.M., and Martin Zucker, *How to Have a Healthier Dog* (Garden City, New York: Doubleday and Co., Inc.), 1981, p. 107.
4. *Ibid.*, p. 108.
5. *Ibid.*, p. 110.
6. *Ibid.*, pp. 157, 158.
7. *Ibid.*, p. 156.
8. *Ibid.*, p. 159.
9. *Ibid.*, p. 141.

CHAPTER FOUR

Arthritis and Other Crippling Disorders

R. GEOFFREY BRODERICK, D.V.M.:
"I haven't had a single case of hip dysplasia since I started using vitamin C for prevention five years ago. Before that, I used to do one or two dysplasia operations every week."

WENDELL O. BELFIELD, D.V.M.:
"In the more serious cases [of ruptured discs], my routine approach is to inject the downed dog with sodium ascorbate [vitamin C] for three to five days. Normally this is all the time it takes to bring the animal back to its feet." [1]

RICHARD J. KEARNS, D.V.M.:
"I believe all cases of spinal myelopathy and wobbler's syndrome are caused by poor nutrition . . . sometimes going back to the mother's nutrition during pregnancy."

ARTHRITIS

As I recounted in the Introduction, two "hopeless" cases of arthritis that responded totally to natural therapy inspired this book. Arthritis can be crippling and it can be extremely painful. It is one of those disorders that seldom occur in animals on the natural diet.

Case Histories of Arthritis

For this chapter, I was treated to a packet of case histories from the practice of Robert Goldstein, V.M.D., and Marty Goldstein, D.V.M., brothers who share offices in upstate New York. Unlike the other case histories summarized throughout the book, these were not written up by the doctors; instead, they were taken from touching letters of thanks from the pet owners themselves. I found it a nice change of pace to read these intensely felt summaries of pets' recoveries written by the people who most closely watched—and were most closely affected by—the recoveries.*

As we have said previously, nutritional veterinarians often do not get to see a pet for the first time until he has already been pronounced "unable to be helped" by orthodox veterinary medicine. Such was the case with Sirius. For several years he had been the victim of hip dysplasia, which was later complicated with arthritis. He also suffered from severe allergic dermatitis, a serious skin disorder. For three years the dog would become so cramped with arthritis that, in the words of his owners, he "could hardly hobble around." In addition, for the last year before seeing a nutritional veterinarian, "he seemed to have constantly had a cold."

Sirius had been treated for three years at an animal hospital that the owners describe ruefully as "well respected (and expensive)." At the end of the three years of expensive treatment, Sirius was "visibly worse." Not only was Sirius deteriorating after the years of multiple blood tests, dips, X rays, and drugs, but the two doctors working with Sirius even gave conflicting diagnoses as to what his problem was.

Finally, Sirius was placed on the natural therapy that the doctors Goldstein recommended after running scientific tests to see what nutrients, specifically, Sirius needed. The owners report that Sirius, who for three years could hardly hobble around much of the time, "will run and play at every opportunity." His skin problem has improved also. Sirius's family writes,

---

*I have had the doctors check over these case histories to prevent mistakes caused by subjectivity and lack of medical knowlege on the part of the owners. The owners' summaries also originally lacked some details that I have had the doctors supply.

with an exclamation point, "This happened in two and a half months!" You can well understand the owners' feelings behind the exclamation point, when you compare two and a half months to the previous three years of spending a lot of money only to see their dog deteriorating before their eyes.

The owners add that friends watching the dog's breakfast being put out in front of him will comment, "I should eat as well as this dog." Sirius's breakfast often consists of oats, fruit, and honey. A typical American human breakfast is a sugar-laden Danish and caffeine-laden coffee. If the friends eat this typical American breakfast, I hope they see the irony in their own statement: They *should* eat as well as that dog.

Alas is a golden retriever, and I wonder if she was named Alas because of the fact that she began her stay in this world with the serious crippling disorder, hip dysplasia. When our present story opens, Alas was thirteen years old and the dysplasia had developed into secondary arthritis. As have virtually all the pets mentioned in case histories in this book, she had been raised on the "nutritionally complete" commercial pet foods.

Alas, at thirteen, found it an impossible task to get up from a lying-down position. She had to be helped to walk; she had to be helped, her owners state, "even to move." You can put yourself in the owners' position. You have an old dog who is in almost constant severe pain. You have to interrupt everything you're doing every time she wants to eat, every time she needs to urinate, almost every time she wants to shift her position. The only "sensible" solution for Alas and for yourself would certainly seem to be to put her to sleep for good.

However, the owners didn't choose this "sensible" solution. They went to Drs. Robert and Marty Goldstein. Six months after the veterinarians put Alas on a natural diet with vitamin and mineral supplements, the owners wrote to the doctors: "We cannot believe she is the same animal we brought to you six months ago."

As we state many times in this book, natural therapies rebuild the total health of the body, rather than attacking individual symptoms, as surgery and drugs tend to do; thus, pets who are treated by nutritional veterinarians for one disorder very often surprise their owners by having other problems clear up as well. After six months under the doctors Goldstein's care, Alas had lost fifteen pounds of overweight; the rash on her skin had cleared up; her coat was better looking; her ear infections had disappeared; and she was no longer hyperactive.

Yes, you may say, but she was being treated because she was so crippled with arthritis that she couldn't even move without help. The owners report after six months that Alas now "actually runs like a pup."

As for her additional bonuses of a new, svelte figure, a new blemish-free skin, and a prettier coat, the owners add an observation that is nonscientific but which, as a writer and as a pet owner, I like: "She appears to be extremely happy with her new image."

Guidelines for Treating Arthritis and
Other Crippling Disorders

As is the case with most disorders, any printed therapy can be used only as guidelines for your particular pet. Every individual body chemistry is unique. For instance, my Shiki has for seven years remained symptom-free of what a veterinarian at one of the country's most esteemed animal medical centers had diagnosed as a case of arthritis for which "nothing could be done." This control has been achieved simply by a return to a natural diet, the addition of a multivitamin and mineral pill, and a bit of apple cider vinegar spread over her food every day.* However, I would not dream of guaranteeing that these three steps alone would achieve a similar control for your particular pet. For one thing, Shiki had youth on her side (she was only a year old); for another, she had been on the harmful commercial foods for only a year, and they had not had time to wreak a general degeneration of her entire body. She also happens to have a particularly spunky, devil-may-care personality that leaves her relatively unsusceptible to psychological stress.

Arthritis Therapy

Here are details of an all-out attack against arthritis used by Drs. Robert and Marty Goldstein. It is the basic regimen applied for all the case histories cited in this chapter from the files of these two doctors. However, these doctors—being men of science and not purveyors of a miracle cure-all—use this regimen only as a guideline. They make modifications for each pet after extensive scientific testing of individual body chemistry (through urine and hair analyses, blood analyses, etc.)

- **Phase out drugs.** Gradual withdrawal of arthritic drugs, under the supervision of a veterinarian, as the natural therapy begins to "take hold." Not only can these drugs produce harmful side effects,** but, as the doctors Goldstein point out, cortisone and aspirin can cover up the painful *symptoms*, while doing nothing for the disorder itself. Thus, the pet may take to using the diseased joint (which he would not do if the pain were not being artificially covered up), thus causing further degeneration to the joint.
- **Phase out old diet.** Gradual elimination of chemical-filled pro-

---

*If you'd like a technical explanation of how apple cider vinegar can be helpful, here is what the doctors Goldstein say: "The apple cider vinegar effects work mainly through the gastrointestinal tract by supporting the hydrochloric acid concentration, aiding in digestion in the stomach and in restoring the proper acid-base balance for proper colon function."

**Ihor John Basko, D.V.M., lists some of the side effects of cortisone: "Weakening of muscles, including the heart; stress on the kidneys, suppression of the immune system—and decreased healing."

cessed foods and replacement by a natural diet over a period of one or two months.

- **Natural diet.** The new diet should contain: 25% finely chopped fruits or vegetables; 50% flaked grains (brown rice, millet, or oatmeal, soaked in hot water until soft)*; 25% ocean fish (lightly steamed), raw milk or cheese, fertile raw egg yolks, yogurt or cottage cheese. Red meat and chicken should totally be eliminated and perhaps gradually added back to the diet as the animal improves. The doctors Goldstein warn, however, that many arthritic animals cannot tolerate the return of red meat to their diet.
- **Pure water.** Pure steam-distilled water only. Distilled water helps remove undesirable mineral salts from the joints. Do not allow your pet access to water during the meal or for one hour before or after.
- **Fasting.** This gives the digestive processes a rest and allows the body to eliminate stored toxins. The doctors recommend a thirty-six-hour fast weekly and a two- to three-day fast every three months. The fast consists of removal of solid foods and the offering of steam-distilled water, fresh carrot and celery juice, or a broth made by adding the skin of four potatoes to one quart of distilled water and simmering for fifteen minutes. A FAST SHOULD BE ADMINISTERED ONLY UNDER THE SUPERVISION OF A VETERINARIAN EXPERIENCED IN PRESCRIBING FASTS.
- **Supplementation.** For a thirty-pound dog, based on two meals a day: brewer's yeast, 2 teaspoonsful per meal; kelp, 1 teaspoonful per meal or 3 tablets per meal; whey (preferably goat's), 2 teaspoonsful per meal; vitamin C, 1,500 mg per day; vitamin E, 200 IU per day; pantothenic acid, 200 mg per day; bone meal or eggshell, 1 tablet per meal; cod liver oil (cold pressed), 1 teaspoon per meal; wheat germ oil (cold pressed), 1 teaspoon per meal; lecithin (granules or liquid), 1 teaspoon per meal; vitamin A/D, 5,000/400 IU, 1 capsule per meal. As the animal improves, these dosages can be adjusted downward to minimum daily maintenance dosages.
- **Massage.** Finger massage of affected joints will increase circulation and therefore help promote healing.
- **Exercise.** Moderate outdoor exercise daily. Perhaps a fifteen-minute walk twice a day.

In addition, veterinarians such as S. Allen Price, D.V.M., and the doctors Goldstein often find SOD (superoxide dismutase) helpful. SOD is an enzyme, produced naturally in the body, that helps destroy harmful free radicals that contribute to degenerative diseases such as arthritis. The

---

*Grains may be replaced by chemical-free dog foods, such as Cornucopia, Solid Gold, or Lick Your Chops. See page 177 for how to obtain these foods.

Goldsteins state that improper diet can deplete the body of its natural supply of SOD, and external SOD supplementation may be necessary.*

Dr. Price is also careful to keep the salt content of the diet extremely low, since salt can help increase pain. This veterinarian also tells me: "I have very good success in pain alleviation with castor oil packs over the joints. This is quite simple to do. Just soak cotton in castor oil, wrap the cotton around the affected limb, and secure it with bandages. Leave the pet's toes outside the bandage; the pet will continue to walk as long as he can feel his toes touching the ground." The castor oil increases circulation, and increased circulation promotes healing. The oil also decreases the inflammation which causes pain.

THE CASE OF THE "MYSTERY" CRIPPLER

The following is a case history of a severely advanced case of collagen destruction. Orthodox veterinarians were not able to offer a clear-cut diagnosis, and neither were the orthomolecular veterinarians I asked. However, this case demonstrates that, if you treat the underlying CAUSE of a problem, you don't always have to know the precise "label" for that problem.

What's collagen? It's a protein substance that acts as the body's cement; it is connective tissue that literally holds the parts of your body together. Frank L. Earl, D.V.M., gave me a vivid description of dogs with severe collagen problems: "They look like they've become unglued; they look like they're falling apart before your eyes." Without collagen, we would all— people and animal alike—literally fall apart. Our bodies would collapse into hundreds of uncoordinated, unconnected pieces. Imagine trying to walk if your body parts weren't connected together. Imagine trying to do *anything*.

Many of us—and many of our pets—are walking around (or trying to) with various stages of collagen disorders. Collagen disorders in human beings include rheumatoid arthritis, rheumatic fever, and a condition characterized by anemia, hemorrhages into the skin, and bizarre central nervous system symptoms (thrombotic purpura).

As you read this case history, you might substitute your pet's name for the name of the dog who actually had to go through all this. I think you will have little trouble empathizing with the frustration and sorrow (and expense) the owner endured for almost two years while a total of six veterinarians attempted to help the dog . . . until the pet was brought to an orthomolecular veterinarian.

At which point in this story would you have put your pet out of its misery?

Heather is a female Doberman pinscher who resides near Annapolis,

---

*Veterinarians: Please see "Of Interest Mainly to Veterinarians," Note 1, at the end of the chapter.

Maryland. Heather was nine years old when everything started to go wrong with her world. In February of 1979 she fell and later began having difficulty walking up and down the steps in her house. A local veterinarian assumed the walking difficulty was the result of the fall; no one questioned whether a physical problem had made her fall in the first place.

Four months later Heather developed a urinary infection. And she started falling when she went outside to urinate. Nine months after that, Heather began to howl and tremble in pain as she walked. She could not see in front of her. If you tossed something at her, she would just stand and let it hit her nose, because she couldn't see it coming.

Heather's personality changed, as will human personalities when we are constantly sick and in pain. Children whom Heather had once considered her "pets," now terrified her. If anyone raised a voice in her presence, she would go into a panic.

While Heather's blindness cleared up in a week, her other problems did not. The next month she was no longer able to perform one of her favorite pastimes, leaping to and fro over a batch of plants. Her rear legs were definitely stiffening.

Nineteen months after the beginning of Heather's ordeal, it had become a terrible chore for her just to walk across the floor; her legs were now slipping out from under her, and she kept falling down in a heap, her legs flailing helter-skelter. At one point, she went into a spasm; her body was contorted into the shape of a "doughnut," as Dr. Earl's file describes it. For a full five minutes her owner stood and watched helplessly as the dog suffered a cramp that glued her nose to her tail.

At this point, an orthodox veterinarian finally thought he had found something wrong: spinal degeneration. Thereupon Heather was taken to a well-known university school of veterinary medicine. However, there they couldn't find anything wrong with her spine.

A month later Heather's limbs started rotating outward in a grotesque manner and her legs slipped out from under her as if they were made of jelly. That last phrase may have rung a bell: yes, Heather's body was becoming "unglued." As we discussed early in this section, collagen is the body's "glue."

In November of 1980 Heather was returned to the university hospital, where a veterinarian (the sixth to try to help the dog) noted something in the X rays that other veterinarians had not seen: damage to part of the spine. The veterinarian prescribed the drug prednisolone. The drug kept the symptoms somewhat in check for a very short period. But when a dosage was missed, Heather would regress rapidly. Even while she was taking the drug, Heather's bladder problems did not improve; she was spending her nights miserably trying to sleep on a bed of wet blankets.

By December, Heather had become progressively worse on the drug and was scheduled for a decompression operation on her spinal cord. As you might guess, operations on the delicate spinal cord are among the most dangerous.

If you took my suggestion and have been substituting your pet's name for Heather's throughout this story, you also would have been substituting yourself for the owner. What would you do at this point? Go ahead with the dangerous, expensive operation? Have Heather put out of her misery with a lethal injection? Give up fighting and let Heather slowly die a "natural" death as a helpless cripple?

Heather's owner chose none of the above. She decided to try the new field of orthomolecular (nutritional) veterinary medicine. As we point out elsewhere, many owners, like Heather's, don't try this new field until they—and their pets—have reached the end of their ropes under orthodox care. The often astounding results orthomolecular medicine achieves become even more astounding when you consider that this field of medicine is very often dealing with the "hopeless" cases of traditional medicine.

Nutritional veterinarian Dr. Earl first saw Heather almost two years after the onset of her disease. His first observation of Heather, which I have from his files, noted a classic appearance of collagen disorder (which had escaped the previous six veterinarians). Dr. Earl wrote on that first visit: "She presents the appearance of a dog whose tendons and ligaments will not support the body; they are very flaccid." On January 5, 1981, Dr. Earl began a five-day treatment of twice-daily intravenous injections of vitamin C (sodium ascorbate), starting with 5 grams twice a day and building to 7.5 grams twice a day by the third day.

On the third day, Heather's bladder incontinence had improved by ninety percent. On the fourth day, it disappeared completely.

As of last report, over a year and a half after Heather happened into the nutritional veterinarian's office, she continues with no symptoms. She sleeps happily in a dry bed; her legs behave themselves, and she walks like a proper lady, instead of flailing and landing in a heap on the floor. And in case you haven't guessed, Heather never did have that "necessary" operation on her spine.*

Heather has been maintained on 1,000 milligrams of vitamin C given by mouth twice a day in addition to a Mega-C Plus supplement available from Wendell O. Belfield, D.V.M., which contains, among other nutrients, 3,000 milligrams of C. (See the Appendix to find out how to obtain this product.) She is also being maintained on Advanced Nutritional Formula, cod liver oil, and four tablets of Dolomite (calcium and magnesium) a day.

Jack Long, V.M.D., reports that, in treating cases similar to Heather's, he uses acupuncture in conjunction with oral vitamin supplements (especially ascorbate zinc and B-complex). He states that the combination

---

*Veterinarians: Please see "Of Interest Mainly to Veterinarians," Note 2, at the end of the chapter.

therapy has resulted in "excellent results in four out of five of these 'wobbler' (or cervical syndrome) cases."

"Most of these animals," Dr. Long says, "have been previously treated with steroids with no improvement. Some have had myelograms showing narrowing of the cervical spinal canal—or a spondylolisthesis. There is usually a noticeable, sometimes dramatic, improvement after the first acupuncture treatment. Only six to eight acupuncture treatments are usually required; the pet is then maintained on the nutritional therapy."

Dr. Long adds that the four out of five pets who respond return to completely normal function.

HIP DYSPLASIA

The orthodox treatment for hip dysplasia is drugs and surgery. It is commonly believed that hip dysplasia is hereditary; this belief, of course, makes hip dysplasia appear to be virtually impossible to prevent. Many of this book's orthomolecular veterinarians do not believe hip dysplasia is basically hereditary; and they have discovered how to prevent it. They believe collagen begins to fall apart and cause hip dysplasia when the tissues are starved for vitamin C. You can see that it is much easier to correct a vitamin C deficiency than it is to do anything for a hereditary condition.*

By the way, it was about two centuries ago that it was first discovered that people who died of scurvy, a disorder now universally recognized as due exclusively to a vitamin C deficiency, had loose joints similar to dysplasia—another example of how medical practice can lag behind available knowledge.

After some five years of using vitamin C as a preventive for his patients, R. Geoffrey Broderick, D.V.M., stated that this "nonpreventable," hopeless disorder had disappeared from his practice. "I haven't had a single case of hip dysplasia," he says, "since I started using the vitamin C five years ago."

Dr. Long reports similar results in his practice. "While I still see many cases of dysplasia in dogs, I do not see it in dogs who have taken ascorbate [a form of Vitamin C] as a preventive from puppyhood."

Breeders from all over the world are also starting to announce that hip dysplasia is disappearing from their kennels. As a matter of fact, breeders have often included with their sales of puppies a certificate saying that if a dog turns out to have hip dysplasia, they will replace it free. Now they are starting to write into their agreements that they will *not* guarantee an absence of this disorder unless the pup is raised by the new owners on the needed amount of vitamin C.[2]

Just in case you have read this far in the book and are still finding it hard to believe that none of those "nutritionally complete" supermarket dog or

---

*Dr. Earl believes that a high metabolic *requirement* for vitamin C may be inherited, rather than the disorder itself.

cat foods is nutritionally complete, take a walk through your nearest super-market today and read all the "nutritionally complete" labels. Unless there is a general enlightenment between my writing of this book and your reading of it, chances are you won't find one mention of vitamin C. That's because the general misconception is that all dogs and all cats produce "enough" vitamin C in their own bodies.

Case Histories of Hip Dysplasia

The following pets were all treated according to the same general therapy guidelines Drs. Robert and Marty Goldstein use for arthritis and other degenerative problems. I detail these guidelines elsewhere. It is important to note that the doctors will modify this therapy after extensive testing of the pet in order to fulfill the animal's individual needs.

Taffy, a six-year-old golden retriever, suddenly began having trouble climbing stairs. In only a few short months, things became so bad that Taffy just simply couldn't "make" the stairs at all; and indeed, as her owner puts it, "Taffy hardly moved at all unless she had to."

X rays showed the dread hip dysplasia.

"Literally within days" after Taffy began the natural therapy prescribed by the doctors Goldstein, not only could Taffy move around again, she could even climb the stairs. Taffy's owner wrote, about a month after the natural therapy was begun: "She now runs as much as seven miles a day with me." All this was accomplished without drugs and without surgery.

More often than not—as we will see throughout this book—a natural diet and supplementation prescribed for one health problem will clear up other health problems as well. This is not surprising, because, while drugs and surgery will attempt to attack one disease, natural therapy aims at rebuilding the total health of the body. In this way the body can cure itself, as a healthy body does naturally hundreds of times a day. Taffy's owner reports that Taffy, who had "always been so fat that people often thought she was pregnant" even though she was never overfed, is now the proud owner of a svelte figure. She now has no fleas, and her coat is richer in texture and color.

We mention elsewhere that many clients of nutritional veterinarians have been led to pursue a natural diet and supplementation for themselves after seeing "unbelievable" changes happening to their pets right before their eyes. Taffy's owner had the opposite experience. She had previously helped herself out of severe arthritis and "total" lack of energy by a similar change in her own diet after finding out that her "mysterious" problems were due to extensive food allergies and low blood sugar. "What I can't understand," says Taffy's owner, "is why I didn't make the connection myself and start Taffy on a healthy diet years ago."

Reggie is another golden retriever. Reggie comes from a long line of AKC champions and his parents were both healthy, so you would not expect Reggie to experience early health problems. The owner bought the puppy from a breeder at the age of six weeks, at which time Reggie already seemed lethargic and tired easily. However, the owners didn't equate this "low-key" personality with diet, just as most animal owners don't equate most problems with diet. Therefore the owners, in all good faith, kept their new pet on the same commercial pet food he already had been introduced to by the breeder. The champion-bred, hardy-stock puppy was thereupon embarked upon trips every two weeks to veterinarians because of frequent vomiting attacks. "Hardly any time at all went by when he was not sick," the owners state.

By the time puppy Reggie was all of seven months old, not only was he vomiting much of the time, he had developed a tumor on his face, which was removed surgically. As if all that weren't enough, he was also having trouble getting up from a sitting position (let alone a lying position). The owners could hear "cracking noises" coming from Reggie's rear legs. X rays revealed a severe case of hip dysplasia.

The owners decided against the expensive operation offered them for the hip dysplasia and opted for the natural therapy of the doctors Goldstein. In a month Reggie had stopped having the crippling symptoms of hip dysplasia; he could now stand on all four of his legs with ease. Several months after that, according to his owners, the previously half-crippled Reggie "turned out to be a terrific swimmer." Also, although it was hip dysplasia he was being specifically treated for, he no longer has the vomiting attacks he had suffered so frequently.

You will notice that Drs. Robert and Marty Goldstein contribute a large proportion of the case histories to this chapter. Interestingly, these two veterinarians tell me that it was a crippling case of hip dysplasia in one of their own pets that was responsible for their shifting the emphasis of their practice from orthodox to orthomolecular.

Leigh, Dr. Robert Goldstein's golden retriever, had developed symptoms of hip dysplasia when he was little more than a puppy. It was rated grade 3, radiographically. (The disorder is rated on a scale from 0 to 5; a grade-3 case is a pretty bad one.) Leigh had been fed exclusively one of the "better"—and more expensive—commercial dog foods. By the time he was six years old, he had "much difficulty in getting up," the doctors tell me, "and was in almost constant pain. He also had chronic skin and ear problems. Leigh was getting long-acting cortisone injections every two to three weeks and topical medicines for his dermatitis." Surgery was being considered "as a next step."

Luckily for Leigh—and luckily for all the animals whose case histories are reprinted in this book from the files of the Goldsteins—the veterinarians were at this time studying human nutrition and were "in the process of transforming our own health. After seeing the tremendous improvement in our own general well-being," the doctors tell me, "we decided to adapt the same basic rules for our own pets."

The results for Leigh, the veterinarians say, "were and are still astounding. Leigh is now a thirteen-year-old dog with relatively no problems. And," the doctors add, "he has been off all forms of drug therapy for close to seven years now."

POSTERIOR PARALYSIS
(SPINAL MYELOPATHY, SPINAL DEGENERATION)

If your pet develops this disorder, your orthodox veterinarian will probably ask you how helpless you are willing to let your pet become before you put him to sleep. It will usually not be a question of *whether* to put him to sleep, but *when*. However, there is hope in•the field of nutritional medicine. Dr. Belfield, for instance, reports healing twenty-five out of thirty cases simply with the use of vitamin C[3] and other nutrients.

As I list the symptoms of this devastating disorder, you will easily see why the orthodox veterinary medical profession often prefers to put dogs with this problem out of their misery. (Dr. Belfield makes the following rueful statement about two dogs with spinal myelopathy that orthodox medicine had decided to euthanize: "The irony of these two cases is that thirty years has elapsed between them and the solution has remained the same, euthanasia."[4]

If your pet gets this disorder, here's what he's in for: pain, progressive paralysis of the back leg muscles, curving of the spine, loss of control of his bowels, loss of control of his bladder. If you just touch him on the hindquarters, he may fall down as if you had hit him with a baseball bat. As his back leg muscles deteriorate, your pet will start pathetically trying to drag himself around on just his two front legs. Simply picture your pet with that last symptom, and you will see why owners seldom fight the suggestion of euthanasia for this disorder.

You might think no one disorder could get worse than all this; but spinal myelopathy can progress further, affecting the front legs, so that the dog can no longer even try to drag himself around at all. Then the disorder can progress even further until it affects the brain.

Having thoroughly depressed you with the description of spinal myelopathy, I'd like to change the mood by describing how a pet with this "hopeless" disorder can be helped by a veterinarian using the field of nutritional medicine.

Case Histories of Posterior Paralysis
Kini was an eight-year-old German shepherd. Dr. Belfield had never been able to interest Kini's owner in vitamins. One day this owner walked into Dr. Belfield's office with Kini, who was having trouble walking, was swaying in the hind end, and couldn't jump or rear up.

Dr. Belfield sent Kini and her owner to an orthodox university veterinary center for the sophisticated testing that is often necessary to diagnose specific spinal problems. The university's diagnosis: spinal myelopathy. Their "solution": euthanasia. Kini's owner, faced now with a *fatal* problem, suddenly developed the interest in vitamins that Dr. Belfield had never been able to instill in him for prevention. The owner refused the university's solution and returned, with his pet still alive, to Dr. Belfield for help.

For three days Dr. Belfield administered vitamin C intravenously twice daily. At the end of that time, Kini was eating better and seemed more "together" in the hindquarters. Kini was then put on oral vitamin C and multiple vitamins and minerals. All of two weeks went by before her owner called to report that his pet had already improved so much that he was going to go out and buy "some vitamins" for himself and his wife. He later reported to Dr. Belfield that his long-term migraine problem had been considerably helped by the supplements.[5]

Bowzer is a seven-year-old beagle mix treated by Michael W. Lemmon, D.V.M. "Bowzer came into my office with such extreme weakness in his rear legs," Dr. Lemmon tells me, "that he could not walk at all." Dr. Lemmon used Dr. Belfield's intravenous vitamin C regimen. "After five days on I.V. vitamin C and other nutrients—such as vitamin E, 400 units, and trace minerals*—Bowzer began to walk well enough to be sent home on a regimen of oral vitamin C and a multiple vitamin-mineral supplement." Soon thereafter, the dog began walking absolutely normally—and, Dr. Lemmon tells me, "After nine months, Bowzer continues to have no paralysis." However, Bowzer also continues to take his supplements for maintenance.

Maintenance is important for spinal myelopathy, as it is for many other disorders. By that I mean you cannot expect a few days' intensive treatment to control completely a supposedly "hopeless" disorder. You will have to keep supporting your pet with smaller amounts of the helpful nutrient(s).

Dr. Belfield, again, gives us a case in point. The part German shepherd and part pit bull was a "junkyard dog," a dog so mean that he is used to guard against thieves' entering junkyards. Perhaps because he was a junkyard dog and not a pet, he did not have a full name, just a letter of the alphabet: H.

When Dr. Belfield first saw him, H was suffering from posterior paralysis; and, as the doctor reports, he "looked considerably less than mean." The doctor hospitalized H for a few days and gave him injections of vitamin C (in the form of sodium ascorbate). As the doctor says, "H had been down two days. C got him up in three."

However, the various employees at the junkyard didn't keep up Dr. Belfield's recommended maintenance program of oral supplements. So, a

---

*Richard J. Kearns, D.V.M., believes that the mineral manganese, as well as vitamin C, is of vital importance in treating this disorder.

short time later, H had the symptoms of posterior paralysis all over again, and Dr. Belfield had to repeat the injections. Again, the dog was on his feet again in a few days.

This time, apparently, the owner had learned the lesson. He maintained H on 3 grams of vitamin C a day along with the other nutrients Dr. Belfield had prescribed. At last report, H was his "bristling old people-eating self again."[6]

Another case in point regarding the importance of maintenance therapy is Heather, a dog who went through such hell with collagen problems and has been symptom-free for a year and a half. Once, during this period, Heather was without her maintenance therapy of Mega C Plus for fifteen hours, while she and her owners were in the midst of traveling. Heather's bladder incontinence returned. The incontinence disappeared, however *thirty minutes* after Heather was given, again, her maintenance dosage of Mega C Plus.

Self-help is Possible
(Although Definitely Not Preferable)

If you cannot get your veterinarian to try orthomolecular therapy or to consult with one of the orthomolecular veterinarians listed in the Appendix—and if you cannot yourself get your pet to an orthomolecular veterinarian—you may be able to help your pet by yourself. Your own therapy will take longer, however, than the intravenous injections a veterinarian would be able to administer and may be less likely to be successful.

A case in point again comes from the pioneering work of Dr. Belfield. Kurt was a ten-year-old Doberman whose owner had been told by a large university veterinary school that Kurt would have to be put to sleep. His owner couldn't find a veterinarian in her area who would attempt vitamin C injections. You may find this particularly dismaying, as I do, in light of the fact that Kurt's owner would not be forsaking successful orthodox treatment to try the less orthodox vitamin C injections; Kurt had already been given up on by orthodox medicine.

Kurt's owner phoned Dr. Belfield, who suggested oral vitamin C plus other vitamins and minerals. Several weeks later, the owner called Dr. Belfield to report a minor "miracle": Kurt could turn himself over. Previously the owner had been obliged to ask some neighborhood children to come around to turn her pet over, because Kurt was too heavy for her to move.

After two months of the simple oral therapy, the owner called Dr. Belfield to report that not only could her "hopelessly ill" pet now turn himself over, he was actually "up and walking about." The owner returned Kurt to the same veterinary school that had pronounced Kurt's death sentence. The doctors examined Kurt and ascertained that he seemed to have recovered from the "hopeless" disorder. Their conclusion: "spontaneous recovery." (Spontaneous recovery is a phrase used not infrequently to "explain away" hopeless animals and human patients who recover through the use of nontraditional medicine.)

Kurt remained free of the crippling disorder for another three years, at which time he died of something quite unrelated to a spinal problem.[7]

RUPTURED DISCS

The symptoms of ruptured discs can include those of spinal myelopathy: paralysis in the hindquarters and legs and inability to control bowels and urine. Dr. Belfield recommends that you try the inexpensive nutritional therapy for this problem before you take your pet for expensive and risky spinal surgery.*

The daily addition of vitamins C and E, as suggested in Chapters 2 and 3, will help prevent this problem. Early cases can be effectively controlled with 1,000 milligrams a day of C. You can give this to your pet yourself at home. More serious cases may require injections of vitamin C (in the form of sodium ascorbate) for three to five days. "Normally," says Dr. Belfield, "this is all the time it takes to bring the animal back to its feet."

If a human member of your family suffers from disc damage, you will be glad to know that vitamin C has been helpful for humans also—and for the same reasons that it helps our pets: C strengthens connective tissue and helps make bones and cartilage strong. It also has an analgesic (or pain-killing) effect.

Dr. James Greenwood, Jr., Professor of Neurosurgery at Baylor University, reports that a "significant percentage" of human patients with disc damage have been able to avoid surgery with 750 to 1,000 milligrams of C a day. Dr. Greenwood has also noted that when the vitamin was used in patients undergoing surgery, it greatly reduced the number of reoperations required. Subsequent operations are a common problem with disc patients.[9]

ACUPUNCTURE

This nondrug, nonsurgery technique of healing has been practiced for five thousand years in the East and since the 1700s in Europe. It wasn't until the 1950s that acupuncture slowly began to be accepted into orthodox medical practice in America.

*Drs. Robert and Marty Goldstein, in checking over this book in manuscript form, added a cautionary note here: "We feel that this is a very delicate decision for an owner to make. In those cases in which the ruptured disc is putting a lot of pressure on the spinal cord (those cases in which surgery would definitely be beneficial), waiting days to see if a nutritional program helps could lead to permanent paralysis." They also add—as does Dr. Lemmon—that recent scientifically conducted laboratory studies indicate that manganese can be of primary help in disc diseases.[8]

Unfortunately, acupuncture is often erroneously thought to be of value only for alleviating pain. The truth is that controlled investigations on dogs have shown that acupuncture can have beneficial effects in treating shock, ulcers, and abnormal heart rhythms. Actual case studies have shown that acupuncture can be of value in a wide variety of nervous, reproductive, urinary, digestive, respiratory, and circulatory problems.[10]

It is because acupuncture can be so successful in many cases of crippling disorders that I have chosen to insert the longest discussion of this technique into this chapter.

Case History Using Acupuncture

Thor is a male miniature poodle. In May of 1977, a veterinarian at the Animal Medical Center in New York City wrote to another veterinarian: "Thor presents radiographically as a classic example of spondylosis (chronic degenerative disc disease)." Before this, Thor had been a very active dog and exhibited the poodle breed's particular penchant for walking around on its hind legs. But in February, Thor had begun finding it difficult to put any pressure on his hind legs, even for "regular" walking. He also started falling down frequently.

For three months Thor was treated with the drugs prednisolone, Valium, and aspirin. The drugs seemed to help alleviate his pain but did little to improve his walking. Also, when the drugs were withdrawn for twenty-four hours on several occasions, the poodle had difficulty controlling his bowels and urine and suffered from vomiting and loss of appetite.

In May and June Thor was taken to Dr. Marty Goldstein for two acupuncture treatments. Thor's owner also gave him several acupressure treatments, after having been taught the technique by Dr. Goldstein. By early July, Thor had returned to nearly normal, except he showed "a slight hesitancy" before jumping up on chairs, according to his owners. Five years later, Thor remains free of problems.

How Does Acupuncture Work?

This has not been agreed upon. And this fact still bothers some members of the medical profession, who find it hard to believe that anything *can* work until they first know *how* it works. (For some reason, the fact that very little has been known about how aspirin works has not stopped the mainstream medical community from recommending huge amounts of it every year.)

It has been observed, however, that both blood circulation and the number of white blood cells are increased around the acupuncture point being stimulated. Also, production of endorphins is increased. Endorphins are natural substances which, it has recently been found, help to reduce the perception of pain.

Does Acupuncture Relieve Only the Symptoms,
as Drugs Often Do?

No. The theory behind acupuncture is that symptoms and diseases are the result of disturbances in the normal strength and pattern of energy through the body. As Ihor John Basko, D.V.M., puts it: "We run tests to determine the underlying *causes* of the symptoms. The chosen acupuncture treatment is designed to correct this underlying cause. Acupuncture actually returns the body to a healthy, balanced state where it will heal itself. Since the healing comes from within, it is self-perpetuating."*

Is Acupuncture Expensive?

The doctors Goldstein, who practice in upstate New York, say treatments run $15 to $30. Sheldon Altman, D.V.M., estimates a cost of $20 for the North Hollywood, California area, about the cost of a regular office call plus one vaccination.

However, acupuncture is often used successfully in dogs and cats who are "hopeless" and set for euthanasia. A course of acupuncture treatments will cost more than putting your pet down. It will cost more in dollars, that is. It will, of course, cost substantially less in guilt and sorrow.

You may be able to cut down the number of acupuncture treatments necessary by applying acupressure. Ask your veterinary acupuncturist to show you this technique. Acupressure is based on the same principles as acupuncture but is done with the fingers rather than with needles. It is less effective than acupuncture, but often can be used as a helpful adjunct.

Will Acupuncture Hurt or
Frighten Your Pet?

One of the uses of acupuncture in both pets and people is to deaden pain during surgery, so it would hardly make sense that acupuncture is painful. As for the needles frightening your pet, dogs and cats do not tend to have the apprehension of needles that we do. Both Dr. Basko and Dr. Altman report that often while the needles are inserted in place the animal will snatch the opportunity to take a nap. Dr. Altman says: "About the only time my patients get emotional is when I have accustomed them to a treat after therapy and then don't give them this treat after one particular session. *Then* they put up a fuss and a racket."

A few words of caution here: When you read in this book of a nutritional therapy you feel can help your pet, you can take him to your personal veterinarian—if you don't live near a veterinarian in the new field of or-thomolecular medicine. Your veterinarian can use information in this book

---

*The doctors Goldstein add that if the condition being treated is due to a degenerative metabolism caused by poor nutrition, acupuncture will effect only temporary relief *when the diet is not altered*.

as basic guidelines and then can ask specific questions of one of the orthomolecular veterinarians listed in the back of the book who have agreed to be available for consultation. The same is not true of acupuncture, however. Please do not badger your veterinarian to use acupuncture if he or she is not specifically trained to do so. The doctor will refuse, and rightly so. All the acupuncture points could have been given here, as well as which points are helpful for which disorders, but all such information in the world will not train anyone how *actually to use the needles*. An acupuncture needle in untrained hands can be dangerous to your pet. (This same danger does not exist, of course, if your orthodox veterinarian uses a hypodermic needle to inject, say, vitamin C for distemper. Every veterinarian has been trained to use this latter type of needle; this book and consultation with an orthomolecular veterinarian will show your doctor simply how much C to use, what form, and how often.)

If you elect to try acupuncture for your pet, you can check the list of nutritionally oriented veterinarians at the back of the book to see if there is one near you who uses acupuncture. Or you may write to the International Veterinary Acupuncture Society, 203 Pembroke Place, Box 958, Thomasville, Georgia 31792.*

What Are the Chances That Acupuncture Might Help Your Pet?

As we have said previously, acupuncture has an impressive success rate with a number of disorders. One of the veterinarians working with me on this book has done a large study of acupuncture used alone as treatment for a number of cats and dogs with crippling disorders. I stress *used alone*, because this means the positive effects achieved cannot be attributed to help from any other therapies. That veterinarian, Dr. Altman, uses acupuncture extensively in his practice. Most of the cases in Dr. Altman's study had been treated by conventional methods for a long time—unsuccessfully. Dr. Altman treated most of the cases with acupuncture eleven times or fewer to achieve his positive results. Some of the doctor's results are as follows:

- Paralysis in the small dog: 11 of 27 cases treated had 75–100% improvement; only 10 showed no improvement.
- Central nervous system conditions such as ataxia (muscle incoordination) and chorea (uncontrollable and ceaseless jerky movements): of 12 treated, 1 had 75–100% improvement; 4 had 50–75% improvement; only 4 showed little or no improvement.
- Hip dysplasia: of 18 animals treated, 7 had 75–100% improvement; 5 had 50–75% improvement; only 1 showed little or none.

*Veterinarians: Please see "Of Interest Mainly to Veterinarians," Note 3, at the end of the chapter.

- Arthritis (chronic): of 19 treated, 5 had 75–100% improvement; 4 had 50–75% improvement; only 2 showed little or none.[11]

Let me repeat that most of these animals had not been helped by long-term conventional veterinary therapy, and most were treated with acupuncture by Dr. Altman only eleven or fewer times. Let me also stress that the National Association for Veterinary Acupuncture, of which Dr. Altman is a member of the board of directors, points out that acupuncture and other techniques of veterinary medicine are not mutually exclusive, and that your pet may benefit even more by acupuncture used in conjunction with another therapeutic approach.

The Association has other impressive statistics to report:

- Intervertebral disc syndrome: a sixty percent success rate *in chronic cases of long duration in which either surgery or conservative treatment has already been tried.*
- Arthritis: "Approximately fifty-five percent of the cases respond. Again, the cases that have been referred to us are usually the worst cases—the cases that have not responded to conventional Western therapy," reports the Association.*

In the beginning of this section, I gave a partial list of disorders—other than crippling disorders—that acupuncture has been shown to help. The Association adds to my list: "Acupuncture has been used to treat a number of other conditions, including certain eye problems, dermatitis, deafness, and general debilitation of old age, and epilepsy. In fact, about the only thing that acupuncture is not recommended for is acute infections."[12]

---

*Dr. Basko states that these successful results for intervertebral disc syndrome and arthritis can be improved by twenty to forty percent when acupuncture is used along with Chinese herbal therapy.

OF INTEREST MAINLY TO VETERINARIANS

NOTE 1. Dr. Price and other veterinarians use Palosein, an injectable form of SOD.

NOTE 2. Here are some more details about this case. One point I believe you will find is that conventional drugs, and vitamins and minerals *used* as drugs (that is, in unnaturally high dosages), can have unexpected results upon one another, both positive and negative.

- The university veterinarians determined that this canine had a 60% calcium deficiency, an underactive thyroid and parathyroid. They prescribed 50,000 IU D_2 b.i.d., 2 g calcium gluconate t.i.d., and 0.5 mg thyroid medication t.i.d.
- The veterinarian who saw damage to the spine (specifically in the area of the third cervical vertebra) prescribed 15 mg prednisolone daily.
- The owner was able to maintain her pet symptom-free with the C-Plus treatment, on 0.6 mg. b.i.d. thyroid medication and 2.5 mg prednisolone every other day. A check four months later with Dr. Earl for an update revealed that the thyroid

medication had been further reduced to 0.2 mg t.i.d., and the prednisolone further reduced to 1.25 mg every other day.

- On days 3 and 4 of the animal's initial I.V. sodium ascorbate treatment, the canine showed relapse symptoms (anxiety, an hour-long seizure of body tremors, and one instance of falling). Dr. Belfield was called for consultation. He believed that the thyroid medication was causing the problem, because of the timing of I.V. medication, thyroid medication, and feeding. Changes were made in the timing of the feedings, and the prednisolone was increased temporarily from 5 mg to 10 mg. This maneuver was successful.

NOTE 3. Veterinarians who might wish to incorporate acupuncture into their practice may attend postgraduate courses offered by this organization or by The Center for Chinese Medicine, 230 S. Garfield Avenue, Monterey Park, CA 91754.

REFERENCES
1. Wendell O. Belfield, D.V.M., and Martin Zucker, *How to Have a Healthier Dog* (Garden City, New York: Doubleday and Co., Inc.), 1981, p. 223.
2. Belfield, *op cit.*, pp. 194, 198.
3. Belfield, *op cit.*, p. 219.
4. Wendell O. Belfield, D.V.M., *Let's LIVE*, December 1981, p. 115.
5. Belfield, *How to Have a Healthier Dog, op cit.*, pp. 218, 219.
6. Belfield, *op cit.*, pp. 220, 221.
7. Belfield, *op cit.*, p. 8.
8. See, for instance, *Veterinary Medicine/Small Animal Clinician*, August 1977, p. 1337.
9. Belfield, *op cit.*, pp. 222–224.
10. M. J. Shively, D.V.M., M.S., Ph.D., *Dog Fancy*, December 1981, p. 17.
11. *Veterinary Medicine/Small Animal Clinician*, September 1981, pp. 1307–1312.
12. *Guide to Acupuncture for Animals*, The National Association for Veterinary Acupuncture, P.O. Box 5181, Fullerton, CA 92635, 1977.

CHAPTER FIVE

Problems of the Eye

ROBERT GOLDSTEIN,
V.M.D., AND MARTY
GOLDSTEIN, D.V.M.:
*"Very often corneal ulcers that
are incurable with standard
drugs will heal with natural
therapy."*

RICHARD J. KEARNS,
D.V.M.:
*"Often, in early cases, a $25
bottle of Vitamin B_{15} drops
will dissolve cataracts. Even in
very advanced cases, cataracts
can be arrested approximately
seventy percent of the time, if
the owner uses a natural diet
along with nutritional
therapy."*

A PLEA NOT TO PUT YOUR BLIND
OR OTHERWISE HANDICAPPED PET
"OUT OF HIS MISERY"

Before we go into ways you can help your pet with eye problems, let me put in a plea on behalf of your pet if he is already blind: Please do not put him to sleep. (I dislike that phrase because I think it is a euphemism that allows some people to do less than they might be able to, to help their pet.) I am not in a position to tell you, of course, that there is never, ever a case where putting your pet to sleep isn't kinder than letting him suffer through a painful, hopeless existence. However, as this book indicates, there are many pets deemed hopeless by traditional veterinary medicine who can, indeed, be helped by the new field of orthomolecular veterinary medicine.

I would say, also, that as a rule a dog or cat who is blind, deaf, or lacking a limb should *not* be euthanized. After all, we don't put a blind child permanently to sleep, do we? And yet cats and dogs are not devastated psychologically by handicaps such as blindness in the way that people often are. In addition, our pets actually need their eyesight less than we do. For instance, when you put your dog in a strange room, he will go about exploring his new surroundings, not with his eyes, but with his nose. And your cat's whiskers act as sensors, alerting him to the slightest change in air pressure around his face. He can "see," partially, through his whiskers.

As one of this book's veterinarians, John E. Craige, V.M.D., puts it: "Blind dogs get along quite well. They can run and play and chase cats and do almost everything a sighted dog can do. They don't have any psychological traumatism as do blind people."

I would like to quote another statement pointing out that not only should you let your handicapped pet live out his life, you might even relax and stop feeling sorry for him. The following is a quote from a book by Pat Widmer. Ms. Widmer is founder and president of Pet Clinicare in New York City. Her clinic is incorporating some of the natural therapies covered in this book.

"My so-called 'handicapped' pets have never demonstrated any overwhelming problems and have in many instances proved that they can be just as obnoxious as anyone else," Ms. Widmer says.

"Blind cats and dogs have no difficulty, provided you don't move all the furniture every day. . . . In particular, my blind street cat (picked up at six months of age at a construction site in the midst of the East River Drive) is the toughest cat I have. He was born blind with congenital cataracts; both eyes have now been removed because of glaucoma. None of which has deterred him in the least. One amusing note: he has obviously learned that when he hears [note, *hears*] the light switch turned off, the other cats are at a momentary disadvantage while their eyes adjust. It is at this very second that he will attack another cat. I have dealt with this situation by warning him *not* to attack anyone as I turn out the light. Also, I note the other cats all watch him as I reach for the switch. No dummies there. . . .

"Lameness or lack of a limb is meaningless to animals. My fastest-moving cat has four legs and three feet, probably from birth. He is named Flash because he always flashes by. His motto is 'Don't walk, *run!*' Unfortunately, he has not grown wings yet, but he is still hopeful."[1]

I know I have often watched with dismay as a three-legged dog came hobbling in my direction, out on his walk with his owner. However, I have watched these dogs continue on, walking as fast as any four-legged dog and enjoying their walk just as thoroughly. I have come to realize that the dogs' handicap does not depress the dogs—only me.

In short, let your handicapped cat or dog enjoy the rest of his life—and stop making yourself unhappy by pitying him.

CATARACTS

When vitamin B_{15} was first discovered, early workers were discouraged. "About all we could find," they reported, "was that it dissolved cataracts on dogs' eyes."[2]

Today Richard J. Kearns, D.V.M., reports that B_{15} drops will help stop the growth of cataracts about seventy percent of the time—in late cases—and will actually *dissolve* advanced cataracts in about thirty percent of the cases.* "One $25 bottle of B_{15} drops," Dr. Kearns tells me, "will dissolve most early cataracts."**

"However," Dr. Kearns warns, "the high success rate for advanced cataracts is based on cases in which people switch their pets to a natural diet. The success rate falls substantially when owners refuse the diet and try to get rid of the cataracts with just the basic therapy of B_{15}, E, and selenium. Some people, oriented toward orthodox medicine, consider these three nutrients the 'medicines' for cataracts—medicines are supposed to do 'everything,' so why does one have to worry about diet, too?"

"In reality," Dr. Kearns continues, "a natural diet has little or no toxins. Cataracts are basically accumulations of toxins in the eyes. A natural diet, therefore, will help keep the accumulated toxins (or cataracts) out of the eyes once they have been dissolved. Without the poisonless diet, the client

---

*Vitamin B_{15} was abundant in our pets' food—and in ours—before we started tampering with foods. B_{15} now is greatly processed out of the new "improved" American diet.

**Veterinarians: Please see "Of Interest Mainly to Veterinarians," Note 1, at the end of the chapter.

has to keep using the three 'medicines' till the end of the animal's life in order to keep controlling the cataracts. This can get to be expensive—for a large dog, maybe $2 a day for the E and selenium, plus $100 a year for the B_{15}."

While even the above "expensive" regimen may be considered to compare favorably with the cost of an operation (approximately $450 for one eye*), I hope you will opt to combine the E-selenium-B_{15} therapy with the natural diet this book recommends throughout. You will be increasing your pet's chances of remaining free of his cataracts; you will be improving the health of his entire being; and you may be able to free yourself—perhaps after a year's time—of the expense of the three therapeutic substances and the bit of effort needed to administer the B_{15} eye drops twice a day. Also, as we have pointed out in early chapters, your pet's natural diet most probably will cost you less than the poisonous foods you buy at your supermarket.

"Of course," Dr. Kearns adds, echoing a point every nutritional veterinarian repeats over and over again regarding most disorders, "if people *start out* their pet with a natural diet, they'll probably never have to worry about cataracts."

Before we continue, I must emphasize something you may or may not know. We have been talking about successfully dissolving cataracts. You may have assumed that dissolving the cataract will in all cases restore sight. Unfortunately, if there is retinal degeneration as well as a cataract, your pet will not regain his sight. In other words, therapy can get rid of cataracts, but it cannot restore a degenerated retina.

However, the retina in all probability will not have degenerated in early cataract formation. Also, if your pet is not already blind, remember that, as Dr. Kearns says, the therapy has a seventy percent chance of stopping further cataract formation in advanced cases. It will preserve whatever sight your pet has at the time. In those cases in which the cataracts are dissolved (most early cases and approximately 30 percent of advanced), and in which the retina has not degenerated, normal sight will be restored.

A Successful Variation on the Above Approach to Cataracts

With many medical problems, there is more than one approach. Your orthodox physician, for example, will often change dosages of a drug, try the drug in combination with another, or switch drugs entirely, depending on what seems to be working or not working for you. In natural medicine, too, optimal success can be achieved by following the effective guidelines for therapy and then modifying them after tests show which particular nutrients your pet's body is most in need of.

---

*By the way, a cataract operation removes the lens of the eye (the cataract is *in* the lens), so that normal eyesight is really never restored.

A veterinarian in Hawaii, Dr. L. O. Brooksby, reports excellent results with cataracts and related eye problems in 300 cases. Like Dr. Kearns, he uses vitamin E and selenium. However, he injects these intramuscularly. He does this once a week for five weeks, and follows this procedure with oral E and selenium twice a week for six weeks. Injections can send a substance into the bloodstream faster than oral administration; and Dr. Brooksby notes that improvement is generally noticed by the third injection.

A particularly dramatic recovery from cataracts was made by a decade-old Shih Tzu. She had lost so much of her eyesight that once, when she was left alone outside, she couldn't see the swimming pool in front of her and fell into it. After only three injections by Dr. Brooksby, the little animal could see well enough not only to sidestep the swimming pool, but to catch Frisbees in midair.[3]

Cataracts in Humans

If you or someone you know requires cataract surgery, please do not be overwhelmed by my discouraging remarks on cataract surgery for dogs. For one thing, dogs, unlike people, are often not recommended for surgery until there is so much damage done to the sight by cataracts that it cannot be restored. Also, human beings can be fitted with thick lenses or contact lenses to compensate for the loss of the lens, which is removed along with the cataract—a compensation not quite so practical for dogs.

At the same time, you should also know that there are natural-therapy alternatives to surgery for human patients with cataracts, too. After citing a number of scientific studies linking nutritional deficiencies to the formation of cataracts—and the correction of these deficiencies to the correction of cataracts—nutritional writer Adelle Davis states: "My files contain dozens of unsolicited letters from persons who have recovered from cataracts after their diets were made adequate, often while they were preparing for surgery. One woman of eighty-six had cataracts on both eyes, yet her daughter reported that after following a good diet for a few months, her mother was again spending most of her time reading her favorite literature—detective stories. . . . An antistress diet high in protein, vitamins B_2, C, and E, pantothenic acid, and all nutrients is essential before good results can be expected."[4]

You might want to look up in a medical library—or perhaps direct your physician's attention to—a study that, as Davis states, shows that people with cataracts often find that the cataracts disappear when stress is removed and they are given an adequate antistress diet.[5]

DRY EYE

In this condition, insufficient tears are produced to help wash away irritants in the eye. The eye will have a thick, stringy discharge. Later, the eye becomes infected and the conjunctiva (lining of the eyelids) looks red. There may also be a discharge of pus. Left untreated, dry eye can lead to major complications, such as corneal ulcers.

In some cases of dry eye, the nostril on the same side may also be dry, and the animal may lick frantically away at his nose in an attempt to keep it wet. Oddly enough, it is often this nose-licking that owners notice and become alarmed by, rather than the eye symptoms.

An operation will transplant one of the salivary ducts from your pet's mouth to the corner of the eye. The eye will then be kept lubricated with saliva rather than with tears. Nutritional veterinarian Dr. Kearns, however, resorts to this operation only when there is no tear-secreting tissue left.

Traditional veterinarians may try controlling the infection and inflammation with antibiotics and steroids. However, John S. Eden, D.V.M., states: "Antibiotics and steroids probably never successfully treat dry eye." Controlling infection and inflammation will not help start the production of tears again, which is what is causing the other two problems.

Dr. Kearns uses pilocarpine to stimulate tearing.* He also has the owner put cod liver oil into the eye. This oil contains vitamins A and D, which are helpful for the health of the eye; and, being an oil, it acts as an additional lubricant. Depending on the case, Dr. Kearns will often put liquid forms of vitamin E and other vitamins directly on the eye. He adds: "I also usually have the owner clean the eyes out with cool tea. The tannic acid in the tea is an astringent, and it will clean the eye out very nicely."

For another successful approach to dry eye, see the regimen following, which is used by Robert Goldstein, V.M.D., and Marty Goldstein, D.V.M.

CORNEAL ULCERS

Ulcers on the cornea of the eye are a serious condition, and books detailing orthodox veterinary medicine warn that without early treatment, the pet may end up having to have his eye cut out surgically. However, Drs. Robert and Marty Goldstein tell me that "a lot of times corneal ulcers that are incurable with standard drugs will heal with natural therapy." Dr. Kearns makes a similar statement: "I just don't have a problem treating corneal ulcers, period."

Surely, a natural therapy potent enough to do what expensive drugs sometimes cannot do must be very costly? "Not at all," the doctors Goldstein state. "The drugless therapy is very inexpensive."

Before we discuss this natural therapy, the point should be made that these two doctors will initially treat corneal ulcers that are in an emergency state with standard treatments for a short while, until the emergency is

---

*Pilocarpine is a drug. As I point out often, orthomolecular veterinarians will use a drug when there is no known effective nutritional therapy.

over. As indicated elsewhere in the book, natural therapies can sometimes take longer to work than, for example, the injection of a drug. In an emergency situation, it is not usually in the pet's interest to make him wait.

The natural therapy used so successfully by the doctors Goldstein includes vitamin E and the herbs eyebright and goldenseal. The eyebright is given alone by mouth, one capsule a day. A combination of the eyebright, goldenseal, and vitamin E is also used directly in the eye.*

When the case calls for it, Dr. Kearns will also sometimes start off with an orthodox technique: a simple operation that brings the third eyelid up over the ulcer. The third eyelid is that membrane you can see at the inner corner of your pet's eye. Why bring this eyelid up over the ulcer? "There is no blood supply to the cornea. That is why corneal ulcers are generally so hard to heal, because there is no way for any healing substance you put into the body to get circulated into the cornea. The third eyelid does, however, have circulation; and, when placed over the ulcer, it will lend part of its circulation to the ulcer."

Dr. Eden adds that this simple operation also protects the ulcerated area from irritation caused by the outer lids passing over the ulcer when the animal blinks. As he states: "This can be of considerable value, when you consider that the lids blink thousands of times a day."

Dr. Kearns will also use vitamins A and E directly on the eye. "There is a combination of A and E that I get from American Biologics. Just one drop of the solution in the eye will give 1,800 to 2,000 IU of A plus E." This powerful combination of vitamins means that less time is spent in giving frequent applications of drops.

OTHER EYE PROBLEMS

Conjunctivitis

Drs. Robert and Marty Goldstein successfully treat this condition with the same combination of vitamin E and the herbs goldenseal and eyebright that they use for corneal ulcers. (They use this combination also as the basis for their therapy for other corneal lesions and for inflammation of the cornea.)

Chronic Blepharitis
(Inflammation of the Eyelid)

Robin Woodley, D.V.M., sends me a case history of a female pointer, Nikki, who was one and a half years old at the time Dr. Woodley first saw her. Nikki had suffered from a discharge of pus from her eyes since she was a puppy. A clinic had subjected her to extensive eye surgery; the surgery had done no good.

The owners then took their pet to a veterinary ophthalmologist (eye spe-

---

*Veterinarians: Please see "Of Interest Mainly to Veterinarians," Note 2, at the end of the chapter.

cialist). There are very few veterinary ophthalmologists in the country;* the owners were obviously going to great expense and effort to help their beloved pet. The discharge was, indeed, controlled by the antibiotics the rare veterinary eye specialist prescribed; but the dog needed frequent treatments, each of several weeks' duration, to control the infection. This was, as Dr. Woodley points out, "very expensive."

In frustration, the owners decided to try a natural, drugless therapy. Dr. Woodley and an associate, C. Clarke, D.V.M., placed Nikki on 10,000 IU vitamin A and 30 milligrams of zinc daily, administered orally. "In the subsequent year," Dr. Woodley writes me, "Nikki has had no recurrence of infection." Were fewer antibiotics needed after the A-and-zinc therapy was started? "No antibiotic therapy has been necessary at all," Dr. Woodley tells me.

Progressive Retinal Atrophy

This condition is a shrinking (atrophy) of the blood vessels in the retina. And it is called progressive because it does just that: it progresses, relentlessly, until the animal is blind. It has been found to be due in some cases (especially in the cat) to the lack of an amino acid, taurine. Taurine occurs abundantly in the cat's natural diet, but has been added to commercial cat foods only in recent years. As a matter of fact, taurine deficiency was discovered only a short time ago. It is for reasons such as this that nutritional authorities urge that we should feed ourselves and our pets natural foods.

While Drs. Robert and Marty Goldstein have treated only one case of this disorder, they have stopped its "certain" progression for a full three years so far. The animal in question is Tina, a ten-year-old poodle. Veterinarians specializing in ophthalmology had previously pronounced that "there was nothing to be done" for the pet. Without the nutritional therapy, Tina could be expected to be "totally blind" by now, the doctors Goldstein state. These veterinarians aren't using magic to make this case of progressive retinal atrophy belie the first word of its name. They tell me that they simply "did an analysis of the dog's body, found out all the ways it was out of chemical balance, and restored the balance nutritionally." Then they repeat an idea all of our nutritional veterinarians have stated to me over and over again: "WE haven't stopped the progressive retinal atrophy from progressing; we have simply helped the animal's body to stop it."

As we say often in this book, there are certain guidelines we can give as to which nutrients are helpful for which disorders, but the ultimate natural therapy for many "tough" disorders can come only after your pet's body has been tested to find scientifically what is lacking in his own body chemistry.

---

*There are currently only about seventy-five animal ophthalmologists certified by the American College of Veterinary Ophthalmology.

The doctors Goldstein do believe, however, that liver imbalance plays a prominent role in all eye problems; and indeed, Tina, our dog with the nonprogressive progressive retinal atrophy, tested out to have gross liver imbalances.

Dr. Marty Goldstein, who is an accredited veterinary acupuncturist as well as a nutritional veterinarian, tells me that in acupuncture it is believed that the energy forces feeding the health of the liver are the same forces feeding the health of the eyes. "I believe," Dr. Goldstein tells me, "that the majority of eye problems are not primarily eye problems, but rather secondary reflections of disorders of the liver. As a matter of fact," he adds, "I have rarely seen a pet with a chronic eye problem who tested out to have a normal liver function."*

Dr. Goldstein mentions that an ophthalmologist (one of the rare veterinarians who specialize in eye problems) once asked him to help treat a dog with abscesses inside the eye. The dog had already lost one of his eyes to abscesses, and two years later the abscesses turned up in the other eye. The ophthalmologist was aware that his orthodox medical approach was not helping with the remaining eye and asked Dr. Goldstein if acupuncture could help. Dr. Goldstein tells me: "It took only two acupuncture treatments before the abscess was completely controlled." Dr. Goldstein adds: "I treated the dog at the acupuncture liver point. When I twirled an acupuncture needle at the liver point, the animal's eyelids quivered, another indication of how closely the liver and the eyes are interrelated."

If Your Pet Is Disabled

I would like to end this chapter, as I began it, by stressing that if your pet is—or becomes—blind (or lame or deaf), please do not feel you must be kind to him by putting him out of his misery. Please realize that your handicapped pet does not suffer because of his handicap the way a person might. Relax; enjoy your pet; and let him enjoy the rest of his natural life.

---

*Dr. Goldstein, referring to the fact that for years it has been shown that vitamin A is of great importance in preventing and treating eye problems, adds: "In actuality, vitamin A helps eye problems because it helps the liver perform its detoxification chores."

OF INTEREST MAINLY TO VETERINARIANS

NOTE 1:   Dr. Kearns uses the product True-15 Optique, obtained from American Biologics, 111 Ellis St., Suite 300, San Francisco, CA 94102.

NOTE 2:   The combination of eyebright, goldenseal, and vitamin E may be ordered from Energy Plus for Animals, 1863 Commerce St., Yorktown, NY 10598.

REFERENCES

1. Patricia P. Widmer, *Pat Widmer's Cat Book* (New York: Charles Scribner's Sons), 1981, pp. 49–50.
2. *Diet Times*, May/June 1979, p. 18.
3. L. O. Brooksby, "A Practitioner's Experience with Selenium-Tocopherol in Treatment of Cataracts and Nuclear Sclerosis in the Dog," *Vet. Med./SA Clinician*, March 1979, pp. 301–302. Cited by Wendell O. Belfield, D.V.M., and Martin Zucker, *How to Have a Healthier Dog* (Garden City, New York: Doubleday and Co., Inc.) 1981, pp. 181, 182.
4. Adelle Davis, *Let's Get Well* (New York: Harcourt, Brace and World, Inc.), 1965, p. 353.
5. I.A. Kurinsky, *National Health Federation Bulletin*, 10, 25, 1964, cited by Adelle Davis, *ibid.*

CHAPTER SIX

Problems of the Skin and Hair

J. KEITH BENEDICT,
D.V.M.:
*"I suppose we veterinarians who
do a lot of work with skin and
hair problems ought to thank
the commercial pet food manufacturers for all the business
they create for us."*

MICHAEL W. LEMMON,
D.V.M.:
*"Popular flea collars often con-
tain powerful nerve gases.
They can kill some fleas. They
can also kill some pets, and can
do damage to children and
adults handling the pet wearing
the poisonous flea collar."*

The following case history is representative of what natural therapy can sometimes do for "hopeless" cases of skin disorders. As we've stated so many times throughout this book, the new field of orthomolecular veterinary medicine is very often not even tried by pet owners until their pet has already been given up on by standard veterinary medicine. Thus, orthomolecular veterinary medicine's often spectacular results might be expected to be even more spectacular if the veterinarians practicing this medicine were presented with a higher proportion of less severe cases.

Lorax, a golden retriever, suffered severely from moist dermatitis for the first three years of his life. He was given a battery of steroid shots which offered him no relief. A specialist in allergies then discovered that Lorax had numerous allergies. However, after many months of allergy shots—and many hundreds of dollars—Lorax still had his skin problems.

He finally found help from a natural regimen prescribed by Robert Goldstein, V.M.D., and Marty Goldstein, D.V.M., that included a fast (with distilled water only) to allow the body to clear out accumulated toxins; and a change of diet, from one of the most popular "nutritionally complete" dog foods to grains, chicken, raw vegetables, and some unsaturated fatty acids. This was supplemented by a poison-free prepared pet food, Cornucopia. Tests had shown that Lorax also had a deficiency of magnesium and the B-vitamins, and he received daily supplements of these.

Lorax had been suffering not only from skin problems, but from paralysis. Not only has he had no skin problems for four years, but the paralysis has also virtually disappeared.

It was J. Keith Benedict, D.V.M., who made the ironical statement: "I suppose we veterinarians who do a lot of work with skin and hair problems ought to thank the commercial pet food manufacturers for all the business they create for us." This same idea is expressed in various other ways by nutritional veterinarians who take a special interest in skin and hair problems. Cats and dogs on natural diets (especially diets supplemented with brewer's yeast and garlic) do not tend to get fleas or ticks; they do not tend to get the other skin problems, some of them life-threatening, that are so common in today's junk-food-fed pets.

You might be surprised to know that a number of veterinarians have told me that problems of the skin and coat are the most common problems they see. This becomes particularly depressing when you realize that several doctors working on this book estimate that ninety percent of skin disorders in dogs are merely outward manifestations of something physically wrong within the animal's body.

Skin problems in the pet can be extremely expensive for the owner.

Sometimes it is possible to spend a small fortune just to get the problem diagnosed. Veterinarians state that—except for skin problems caused by parasites—it can require endless medical testing and detective work just to give the disorder its proper name.

That's the bad news about skin problems. The good news is that you probably won't ever need the information in this chapter if your cat or dog is on a natural diet; and you may not need the endless testing to give a disorder its proper name if you follow nutritional therapy. Since good nutrition can rebuild the total health of the body, it can heal a problem sometimes even when the proper technical name has not been found for it. Indeed, Wendell O. Belfield, D.V.M., states that seventy percent of skin problems can be cleared up simply by putting the pet on a chemical-free food preparation (see page 177 for recommended products), and by adding vitamins and minerals.[1]

GUIDELINES FOR TREATING
SKIN AND HAIR PROBLEMS

Please see the text of this chapter for important details.

Natural diet as described in Chapter 2

Initially, however, a diet of lamb and well-cooked brown rice may be tried, as recommended by Dr. Benedict. (The lamb and rice should not be served at the same meal.) This diet is free of foods that commonly cause allergies in pets. (Food allergies are frequent causes of skin disorders in dogs and cats.) Additional foods may be added to the diet one at a time; if any one addition causes a flare-up of the skin problem, it may be an indication that your pet is allergic to that particular food.

A multivitamin, multimineral supplement formulated for dogs or cats

Additional vitamin C

Additional vitamin E

Nontoxic shampoo

The following are suggested amounts of supplements for a fifty-pound dog with skin problems. These guidelins are from Drs. Robert and Marty Goldstein, who adjust the recommended amounts for their patients after nutritional testing for individual needs.

—Cold pressed oil (sunflower or sesame) initially: 2 tablespoons per meal

—Vitamin C: 1,000—2,000 mg a day

—Vitamin E: 400 IU a day

—Vitamin B complex with B_{12}: 50 mg per meal

—Kelp: 2 teaspoons a day or 3 tablets per meal
—Zinc: 30 mg a day
—Multivitamin and mineral supplement formulated for pets
—Bone meal: 1 tablespoon a day or 2 tablets per meal
—Selenium: 50 mcg a day
—Wheat germ oil capsules: 2 per meal

An initial fast, with distilled water only, may be helpful in aiding the body to rid itself of stored-up toxins. A FAST OVER TWENTY-FOUR HOURS MUST BE DONE UNDER SUPERVISION. Do not fast a diabetic animal.

Before we discuss specific skin disorders, here is a very sketchy, very incomplete synopsis of some of the studies that show how nutrition can prevent—and cure—skin problems in our pets and in ourselves.

Human volunteers kept on diets just slightly lacking in only one vitamin (B_2) developed overly oily hair and skin.[2] Studies detailing this go back close to half a century ago. The reverse problem, skin that is too dry, has been caused in human volunteers by giving too little vitamin A or C, linoleic acid, or any one of several B-vitamins.[3]

Do a couple of hours' sunbathing turn into a nightmare for you because you are one of those people who get sunburned easily? You might be interested in research showing that people like you can sometimes tolerate *fifty to one hundred times* more sun exposure when taking 1,000 milligrams a day of PABA (a B-vitamin) or when applying a salve containing this vitamin.[4] This study was done thirty years ago. Today many suntan lotions contain PABA. As usual, I am against self-prescription of vitamins; please do *not* prescribe for yourself 1,000 milligrams a day of PABA. You will upset the balance of the B-complex and may do yourself serious harm. The study cited was done for experimental purposes only.

Imagine the following "mysterious thing" happening to your body and you will probably conclude that nothing on earth could possibly help you. You're a fair-skinned person, but your skin begins turning dark. (This condition can be caused by exhausted adrenals, as in Addison's disease.) Eventually, your skin becomes nearly black. An adequate nutritional program can reverse the process and restore your natural skin tone.[5]

A study done with 254 persons showed that four to eight tablespoons a day of lecithin (a natural food substance) healed even the most severe cases of psoriasis within five months.[6]

Gray hair? Nothing can be done about that, right? It can occur "naturally" with aging, or it can occur "unnaturally" without aging. In either case, it's God's or nature's will. Yet, gray hair has been produced in studies by giving too little copper, too little folic acid, too little pantothenic acid, and too little PABA. Conversely, hair has been restored to its original color sometimes by giving only PABA every day.[7]

So much for a brief overview of how laboratory studies have for years linked skin and hair problems to nutrition. Now for the practical applications that can help your pet.

FLEAS

A DO-IT-YOURSELF
NONTOXIC FLEA TREATMENT

The following is a nontoxic treatment suggested by Drs. Robert and Marty Goldstein for a cat or dog with a moderate case of flea infestation. A pet who is bleeding or chewing excessively should be attended to by a veterinarian.

- Bathe your pet in a nontoxic shampoo and dry him thoroughly.
- Apply a natural healing ointment (vitamin E, A, or D) to the reddened areas and deter your pet from licking it off.
- Give a fifty-pound dog one tablespoon of brewer's yeast a day. An adult cat might be given one teaspoon. The doctors recommend imported brewer's yeast, called Petzymes, and Lick Your Chops yeast tonic. The average brewer's yeast, they believe, is not concentrated enough to work against an already existing parasitic condition.
- Add one to two cloves of fresh garlic per day to your pet's food. Use a garlic press or chop the garlic finely.
- Cats and small- to medium-sized dogs may use an herbal flea collar. Larger dogs may have a drop of pennyroyal added to their mesh collars.
- Sprinkle brewer's yeast onto your pet's coat and skin every two to three days during heavy infestation. Then use once every two weeks.
- Change the diet to a chemical-free health food diet. See Chapters 1 and 2.

How Not to Poison Your Pet
With Flea Collars

Writers concerned with natural approaches to animal health often refer to a flea collar as "a necklace of poison." Perhaps the following two paragraphs will help explain why.

The flea collars you buy at most stores kill fleas by poisoning them. It would be comforting to think that the manufacturers of these collars have found a way to poison the fleas without the risk of poisoning your pet; but this is not not true. The label may state that children should not touch these collars. If they are harmful to your child's skin, what about the even more sensitive skin of your dog or cat? And just how does your child manage to play with your dog or cat without coming into contact with the collar? And how do *you* manage this?

You may be thinking that perhaps these collars do contain poison, but surely it can't be a very serious poison or the manufacturers wouldn't use it. Yet, best-selling brands may contain powerful nerve gases.* "Powerful nerve gases" is not a misprint. These can be absorbed into the bloodstream and, according to animal nutritionist Kathy Berman, "can lead to nerve damage, paralysis, severe internal poisoning, and a case of dermatitis for pets, their owners, and even children who play with the pet."[8]

Give your pet a harmless flea collar filled with natural herbs such as pine, cedar, citronella, or eucalyptus. John E. Craige, V.M.D., states: "A necklace made of eucalyptus nuts seems to be more effective for getting rid of fleas than all the highly touted chemical flea powders and flea medallions." These herbs are not poisons and so they will not kill the fleas; but they won't kill your pet either. The herbs help rid your pet of fleas because fleas hate their herbal aroma and will abandon your pet's body in droves.**

Another simple, inexpensive measure you can take to help your pet ward off fleas is to include brewer's yeast and/or raw grated fresh garlic in your pet's food.*** Both of these give the pet's skin a smell that nobody notices—except fleas, who can't bear it. The yeast and garlic also contain nutrients that are extremely healthful for our pets (and for us). As a matter of fact, many nutritional experts recommend that brewer's yeast and garlic be a part of your pet's (and our) daily diet—fleas or no fleas.

You might also dust brewer's yeast directly onto your pet's body, a good ploy for a cat who is a finicky eater and may take a while to accept strange new foods that appear in his food bowl. In bathing himself the cat will lick up the yeast on his coat and will thus benefit from the good internal effects of the yeast. By the way, it's best to put your cat outside for a while after the "dusting," because the yeast is not a poison and therefore does not kill the fleas (or your cat). It merely sends the fleas scampering off your pet's body.

You can see the contrast: On the one hand, we are worried about the poisons in commercial flea preparations getting on or into your pet; on the other hand, we are worried about natural flea retardants not getting on and into your pet—even to the point where we have had to play a sneaky trick on your cat to get him to swallow brewer's yeast.

---

*For a discussion of several studies showing harm in both human beings and pets caused by one nerve gas, see "A Necklace of Poison," *Prevention*, August 1975.

**Michael W. Lemmon, D.V.M., adds here: ". . . if the body is relatively healthy and not on commercial foods." Of course, we have recommended that commercial foods be withdrawn, or, preferably, never be given at all.

***Dr. Benedict reports that he has little success with the herbs mentioned in the preceding paragraph when they are used alone. "When I have my clients add either brewer's yeast, garlic, or desiccated liver, the results improve markedly."

Most important, placing your pet on a natural diet, supplemented with a multivitamin and multimineral pill (as detailed in Chapters 2 and 3), will rebuild the total health of your pet. Fleas are parasites, and as such their role in life is to scavenge the blood of sick bodies—and sick bodies only.* (Remember, we said earlier that more often than not skin problems are a sign of internal sickness?) When you have rebuilt your pet's total health, he will no longer fit the category of a sick host. At that point, your dog or cat probably can come into contact with fleas a hundred times a day (from other dogs, from the yard, from newly hatched eggs hidden in your house), and the fleas will snub his body as being "unfit" for their scavenger purpose in life.

In addition, some of the orthomolecular veterinarians who have a special interest in skin problems recommend nontoxic rinses as helpful for the control of fleas. Dr. Benedict will often use Green, a nontoxic (and biodegradable) kelp-based product that gets rid of fleas and also soothes irritation from the scratching that fleas cause. "One of the nice things about Green," Dr. Benedict tells me, "is that—since it is nontoxic—you can use it every day, thus increasing its effectiveness." It is okay to use Green on your cat. Since it is nontoxic, he can lick it off his skin without harm while he grooms himself. Dr. Benedict adds that Green can be used by people as an effective, nontoxic shaving lotion, shampoo, and soap. "When I travel," he says, "Green is the only soap-type product I carry with me. And," he quips, "no fleas!"**

So you see, there are inexpensive means you can use to help your pet with his flea problem—ones that not only do not poison him, but actually can enhance his overall health.

FLEA-BITE ALLERGY
(OR FLEA ALLERGY DERMATITIS)

This is an extension of the general problem of flea infestation. Flea-bite allergy shows itself in bald spots and in swollen, inflamed (and painful) skin, the result not only of the flea bites but also of the afflicted pet's biting and scratching. Just as we do when we are in constant discomfort, your pet may lose his appetite and change from a sweet, happy being to an irritable, mean one.

---

*All the veterinarians who read this chapter before publication agreed with this statement. John S. Eden, D.V.M., added, however: "Fleas will infest and parasitize *any* body. They are *dangerous* only to the sick."
**Have you been driven to using vast amounts of poisonous insecticides in an attempt to save your trees from the recent invasion of gypsy moths? I have a friend who spent many hours last year spraying and gagging on the poisonous fumes and didn't manage to save too many of his trees. You might be pleased to know that Dr. Benedict reports that the nonpoisonous Green may do the job for you.

Orthodox medicine's treatment involves corticosteroid drugs. Some of this book's veterinarians, such as George M. Thue, D.V.M., will also use these drugs for this condition. However, Dr. Thue will add to the drugs—when he feels he must use drugs at all—a good diet and additional nutritional supplements. He will use high doses of a B-vitamin, pantothenic acid. "This vitamin," Dr. Thue states, "is thought by many to support the adrenal glands."

Dr. Craige has been working closely with the problem of flea-bite allergy since the 1950s. He has found "excellent results" by using a combination of acupuncture, vitamin C, and the B-complex vitamins. He will also sometimes use a flea antigen made from an extract of dog fleas. The antigen Dr. Craige uses has been employed successfully to help people allergic to fleas. It works basically on the same principle as do vaccinations, building up the body's natural immunity to fleas. Dr. Craige adds: "I have found that many animals given this antigen not only lose their allergy to fleas—but also never again have fleas on their bodies."*

HAIR LOSS

"You have to determine what's causing the hair loss," says Dr. Benedict. "But no matter what is causing it, it is imperative that you improve the animal's nutrition." Dr. Thue, like Dr. Benedict, will check for such things as hormonal deficiency, parasites, and pressure wounds that might be causing the hair loss. "When there is no indication for specific treatment, I will occasionally use cider vinegar, in addition to a natural diet plus supplements," Dr. Thue tells me. "Daily application of cider vinegar rubbed in thoroughly on small areas of hair loss can do wonders to stimulate dead or weak hair follicles and restore natural hair growth."

I have on hand a set of pictures of an eight-year-old dog that was a patient of Dr. Thue's, and the before-treatment pictures show the dog with a large, erratically shaped bald spot on her back. Her hair had also turned gray around her eyes and mouth. The after-treatment picture shows the bald spot completely grown in. The gray hair on her face is now dark. The before-and-after pictures were taken a little over two months apart. Dr. Thue treated the dog with a liquid B-complex, vitamins C and E, lecithin, unsaturated fatty acids, and Viokase (a mixture of natural pancreatic enzymes).

To sum up, let me repeat that hair loss in your dog or cat should be checked out by a veterinarian to find its exact cause. However, no matter what the cause is, you should make sure your pet's nutrition is optimal (see Chapters 2 and 3).

---

*Veterinarians: Please see "Of Interest Mainly to Veterinarians," Note 1, at the end of the chapter.

SKIN ULCERS

This is a case history reported in a personal communication to Dr. Wilfrid E. Shute, one of the world's major pioneers in work with vitamin E. At six months of age the puppy developed skin ulcers and lost so much hair that literally half his body was bald. The owners dragged the young animal to half a dozen veterinarians. The doctors could not help the dog. Two years—and $800—later, the owners were told to give up and put the young dog to sleep. At this point, luckily, the breeder who had sold the dog to the owners suggested they try vitamin E. The owners gave the dog 200 IUs a day for two and one-half months. The breeder reports: "When I saw the dog again I couldn't believe my eyes. The coat was long and the dog was in beautiful condition, with no trace of ulcers or rash."[9]

Other veterinarians have reported success with vitamins C and A. As is the case with many disorders, there are certain nutrients that are known to be generally helpful, but often the specifics for an individual therapy depend on which of the generally helpful nutrients are most deficient in the particular animal's body.

Dr. Thue will use a medicated shampoo and ointment and will shave the area to help keep it clean. In addition to bathing the pet, he will give B-complex and vitamin C. Then he will have the owners continue giving their pet multivitamins, with additional C and E. Of course he will ask the owners to place the animal on a natural diet.

Jan Bellows, D.V.M., adds that the mineral zinc is often helpful in treating skin ulcers.

DEMODECTIC (RED) MANGE

This skin disorder usually affects dogs and cats under two years of age. Hunks of hair disappear from around the muzzle and the eyes. The bald areas are red and a bit swollen. When you see these symptoms, you should obtain immediate veterinary aid for your pet. Red mange can spread quickly. A strong chemical insecticide is needed to kill the mites that cause the disorder. Be absolutely certain to increase your pet's vitamin and mineral supplementation at this point, to help detoxify the insecticide.

For generalized red mange (that is, red mange that has already spread over the body), every source I turned to—whether orthodox or orthomolecular—offered mainly despair. I persisted, however, until I found Dr. Bellows, who told me: "First the pet must be supplemented with vitamins to get him in a positive nitrogen balance, using megadoses of the B-complex, C, and E. Also, any infections must be cleared up with antibiotics. Then amatraze (a peach insecticide) must be used as a rinse." Rather than despairing of healing generalized red mange, Dr. Bellows tells me, "This works on almost all cases." Dr. Bellows can be reached for consultation (see the List of Nutritionally Oriented Veterinarians).

Animal nutritionist Pat Widmer adds that in her clinic all animals with generalized red mange have tested out to have very low levels of zinc in their bodies. "With the use of zinc," she says, "we have seen the entire coat grow back within a week." Ms. Widmer also states that relieving stress is very important with this disorder. (See elsewhere her remarks on stress in the leukemic cat.) "When I find a pet has a very stressful home situation," she tells me, "I persuade the owner to let the animal stay with me at the clinic, where I make sure to give him a calm environment and a lot of loving attention."

PYODERMA

Pyoderma attacks young puppies.* Eruptions appear on the bodies and start oozing pus. The standard treatment is antibiotics and steroid cream, but it works slowly for pyoderma—when it does work at all. It is not uncommon for puppies on this standard treatment to end up having to be destroyed.

Dr. Benedict states that antibiotics alone are not the best way to treat pyoderma. "You've really got to get the nutrition up," he states emphatically. "As a matter of fact, there is no contest between the standard antibiotic treatment and the combined antibiotic-and-nutrition therapy." Dr. Benedict stresses high amounts of vitamin E, which helps promote healing and prevent scarring.

John S. Eden, D.V.M., states: "Only in severe or intractable cases do I use antibiotics." Besides nutrition and supplementation, Dr. Eden stresses cleansing of the skin, using either an iodine-based or chlorhexidine shampoo. "I recommend that the owner, while bathing his or her pet, open the pustules and remove scabs to allow the shampoo (surgical scrub) to get at the bacteria."

One reason antibiotics used alone are not the best solution for pyoderma is given by Drs. Robert and Marty Goldstein. The substances that come out through the skin in the pus "are built-up toxins from within the body. Antibiotics stop the elimination of these toxins. This, of course, causes a buildup of toxins within the body and eventual recurrence of the pyoderma. Therapy must include some detoxification in order to achieve a cure. This detoxification is a nutritional program."

Dr. Thue states that vitamin C is especially valuable in helping skin to heal. "For instance," he tells me, "I've done surgery on animals whose bodies simply couldn't heal the skin. Two whole weeks after surgery, there would be no healing whatsoever. Then I've given vitamin C, and in another week or two the skin was completely healed."

In short, nutritional veterinarians question the standard antiobiotic-steriod treatment, which often ends up with the pet having to be destroyed.

---

*Dr. Bellows states that young cats, too, can get pyoderma, especially in the chin area. This tends to "respond very well to routine cleaning with alcohol."

A more natural therapy must be used—even if just as an adjunct to standard therapy—to help your pet.

OF INTEREST MAINLY TO VETERINARIANS

NOTE 1: Dr. Craige uses the flea antigen available from Hollister-Stier Laboratories in Spokane, Washington.

REFERENCES

1. Wendell O. Belfield, D.V.M., and Martin Zucker, *How To Have a Healtheir Dog* (Garden City, New York: Doubleday and Co., Inc.), 1981, p. 205.
2. W. H. Sebrell *et al.*, *Pub. Health Rep.*, 53, 2282, 1938; 54, 2121, 1939.
3. V. Ramalignaswami *et al.*, *Brit. J. Derm.*, 65, 1, 1953; F. Bicknell and F. Prescott, *The Vitamins in Medicine* (Milwaukee, Wisconsin: Lee Foundation for Nutritional Research), 1953.
4. C. J. D. Zaraponetis, *J. Invest. Derm.*, 15, 399, 1950.
5. Adelle Davis, *Let's Get Well* (New York: Harcourt, Brace and World, Inc.), 1965, p. 155.
6. P. Gross *et al.*, *NY State J. Med.*, 50, 2683, 1950. Cited by Davis, *op cit.*, p. 156.
7. Davis, *op cit.*, p. 166.
8. Kathy Berman, "Herbs and Your Pet," *Herald of Health*, November 1978.
9. Personal communication to Dr. Wilfrid E. Shute, cited by Wendell O. Belfield, *op. cit.*, pp. 205, 206.

CHAPTER SEVEN

Infectious Diseases

RICHARD J. KEARNS,
D.V.M.:
"The only time I use an antibiotic is when the client insists on it. With drugs, the animal has less of a chance of being cured than he has with natural therapy. Also, even in those cases where the drug does cure, the poor animal can be suffering for a week or two; whereas with vitamin C and other nutrients, he can be well in three days."

H. H. ROBERTSON,
D.V.M.:
"Bacteria do not attack a healthy body. Most doctors worry about the bacteria. I do not treat the bacteria; I treat the animal."

MICHAEL W. LEMMON,
D.V.M.:
"With . . . upper respiratory tract diseases, I get ninety percent cure in early cases. However, if the animal has already been treated with antibiotics and other drugs when I get to see him, my successful results drop to about seventy-five percent."

You will read in this chapter what may seem like an astounding fact: that often, if your veterinarian tells you there is nothing to be done for your pet in the final stages of a viral disease, that same dying pet can be back to all his old mischief within days after administration of nutritional therapy.

The skeptics among you at this point may be thinking I am talking about "miracles." I am not. The "miraculous" results of the basic nutrient used in this therapy—vitamin C—have been documented for many years in orthodox medical studies (but not known by, or accepted by, most doctors); and these same results have been well proven in many, many cases in the daily practice of the pioneering veterinarians whose work is covered in this book.*

Bear in mind that *every* disease was once "incurable"—until medical science found the cure for it. Bear in mind also that it took a number of years for many of today's totally accepted cures to come to the attention of most doctors and even more years before most doctors accepted them. (In this book you are reading about new cures and controls for pet disorders before most veterinarians have found out about them and accepted them.) The following are just a few instances of how long it sometimes can take for new medical knowledge to become known and accepted:

- For about two centuries (the late 1500s to the late 1700s) some sailors cured themselves of "incurable" scurvy by eating foods containing a high amount of vitamin C, the same nutrient that is so helpful in curing the infectious diseases discussed in this chapter. No one paid any attention to these cured sailors, while for some two hundred years the still-"incurable" scurvy often wiped out as many as fifty percent or more of the sailors at sea. Finally, in 1747, Dr. James Lind, who had been compiling data for years, ran a controlled scientific study. Dr. Lind concluded that a bit of lemon or lime juice (both high in vitamin C) should be given to crews. The navy officials attacked him. The medical community attacked him. After all, how dare anyone suggest that an incurable disease was curable? Doesn't common sense tell you otherwise?

  It was about half a century later that Dr. Lind's recommendation was finally taken. Lemon juice (at that time called lime juice) was prescribed as part of the regulation diet for British sailors—and the "incurable" scurvy disappeared. (The fact that the sailors drank lime

---

*These veterinarians tell me, by the way, that the dread diseases covered in this chapter very seldom occur in dogs or cats raised according to the suggestions made in Chapters 2 and 3.

juice led to their being nicknamed "limeys," which they are still called today.)

Today every doctor knows and agrees that scurvy is due to a vitamin C deficiency, but it took hundreds of years for that basic information to get disseminated to everybody. I hope this book will help cut down on the time otherwise needed for the newer uses of vitamin C to become generally known.

- There was once a Dr. Harvey who was considered a quack by the medical profession for a full century. Dr. Harvey had this absurd notion, you see, that blood circulates throughout the body.

- A more recent "quack" thought he had found the cure for not just one but a number of "incurable" diseases from—of all things—a substance derived from molds. The medical profession denigrated him for a decade. The quack was Sir Alexander Fleming, and the substance is penicillin.

Let's investigate briefly the history of vitamin C, the nutrient that our pioneering veterinarians use as the basis for their sometimes "impossible" cures of infectious diseases. I know of medical studies going back to 1937 that show the "new notion" that vitamin C can kill bacteria.[1] Dr. Fred R. Klenner, Chief of Staff at the Memorial Hospital in Reidsville, North Carolina, began his work with vitamin C in the late 1940s and continues with it today. Dr. Klenner's work, published extensively in the medical literature, was often done with human patients who were by all rights supposed to die. Many of them had been previously treated with penicillin, aureomycin, and other antibiotics with no success. Often these terminally ill people, with fevers of 103 to 105 degrees, had a normal temperature within a few hours after the administration of vitamin C—and were able to enjoy the next meal offered at the hospital. Two or three days later—when they would otherwise have been lowered into the earth—they left the hospital in good health.[2]

Later we will see how orthomolecular veterinarians have been getting the same kind of results with pets.

The diseases Dr. Klenner has successfully treated with vitamin C include hepatitis, herpes simplex, measles, chicken pox, mononucleosis,[3] meningitis, encephalitis, polio, viral pneumonia, and lockjaw.[4]

The well-known nutritional writer Adelle Davis cites a number of studies, conducted in the years from 1938 to 1960, which reported that vitamin C is deadly to all types of bacteria and viruses.[5] Why *all*? Because vitamin C doesn't waste its time racing through the body trying to attack the viruses and bacteria per se; it rebuilds the immune system. And the immune system kills the viruses and bacteria, just as it does, when it is strong, many times in the course of a normal day.

Some veterinarians who don't have a special interest in nutritional therapy wonder how vitamin C can help a pet, because dogs and cats (unlike people) produce vitamin C in their own bodies. This argument overlooks the fact that what the animal can produce does not approach the huge amount necessary for a therapeutic dosage. Dr. Klenner's excellent results with people, for instance, were sometimes achieved with well over 4,000 times the recommended daily allowance of vitamin C.

Robert Goldstein, V.M.D., and Marty Goldstein, D.V.M., add: "In order for the animal to produce vitamin C in his body, he must have proper nutrition. And most animals on commercial foods do not get proper nutrition."

BASIC THERAPY FOR ALL INFECTIOUS DISEASES

As we've said, orthomolecular veterinarians use high dosages of vitamin C, usually in the form of sodium ascorbate, as the central part of their therapy for all infectious problems. In times of crisis the C will be given intravenously, often at the rate of 1/2 gram or more per pound of body weight, twice a day.*

The difference between a shot of vitamin C and a vitamin C tablet can very probably be *the* difference between life and death for your pet with a very serious infectious disease. It is for this reason, among others, that I urge you not to make up your own treatment for your pet. Once the dog or cat is past the crisis, the amount of the vitamin will be reduced, and the vitamin will be given by mouth.

Often, in crisis cases, intravenous fluids also will be administered to offset existing dehydration. And solid foods will be withheld.

Nutritional veterinarians (such as Richard J. Kearns, D.V.M.; Michael W. Lemmon, D.V.M.; the doctors Goldstein; and S. Allen Price, D.V.M.) use thymus extract also. The thymus gland is a major part of the all-important immune system; and, as Dr. Kearns states, "The amount of thymus gland hormone in the blood can be just about destroyed in twenty-four hours with infectious problems."

Calcium and the B-complex and other vitamins also are often used as part of the natural therapy for viral diseases.

To combat phlegm, discharge, and lung congestion, various herbs and homeopathic remedies are very helpful. However, as the doctors Goldstein point out, if discharges are not adversely affecting the pet, they should not be stopped, because they are the body's natural way of getting rid of toxins.

Vitamin A not only helps rebuild the immune system but also helps directly in problems of the mucous membranes common in such infectious diseases as pneumonia and distemper. Using the newer, nontoxic form of

---

*Veterinarians: For further details of the I.V. administration, please see "Of Interest Mainly to Veterinarians," Note 1, at the end of the chapter.

A,* as Dr. Kearns points out, up to 200,000 units a day can be given to an animal weighing ten pounds or more. Being able to use such massive amounts helps the body to flush out the poisons very quickly: "Much more quickly than with drugs," Dr. Kearns adds. The reason for this is that huge amounts of toxic drugs can't be used without killing the animal.

Unlike many orthodox veterinarians, nutritional veterinarians will seldom try to fight the symptom of fever, unless the fever is excessively high. A fever is a sign of increased body metabolism; the high metabolism results from the fact that the body is in the middle of intense activity—fighting off its invaders.

CANINE DISTEMPER

Distemper and the secondary bacterial infections that accompany it are sometimes estimated to kill ninety to ninety-five percent of the dogs that are brought to veterinarians. Orthomolecular veterinarians achieve eighty-five percent cure. You did read those numbers right.

Early symptoms of distemper are loss of appetite, depression, and fever. Often these symptoms disappear for a few days—and then the disease manifests itself again with a vengeance. There may be watery or puslike discharge from the eyes and the nose. The dog's eyes may become sensitive to light, and he may try desperately to keep himself in a dark place. There may be diarrhea and a skin eruption on the abdomen and on the insides of the hind legs. There may be a hardening of the foot pads.

R. Geoffrey Broderick, D.V.M., was perhaps one of the first nutritional veterinarians to use vitamin C to cure a "terminal" case of distemper. He tells of his first effort: "When the dog was brought in to me, he had been given up on by orthodox veterinarians. He had a temperature of 105 degrees. He was foaming at the mouth. He had not eaten in a week. He had not touched water in two days. He couldn't stand up. The other veterinarians who had seen him were quite right: he was dying.

"The question was," said Dr. Broderick, "should I follow all the rules of orthodox veterinary medicine? If so, I too was going to have to put this little dog permanently to sleep. Or was I going to try a treatment for which there were at the time few or no precedents?"

Dr. Broderick asked the owners: "Will you be willing to try a bit of medical pioneering with me? Will you let me try vitamin C?" They agreed.

"As I filled the needle to inject the vitamin C into the dog," Dr. Broderick says, "I could just hear all my colleagues uttering, 'Preposterous! This dog is dying, by all rules of medicine—and you are going to cure him with a vitamin?'

"Nevertheless, I couldn't take the easy way out and destroy this dog. I

---

*This is a water-soluble form of vitamin A, which does not tend to be stored in the body as the fat-soluble form does.

gave him 25,000 milligrams of vitamin C, intravenously, main line. Then, with perhaps more hope than I really felt, I put a bowl of food in front of this dog who had been too sick to eat for a week—and left him alone for an hour in quiet.

"An hour later, I came back to see what I would find. The puppy, who had come in an hour before in a crumpled heap, was now standing up. He had his head in the bowl of food and was eating away ravenously. His tail was wagging up a storm. The tail wagging is not a scientific indication; but it certainly affected *me* at the time. There was a scientific barometer, though. His temperature was now absolutely normal. The doomed puppy had been cured in an hour."

Not all dogs respond so completely to a single shot of vitamin C, of course. Often the pet has to be given twice-daily shots for four or five days. That was true of a nine-month-old beagle that H. H. Robertson, D.V.M., treated. The puppy, named "Sooner," had not been eating when Dr. Robertson first saw him. He had a temperature of 104.5 degrees. His pharynx was severely inflamed and he had swollen tonsils. A purulent discharge oozed from his eyes and from his nose. Sooner required six shots (5 grams each, given every twelve hours) of sodium ascorbate (vitamin C) before he was cured. These six shots allowed him to fare much better than his brother and sister, both of whom had died the week before—not having been given vitamin C—of the same disease.

According to the severity of the case, such veterinarians as Dr. Lemmon and Dr. Kearns report that they will sometimes add the following to the intravenous vitamin C: DMSO (dimethyl sulfoxide) and a mixture of sodium chloride, potassium chloride, calcium chloride, and water. (This mixture is more technically known as lactated Ringer's solution. It is helpful in replacing the body's electrolytes and in combating dehydration.) Also, these doctors will often add a multiple vitamin-mineral supplementation and a combination of raw glandular extracts.*

When orthodox veterinary medicine does achieve a cure of distemper, the dog is often left with debilitating neurological problems, if the disease has progressed to the central nervous system. Dr. Lemmon is one of our veterinarians who uses acupuncture. He recently was presented with two dogs who had been having chomping fits for several days. A dog with chomping fits will look as if he is chewing gum furiously, and often a bubbly froth will come from his mouth. (By the way, vaccinations are not one hundred percent effective in preventing diseases, and these two dogs serve as proof: They had both come down with distemper shortly after receiving the distemper vaccine from other veterinarians.)

Dr. Lemmon used a single fifteen-minute acupuncture technique, and the

*Veterinarians: Please see "Of Interest Mainly to Veterinarians," Note 2, at the end of the chapter.

fits in both dogs stopped within twelve hours. "One dog had no relapse, even though we checked him periodically for months," Dr. Lemmon tells me. "The other, who had been more ill and was having many fits throughout each day, had no fits at all for a week, then had a relapse. I feel another treatment would have helped this animal toward a total cure, but the owners declined further treatment and chose to have their dog euthanized. I know that other veterinarians, using acupuncture for this 'incurable' neurological aftereffect of distemper, have very high success—when the owner cooperates."

Drs. Robert and Marty Goldstein add to this statement: "Acupuncture is very successful in the alleviation of seizures secondary to distemper, *even when permanent damage has been done to the central nervous system.* With permanent damage, seizures can be controlled (but not cured) with injections of vitamin B_{12} or C at the proper acupuncture points . . . or with surgical implants at these points. The owner can choose: the B_{12} or C injections have to be repeated; the implants do not."

Dr. Kearns has also dealt successfully with the neurological aftereffects of distemper, as this case history recounts. "I first saw the German shepherd when he was a nine-month-old puppy. He had been treated at one of the most prestigious animal hospitals in the Northeast for distemper; and, while they saved his life, he was left with encephalitis and massive seizure activity. I used vitamin C intravenously daily on this dog—starting out with 30 to 40 grams a day. Within ten days the seizures had stopped. The dog never again had a seizure—although he lived to the rather ancient age of fourteen. Not only that, but his long life was completely disease-free. He was maintained on 3 grams vitamin C a day given orally, which was 'upped' to as much as 10 grams daily when he showed the first signs of another infectious disease." Dr. Kearns adds: "Vitamins C and A, a natural diet, calcium, magnesium, selenium, vitamin E, and the B-vitamins will control most aftereffects of distemper—or other central nervous system virus."

FELINE DISTEMPER
(FELINE INFECTIOUS ENTERITIS,
FELINE PANLEUKOPENIA)

Several of the orthodox veterinary books I consulted used exactly the same phrase for this disease: "the most deadly of all cat diseases." The death rate is described as "enormous"; one estimate sets it at eighty percent. Yet, Dr. Kearns reports: "I do not lose these cats—unless they are brought in already in a coma."

Before we discuss the specifics of Dr. Kearns's treatment, there is more you should know about feline distemper. This disease takes its toll extremely rapidly. Your cat may start out one morning in apparent good health and may be dead the next morning. Time is of the essence; and, indeed, the enormous death rate reported by traditional veterinary medicine may be due in no small part to the fact that owners don't get treatment early enough. Since this is such a fast-acting disease, keep your pet vaccinated against it and give him the recommended preventive amount of vitamin C (Chapters 2 and 3).

I said in the Introduction that for most disorders you can use the information provided by this book to find an orthomolecular veterinarian, or you can ask your own veterinarian to read the details in this book and then consult with an orthomolecular veterinarian if your doctor needs more details. However, since time is so crucial to saving your cat with distemper, you cannot afford to waste it. GET TO YOUR OWN VETERINARIAN IMMEDIATELY. As a matter of fact, that might be amended: GET TO THE NEAREST AVAILABLE VETERINARIAN IMMEDIATELY. Show the doctor these pages; but if he or she is skeptical, you must either DEMAND that Dr. Kearns's treatment be tried (as a client, you have this right), or you must let your doctor try traditional medical techniques. A further word of caution; it won't save your pet if you decide to take your cat back home from a skeptical veterinarian and try calling Dr. Kearns so you can institute his treatment yourself. Only a qualified veterinarian, with the proper "tools," can use this particular technique.

Why do I keep referring to Dr. Kearns—and Dr. Kearns only—rather than nutritional veterinarians in general? Because, with this disease, Dr. Kearns has had more success than the other nutritional veterinarians I asked about feline distemper. Of course, if you live near another orthomolecular veterinarian named in the List of Nutritionally Oriented Veterinarians, you might call and check. Even if he or she is not at the time having the success Dr. Kearns has, the nutritional veterinarian very likely will be happy to read about Dr. Kearns's treatment and apply it. Make sure you specify on the phone, however, that the optimal treatment requires vitamin B_{17} (laetrile); the doctor may not have it on hand. Dr. Kearns states that with B_{17} the successful results are close to 100 percent; but without it, the success rate is still high: fifty to sixty percent.

Symptoms of Feline Distemper

The first symptom is refusal of food. Since I am owned by a cat, as are you, I am well aware that we cannot drag our pets to a veterinarian every time they turn up their noses at food. However, if you take your cat's temperature at this point, you may find it to be 104 degrees or more. TAKE YOUR CAT TO A VETERINARIAN RIGHT AWAY. Another very early telltale sign is when your cat sits hunched up and looks generally "miserable."

You may not take your cat's temperature every time he refuses food. So, if your cat has distemper, you may miss this early opportunity. Still, you have another chance to catch feline distemper before it is too late. An hour or two after refusing his food, your cat will start to vomit violently. Only liquid will be brought up, not solid foods. The vomit will at first be white in color; later it will turn yellow. AT THIS POINT, YOU MUST TAKE HIS TEM-

PERATURE. IF IT IS HIGH, YOU MUST GET HIM TO A VETERINARIAN IM-MEDIATELY. The violent vomiting produces severe dehydration; and very quickly your pet will have lost so much weight, that he may be unrecognizable. The progress of feline distemper is so rapid that all I have mentioned—including the extreme weight loss—can happen within a few hours.

Dr. Kearns's Nutritional Therapy

I hope you have read the preceding section thoroughly before reading this one.

As I said earlier, the orthodox books I consulted described the death rate of feline distemper as enormous. However, when I asked nutritional veterinarian Dr. Kearns about this disorder, he told me:

"I do not lose these cats at all—unless they are brought to me already comatose. I just have really good luck with them. I think laetrile was 'made' for cats.* When you get a cat in with distemper, you get tremendously high fever and tremendous wasting; and the poor cat is in absolutely terrible shape. Laetrile [vitamin B_{17}] gets their temperature down, makes them feel good, gives them a sense of well-being—so that they will start to eat.

"However, laetrile is not in and of itself a cure for feline distemper, and is actually a very small part of the total treatment. It might be more accurately called a 'trigger' that 'turns the animal around.' It gets the temperature down; it makes them feel good; and they start to eat. Once they start eating, you can give them vitamin and mineral supplements and bring them right back to health.

"Laetrile, though, is a very small part of the treatment. The first thing we use is fluids, because the animals are dehydrated. In the fluids we put amino acids (proteins), to supply all the amino acids they're missing; and then we add sodium ascorbate (a form of vitamin C) and the B-complex to the fluid solution. We pass a tube orally down into the cat's stomach, and we give them vitamins A and E that way, and we give them a little egg yolk. So that it all gets optimally absorbed. We also give pancreatic enzymes this way.

"With orthodox techniques, you might as well give up on your cat if he has feline distemper. With more natural techniques, it is a big job and an expensive one. But the more natural techniques save a lot of otherwise 'doomed-to-death' animals."

PARVOVIRUS
(MORE COMMONLY KNOWN AS PARVO)

This is an infectious disease generally believed to attack dogs only. It is thought to be a mutant of a cat virus; it can overrun your puppy's body and

---

*If the word "laetrile" immediately makes you skeptical, please read the "laetrile" section in the chapter on cancer.

kill him—even before you have a chance to notice any symptoms. It is also serious in the adult dog. It is a disease you can prevent easily—and treat successfully—if you follow the recommendations made by orthomolecular medicine.

I first came upon this new and often fatal disease when I accompanied a friend and his dog to the Animal Medical Center in New York City for a simple medical checkup. The large waiting room of the Center looked as though a bomb had hit it. The casualties—scores of dogs—were lying around in various states of near-death.

"What on earth happened?" my friend asked a woman who was sitting glassy-eyed beside her pet, a dog who looked as if he had perhaps minutes of life left in his small brown body.

"Most of us here," she said, "think it's an outbreak of parvo."

It *was* parvo, a harried veterinarian at the Center told me. The disease was sweeping the country; and before this particular epidemic had died down, it had snuffed out thousands of animal lives.

As I was coming home from the Medical Center, I ran into a neighbor who was raising ten new puppies her champion standard poodle had recently presented to the world. "Come see the beautiful little ones," she said.

As I accompanied her on the elevator, the woman talked happily about the new pups. Champion-bred. Hardy, healthy stock. Sell for a fortune. Liveliest, most mischievous little things you ever saw. Been alone all day today; wait'll you see the big greeting we get.

There was no greeting when we opened the door. Lady, the mother, sat in the middle of the living room, whimpering piteously. Beside her lay seven inert little forms, her dead pups. Across the room, her three still-alive puppies lay huddled together, echoing their mother's cries in smaller voices.

In her instinctive wisdom, the mother apparently had separated her still-living pups from the dead ones, so that her healthy babies might not catch whatever the terrible, fatal "it" was.

"It" was parvo.

Veterinarians told me: "People are calling us up in the morning, right after noticing the more alarming symptoms. We're giving them appointments for several hours later, just giving them enough time to *get* here, really. But the people are calling back, saying, 'Never mind the appointment. My puppy is dead.' "

Prevention of Parvovirus

You can prevent parvo simply by giving your dog every day the amount of vitamin C recommended in Chapters 2 and 3. This will keep your pet's immune system strong and at the same time will help prevent other infectious diseases, too. As Wendell O. Belfield, D.V.M., often considered *the* pioneer in the use of vitamin C for pets, says: "I have not heard of a single case of parvovirus among dogs receiving either the vitamin C alone or vitamin C along with a general vitamin-mineral program." Dr. Belfield adds:

"These are dogs who for the most part did not receive any vaccine."[6] (Drs. Lemmon and Kearns tell me that they also know of no cases of parvo when vitamin C has been used as a preventive.)

Symptoms of Parvovirus

Sometimes there are few noticeable symptoms before a puppy suddenly dies. The principal signs are high fever and protracted vomiting. There is diarrhea, with grayish or yellow-gray stools. Later the stools become bloody.

Treatment for Parvovirus

Intravenous vitamin C, in the sodium ascorbate form, is the basis of the treatment. Because of the swiftness of this disease, orthomolecular veterinarians such as Dr. Kearns, Dr. Robert Goldstein, and Dr. Marty Goldstein have quadrupled the amount of vitamin C they use for many other viral conditions, raising the dosage from a half-gram of sodium ascorbate per pound of body weight to two grams per pound. Dr. Kearns will sometimes use even more according to the particular case. Our veterinarians find that the virus is usually controlled in about two days.

Dr. Kearns adds a dramatic statement here: "I have lost only one dog to parvovirus. That was a dog who had been treated by another veterinarian. When the puppy was brought into my office, he was literally one hour away from death. He did not have enough time left for the vitamin C to take effect."

Depending on the particular case, many nutritional veterinarians will use an antibiotic at the beginning of treatment, as an adjunct to the natural therapy. They will usually administer a high volume of fluids to prevent dehydration. Recovering patients are sent home with vitamin C that can be taken by mouth.

Other additions to the treatment vary according to the particular doctor's special areas of study within the field of natural medicine. Dr. Lemmon and Dr. Kearns, for instance, will use DMSO. John B. Limehouse, D.V.M., who has made a study of the field of herbology, will often use Kyolic garlic, which contains built-in antibacterial and antibiotic agents. Sometimes he will use a combination of herbs that contain nutrients that help build up the liver, such as dandelion, red beet powder, and parsley.

If you have never studied the field, the use of herbs may sound like just another old wives' tale. Yet, herbs are *not* "strange little things" to which uneducated people hundreds of years ago attributed mystical powers. Herbs are often powerhouses of healthful nutrients; and our veterinarians who use herbs as part of their therapies have made a study of herbs and know just what nutrients are in what herbs. Therefore, they know just which herbs are likely to help any given condition.

For instance, it was just mentioned that Dr. Limehouse sometimes uses dandelion to help rebuild the liver. How can a pesty weed that clutters up your garden help rebuild health? Well, that "pesty weed" contains five times more vitamin A than do carrots (which are one of *the* best sources of A). It contains vitamins B₁, B₂, B₃, C, E, and P. It also contains the minerals calcium, iron, magnesium, potassium, silicon, and sodium.[7]

Veterinarians such as Dr. Kearns also will use vitamin E to help prevent scarring of the heart. Scarring of the heart kills some animals even after they have recovered from parvo; a number of scientific studies have shown that vitamin E helps prevent scarring. Dr. Kearns also uses proteolytic enzymes to reestablish normal intestinal flora.

When the dog is well enough to eat again, our veterinarians are careful not to let him go right back to his normal foods. Dr. Limehouse, for instance, likes to keep the dog for the first few days on a liquid diet, such as chicken and vegetable broths. Then he will switch the animal for three to five days to a rice and cottage cheese diet. These two foods are easily digested and therefore "go easy" on the intestines, which are often severely affected by infectious diseases.

A Word of Warning

Since parvo has not made the headlines for a few years, you might assume that the disease has disappeared. Unfortunately, parvo has *not* disappeared. Our veterinarians report local outbreaks in their parts of the country, as well as additional isolated cases. And, as Dr. Lemmon states, "No one knows when there will be another major epidemic." Dr. Lemmon recommends, therefore, that you don't get lax either about giving your pet periodic vaccinations against the disease or about giving him the recommended amount of vitamin C (see Chapters 2 and 3) to help prevent all infectious diseases. As Dr. Lemmon says, "The vaccination itself is helpful, but far from perfect, in preventing parvo. However, the combination of the vaccine and the recommended amount of C is just about a one hundred percent preventive." Of course, when Dr. Lemmon talks about virtually total prevention, he is counting on your also giving your pet a natural diet (see Chapter 2).

RESPIRATORY DISEASES
(INCLUDING PNEUMONIA AND PNEUMONITIS)

Dr. Kearns reports approximately ninety-five percent successful results in treating respiratory disorders if the animal has not been treated with antibiotics.

Symptoms of Pneumonia and Pneumonitis

These diseases are characterized by high fever, coughing, rapid breathing, and rapid pulse. In severe cases, there will be a blue cast to the lower eyelid.

This is due to the fact that the dog or cat is suffering from oxygen starvation. You may notice your pet trying hard to avoid lying down. He may take up an odd new sitting position, with his neck extended forward and his elbows turned out. This strange behavior is his attempt to give his constricted chest cavity literally "more room to breathe."

Nutritional Therapy for Respiratory Diseases

Vitamin A (perhaps 10,000 units daily) and, again, vitamin C are the basis of treatment, with doctors adding various adjuncts according to the particular case. Dr. Kearns and Dr. Lemmon, for instance, will sometimes make a solution of sodium ascorbate (vitamin C) or DMSO with sterile distilled water and put drops of this solution directly into the nose to relieve nasal congestion. They may also make a dilute solution of either of these two substances to use as eye drops. Dr. Kearns adds that this solution can also be used intravenously.

Sometimes Dr. Lemmon and Dr. Limehouse will use the herb garlic, which has a great mucus-destroying effect. Mucus in the lungs, of course, is a prime problem in respiratory diseases. The doctors will also sometimes use the herbs fenugreek and comfrey. As Dr. Lemmon states, "I don't use all of these things all of the time. If one substance doesn't seem to be working quickly for the particular dog or cat, I'll use another one."

With rhinotracheitis and other upper respiratory tract diseases, Dr. Lemmon reports a ninety percent cure rate in early cases. "However, if the animal has already been treated with antibiotics and other drugs when I get to see him, my successful results drop to about seventy-five percent." Dr. Kearns reports similar statistics. Why should the antibiotic-treated pet have a lesser chance of being cured? Dr. Lemmon states: "While antibiotics may inactivate or kill bacteria, they also suppress the immune system." The immune system is vitally important in fighting off diseases. "The vitamins C and A used by nutritional veterinarians," Dr. Lemmon states, "do the opposite: They improve the immune system."

SEPTICEMIA

Septicemia is blood poisoning throughout the entire body of the dog or cat. I think the definition tells you it can be a very serious disease and is often fatal. Septicemia, for instance, is said to kill many more new puppies than does any other disease. However, nutritional veterinarians (such as Drs. Limehouse, Kearns, Robertson, and Marty and Robert Goldstein) report "excellent results" with this disease.

Symptoms of Septicemia

It is imperative that an owner keep a sharp eye out for symptoms of septicemia, especially in a newborn pet, because once the disease gets hold, it can spread like wildfire. The pup or kitten may have started out his new life looking well and nursing well; but then, perhaps a week after birth, he may withdraw from the rest of the litter and even from his mother. His cries become piteous and grow fainter. The name given to septicemia in puppies is descriptive of the symptoms: fading pup syndrome. When the symptoms start, the animal should get immediate veterinary help, or he will die within twenty-four to forty-eight hours.

Symptoms in the adult pet will be listlessness, poor appetite, and fever.

Dr. Lemmon adds a point that we make for all other disorders in this book: this dread disorder can be prevented by the natural diet and supplementation detailed in Chapters 2 and 3. However, to stop septicemia from striking your newborn pet, prevention must begin with the mother at the start of pregnancy or before.

Nutritional Therapy for Septicemia

Dr. Limehouse gives vitamin C intravenously and four capsules of Kyolic garlic four times a day (sixteen capsules daily). He also uses herbs such as burdock to purify the blood. The doctor also withholds all solid foods, giving liquids only, until the pet is cured. "Sometimes," Dr. Limehouse adds, "we'll give them enemas, to help clear the system faster of toxins, especially when we feel the poisoning has come from food." (Dr. Limehouse calls such poisoning "garbage gut.")

In addition to the intravenous C (1/2 gram per pound of body weight), Drs. Lemmon and Kearns often use a small amount of DMSO.*

When Dr. Lemmon finds, through blood tests and acupuncture testing, that there is an accompanying problem in an internal organ such as the liver or kidneys, he will often use vitamin B_{12} injected in the acupuncture trigger points to that organ.**

A FEW WORDS ABOUT VACCINATIONS

If you are against introducing drugs and other unnatural substances into the body, you may also be against vaccination. A few of this book's veterinarians agree with you. However, Dr. Limehouse seems to me to sum up the belief of most of this book's participating veterinarians. "Ideally," he says, "I would like *not* to vaccinate; because, of course, when we vaccinate, we're introducing a small amount of the virus into the system." A number of nutritional authorities believe there is always a chance that a weak immune

---

*Veterinarians: Please see "Of Interest Mainly to Veterinarians," at the end of the chapter.

**Why B_{12}? You may have heard that Hollywood and sports stars sometimes get B_{12} shots for energy. While this is a gross oversimplification of what B_{12} can do, the vitamin does act as a stimulant on acupuncture points that are deficient in energy.

system will not be able to fight off even this small amount of virus, and that the vaccination might cause the very disease it's meant to prevent. "However," Dr. Limehouse continues, "today's dogs and cats are fighting so many new toxins—in their food, in their water, even in the air they breathe—that I'm afraid vaccinations are a necessary aid."

Dr. Lemmon states that the combination of vaccinations, natural diet, and supplementation, particularly with vitamin C, forms virtually one hundred percent prevention for the often deadly infectious diseases.

You can take some easy steps to prevent the two major shortcomings of vaccinations: the fact that they sometimes cause the disease they're meant to prevent, and the fact that they sometimes just don't work to prevent it.

First, don't vaccinate your dog or cat when he is showing any signs of illness. If your pet is already ill, his immune system may not be able to produce the antibodies the vaccination is supposed to stimulate; and he stands a chance of being overwhelmed by the small amount of virus in the vaccine, and succumbing to the illness he's being vaccinated against.

Second, take the recommendations of Drs. Robert and Marty Goldstein. They suggest you make sure your pet receives the following supplements two to three weeks before and after vaccination:

- Vitamin A. 10,000 IU a day for a fifty-pound dog; 2,500 IU a day for the adult cat.
- Vitamin E. Dog: 400 IU a day; cat: 200 IU a day.
- Vitamin C. Dog: 5,000 mg a day; cat: 2,000 mg a day. Start the C at 500 mg a day and increase every second day until the recommended dosage is reached. Give the dosage in stages two to four times a day.

Third, please realize that *vaccinations do not take effect overnight.* Don't take your cat or dog to a groomer, kennel, or other animal gathering place for two weeks after the immunization shot.

You may have always thought you were doing all you could to prevent infectious diseases in your pet by vaccinating him; you have already read about two major ways in which vaccines can be imperfect. You will realize, also, that there are vaccinations for only a comparatively few infectious diseases. What good is it to protect your pet from these few diseases, if you end up losing him to another infectious disease? As we showed early in this chapter, there is one substance that can protect against all viruses and all bacteria. We are back where we began—with vitamin C.

OF INTEREST MAINLY TO VETERINARIANS
NOTE 1. *Re I.V. sodium ascorbate:* Nutritional veterinarians such as Dr. Kearns, Dr. Robertson, and Dr. Belfield use sulfite-free injectable 25% sodium ascorbate (Cetane-Injection) prepared by Fellows Medical Mfg. Co., Inc., Anaheim, CA

92806. Sodium sulfite used as a preservative has caused side reactions resembling the neurological signs of beriberi.

The cephalic vein is the route of choice. .

If the 25% sodium ascorbate solution is administered undiluted, it can cause weakness or vomiting; these can be prevented by slow administration, at least two minutes for the injection.*

Ideal strength is that of an isotonic solution, 3%.

Multivitamin and mineral preparations are important with continued administration, since megadoses of sodium ascorbate are diuretic. Calcium, magnesium, potassium,** and the water-soluble vitamins must be replaced.

Collapsed veins may sometimes occur in cats and smaller dogs being treated I.V. b.i.d. The required dosage can then be injected subcutaneously by diluting the 25% injectable sodium ascorbate solution with approximately 2 parts of sterile water, giving approximately an 8% solution. The injected ascorbate will take thirty to forty minutes to be absorbed into the body.[8]***

NOTE 2. Drs. Lemmon and Kearns obtain the glandular extracts from Seroyal in Concord, CA. These extracts are obtained from animals fed organically raised foods.

NOTE 3. Drs. Lemmon and Kearns use DMSO at 2 to 3 cc for the 40- to 60-pound animal once or twice a day in lactated Ringer's solution, with I.V. drip.

REFERENCES

1. C. W. Jungeblut et al., *J. Immunol.*, 33, 203, 1937; see also I. J. Kligler et al., *J. Path. Bact.*, 46, 619, 1938; and C. W. Jungeblut, *J. Expt. Med.*, 70, 315, 1939. Cited by Adelle Davis, *Let's Get Well* (New York: Harcourt, Brace and World, Inc.), 1965, p. 141.
2. Adelle Davis, *Let's Eat Right to Keep Fit* (New York: Harcourt, Brace and Co.), 1954, p. 142.
3. Wendell O. Belfield, D.V.M., and Martin Zucker, *How to Have a Healthier Dog* (Garden City, New York: Doubleday and Co., Inc.) 1981, p. 328.
4. Adelle Davis, *Let's Get Well* (New York: Harcourt, Brace and World, Inc.), 1965, p. 142.
5. *Ibid.*, p. 141.
6. Belfield and Zucker, *op. cit.*, p. 254.
7. Kathy Berman, "Herbs and Your Pet," *Herald of Health*, November 1978.
8. Wendell O. Belfield and Irwin Stone, *J. Internat. Acad. Prev. Med.*, Vol. 2, No. 3, third quarter 1975, p. 16.

*Dr. Kearns comments: "Especially for cats, I will often add the sodium ascorbate solution to lactated Ringer's or distilled water, and administer it by I.V. drip."

**Dr. Kearns: "Chelated minerals are preferable."

***Dr. Kearns: "In my experience, ... some animals have not absorbed subcutaneous fluids after twenty-four hours. I try to instill an I.V. catheter in these very sick animals at the beginning of treatment. In this way, of course, I can administer fluids, sodium ascorbate, etc., at will."

CHAPTER EIGHT

Some Problems of Internal Organs

NORMAN C. RALSTON, D.V.M., AND RICHARD J. KEARNS, D.V.M.:
"Just by adding vitamin E in high enough doses for diabetic pets, you can cut insulin down to only ten to twenty percent of what the animal needed before taking the vitamin. If you add a natural diet and pancreatic enzymes, you can get even better results."

NINO ALORO, D.V.M.:
"Diet seems to be at the base of about ninety percent of the cases of cystitis that I see. . . . When my clients observe the proper diet after initial treatment, there are rarely any of the 'normal' relapses. If they put the pet back on commercial food, then the cystitis comes back."

RICHARD J. KEARNS, D.V.M., AND NORMAN C. RALSTON, D.V.M.:
"Bladder stones and kidney stones are completely a nutritional problem. [We] have never seen a recurrence once an animal is put on a natural diet. Never."

In this chapter, nutritional veterinarians discuss therapies for several serious problems of internal organs. These therapies involve little or no surgery or drugs and are often much more successful than the more toxic therapies that are in wider use.

DIABETES

Diabetes occurs when the pancreas becomes unable to secrete enough insulin to maintain a normal blood sugar balance. Diabetes can cause convulsions and death. Traditional treatment is successful in controlling the disease: but, as will be discussed, this traditional treatment has drawbacks that often lead orthodox veterinarians to suggest that owners consider euthanasia. The newer therapies detailed here do not tend to have these drawbacks.

Symptoms
It is imperative that you not ignore the symptoms of diabetes. Not only can diabetes be a killer in its own right, as we've said; it also can lead to liver enlargement (the liver can actually double in size), kidney damage, and cataracts, among other things.

Your pet's appetite can be a symptom: the animal may become a glutton. At the same time that he's eating more, however, he may start losing weight. This does not mean an obese animal cannot develop diabetes. This disease is as common in the obese pet as it is in the obese person. He may also develop increased thirst, spending a lot of time at his water bowl, lapping furiously. If these symptoms appear, don't think of them as "odd changes in habits"; they could be the only warning you'll ever get that your pet has diabetes.

A number of veterinary cat books written for the public do not mention diabetes among the list of disorders. Don't let these omissions lead you to think diabetic symptoms in your cat can't mean diabetes. They can. As Margaret Reister, D.V.M., states: "Diabetes mellitus is not common among cats, but if not treated promptly, it can cause irreversible organ damage and eventually death."[1]

The Difference Between Orthodox and
Orthomolecular Approaches
Standard medical treatment involves introducing insulin from outside the body for the lifetime of the pet. Nutritional veterinary treatment involves rebuilding the total health of the body so that it can again produce enough of its *own* insulin, just as it always did before it "got" diabetes.

Insulin shots are expensive and have to be maintained throughout the pet's life. They do not always work. (Or, as Norman C. Ralston, D.V.M., comments: "They *many times* do not work.") Their rigid scheduling can make an owner a slave to his or her pet's sickness. (Scheduling of nutritional supplements is not so crucial and allows the owner more freedom.) For these reasons, some orthodox veterinary books and articles written for the public state that you might be "better off" putting your diabetic pet to sleep.

Insulin introduced artificially into your pet's body makes him continually vulnerable to diabetic shock, which can be fatal. This is called an insulin reaction; if you are not around to give your pet immediate emergency help, he may die.* This is another fact that leads an owner either to become a slave to a diabetic pet, sometimes rearranging work and sleep schedules to be nearby when diabetic shock can be expected—or to dispose of the pet entirely.

Once a natural therapy allows the pet to be removed completely from insulin, of course, the owner need no longer worry about the possibility of diabetic shock. (Unless, of course, you let your pet binge on products containing sugar.)

At its best—when insulin controls diabetes without side effects—it does only that: it controls the diabetes. It does nothing for the degenerative changes in the body that caused the diabetes in the first place and that are probably causing other health problems as well. An overall orthomolecular approach will attack the cause of the diabetes (a chemically imbalanced body), rather than just trying to control the symptom (diabetes). In this way the body usually will again be able to create enough of its own insulin, just as it did before it started to degenerate. You may also very well find your cat or dog suddenly recovers from other, seemingly unrelated, health problems as well.

Therapy

For a recommended diet for diabetes, see the box at the end of the section on pancreatitis, page 131.

Medical studies testing human beings have shown that vitamin E can cut out completely a diabetic's need for insulin, or cut down significantly the amount needed. In one study, *half of the diabetic people tested required no insulin at all, and another thirty percent needed less.* This was accomplished by giving approximately 300 IU a day.[2]

Drs. Evan V. and Wilfrid Shute of Canada, whose many years of work with vitamin E have established them as experts, report that vitamin E in high enough doses will allow eight out of ten diabetics either to go off insu-

---

*If your pet is on insulin, *please be sure* your veterinarian tells you when insulin shock is most likely to occur, what signs to look for, and what emergency help you can give.

lin entirely or to drastically cut down its use. A number of other studies around the world back up the doctors Shute's findings on diabetics.[3]

If you are interested in the implications of these studies for the treatment of human diabetes, discuss them with your doctor or seek out a nutritional physician. ABSOLUTELY DO NOT EXPERIMENT BY YOURSELF. Death will result.

For the treatment of diabetes in pets, Richard J. Kearns, D.V.M., says "Just by using vitamin E in high enough doses, you can cut insulin down to only ten to twenty percent of what the animal needed before taking vitamin E. If the clients will add to the E a natural diet and pancreatic enzymes, we can get seventy to eighty percent of the cats completely off insulin; and we can get dogs to the point where they need 'next to nothing.'"* Pancreatic enzymes are prescribed by the veterinarian to help restore the ability of the pancreas to function on its own and produce insulin.**

Dr. Kearns also uses the proteolytic enzyme bromelain. This helps break down much of the harmful fibrous scar tissue that clogs the pancreas.

You cannot gauge your pet's insulin level or the correct amounts of vitamin E yourself. That work is strictly for a veterinarian. I repeat my earlier warning: DO NOT EXPERIMENT BY YOURSELF. You will kill your pet.***

Note that an orthomolecular veterinarian such as Dr. Kearns will not abruptly withdraw your pet from insulin. He or she will institute nutritional therapy while keeping the pet on insulin. As the nutritional therapy increases the pet's ability to produce his own insulin, the doctor will gradually decrease the amount of insulin introduced artificially into the body. It is imperative that there be at no time either too much or *too little* insulin introduced from outside the body, to balance the new amount your pet's body is producing. Monitoring the insulin level requires periodic scientific testing.

If your pet is diabetic, you cannot read the paragraphs above quoting Dr. Kearns, whisk your pet off insulin, give him some vitamin E, and expect him to be alive a few weeks from now. You must also expect the same

---

*Most of the small percentage of animals to whom Dr. Kearns has to continue giving any insulin at all are those who were so deteriorated when he first saw them that there was "literally no insulin-secreting tissue left in the body." Even in these "hopeless" cases, however, insulin can be given in lower doses than would be needed without nutritional therapy.

**Veterinarians: Please see "Of Interest Mainly to Veterinarians," Note 1, at the end of the chapter.

***Although my magazine articles specifically warn against self-prescription, some people try it anyway. For instance, I once wrote an article mentioning the help curare could give for a particular disorder. I cautioned that although curare was derived from a natural source, it was a powerful drug; it could be administered only by a physician. If it *were* self-prescribed, I warned, it could be so lethal that it could "cure whatever ails you—forever."

I received a letter from a sincere lady who reported she could not find curare in her local health food stores. Could I please help her find this miracle substance that—in her words—"cures everything."

disastrous result if you are diabetic and start giving yourself vitamin E and taking yourself off insulin. What you *can* do to use the information on E and insulin for yourself is to see "How to Use This Book" in the Introduction, regarding how to find a nutritional physician.

In reviewing this chapter Dr. Ralston commented here, "Please reemphasize this point. I just lost a wonderful cat. The owner decided to treat her animal herself because what I did seemed so simple. And it *was* simple—but she depended too long on her own treatment, without having the insulin level professionally checked. The cat was rushed to emergency and died."

Robert Goldstein, V.M.D., and Marty Goldstein, D.V.M., also have good results with diabetes, using basically the same therapy as does Dr. Kearns. They too will keep the animal on insulin while they rebuild the body's natural ability to produce its own. They will use a complex carbohydrate diet.

Complex carbohydrates are not to be confused with simple carbohydrates. Sugar is a simple carbohydrate, and of course the last thing you want to feed your pet is sugar, if he has diabetes (or even if he doesn't).*

The doctors Goldstein will also use the herb goldenseal, which, as they tell me, "aids in lowering blood sugar and has an insulinlike effect on the body." Dr. Ralston adds: "Goldenseal also has the great quality of healing the gut wall. This healing is badly needed by the diabetic animal."

Regarding goldenseal, several nutritional veterinarians urged me to repeat the warning just made about vitamin E: Treating an animal without veterinary supervision can be dangerous, whether the treatment is with drugs or with nutrients. Dr. Kearns states, "Many herbs, including goldenseal, can be extremely dangerous if given in the wrong amounts."**

PANCREATITIS

If you're like most people, you never worry about your pet's pancreas (or your own) unless diabetes strikes. Yet pancreatitis—inflammation of the pancreas—can kill. If your pet doesn't die, he may, with standard treatment, have recurring bouts of the disease, any of which might kill. With the newer therapy detailed here, pets do not tend to have these recurring bouts.

As Drs. Marty and Robert Goldstein state, "Pancreatitis is the root of many, many other conditions [including diabetes]. Once the pancreas starts deteriorating, other organs often follow." They add: "A diseased pancreas is usually the result of an improper diet."

---

* Dr. Ralston warns that many drugs contain sugar. So, of course, do many processed foods (for pets and people), as stressed in Chapter 1. "Even ordinary table salt," says Dr. Ralston, "now sometimes contains sugar."
** Veterinarians: Please see, "Of Interest Mainly to Veterinarians," Note 2, at the end of the chapter.

Prevention

You can prevent pancreatic deterioration (as well as most other disorders) by following the recommendations in Chapters 1 to 3; you will be avoiding the improper diet the doctors Goldstein refer to as the major cause of a diseased pancreas. In those early chapters, "combining foods properly" is also recommended. "Combining foods properly" might more aptly be described as *not* combining foods. Give meat only at one meal, grains and fruit at another feeding. (Vegetables, however, may be given with either grains or meat.) Why? Because the pancreas is our great enzyme-producing organ. It secretes one set of enzymes to help digest heavy proteins (such as in meats) and another set to help digest carbohydrates (such as in grains). You can see how asking the pancreas to produce two differing types of enzymes at the same time—to digest two different categories of food—can cause the pancreas much distress over a period of time. (It can also cause the rest of the body much distress, as mentioned in Chapter 2.)

(Is all this true for human beings, too? Yes, it is. Rather than eating cereal, toast—carbohydrates—ham—heavy protein—and eggs for breakfast, you might be just as happy with cereal, fruit, and toast—all carbohydrates. If you are troubled by puzzling bouts with "gas," you might want to see if proper food combining puts an end to them.)

Symptoms

The acute form of pancreatitis manifests itself in sudden vomiting, depression, abdominal pain, and fever. These are symptoms of a number of other problems also; and only a veterinarian can competently give the diagnosis of acute pancreatitis. Since this disease can kill very rapidly, you cannot spare time to search around for orthomolecular help—unless, of course, you live close to a nutritional veterinarian. Nutritional veterinarians start with orthodox therapy, anyway, for this disorder. Get your pet over the emergency first, and then seek orthomolecular aid to promote further healing and to prevent the common recurrences.

Chronic pancreatitis (or pancreatic insufficiency) is frequently marked by voluminous putty-colored stools. These stools have a rancid odor. Your pet may have a great appetite but lose weight. Why? He may be losing weight because his diseased pancreas is not digesting (that is, not allowing his body to use) the food; he may have a "great" appetite for exactly the same reason.

As we have said, the unfortunate animal with chronic pancreatitis is subject to bouts of the acute form. Indeed, chronic pancreatitis *is* the "recurring bouts" that are common when acute pancreatitis is treated by traditional means. Chronic pancreatitis is very uncommon when acute pancreatitis is treated with nutritional therapy.

Therapy

As I have said, under standard veterinary treatment, pancreatitis tends to recur or to lead to other problems. But the nutritional veterinarians I talked with about pancreatitis report excellent results in treating this disorder. Dr. Kearns tells me: "As long as my clients keep their pets on a natural diet, with pancreatic enzymes, we just have no further problems."

Orthodox therapy must always be used at the beginning for acute pancreatitis, according to Dr. Kearns. The traditional therapy involves antibiotics and steroids and fasting with water only for three to seven days.

As Dr. Kearns states: "With acute pancreatitis, the animal often has a white blood count so abnormally high that it literally runs off the scale of any testing machine. It is a life-threatening situation. Hours make a difference in life and death."

Once the medical emergency is over, the pet will be shifted to the diet he should have been on in the first place: a nonpoisonous, nonsupermarket diet with proper combining of foods.

Dr. Kearns and the doctors Goldstein also use pancreatic enzymes and extracts to help prevent the recurrences and further complications that often occur with more standard treatment. As "pancreatic enzymes and extracts" might imply, these substances aid the sick pancreas in fulfilling its function in life. In helping the pancreas do its job without strain, of course, they are helping to keep healthy the rest of the body, which is so dependent on a fully functioning pancreas.

For the pancreatic enzymes, Dr. Kearns uses something a bit different from Viokase, used by a number of other nutritional veterinarians. He uses the raw tissue before it is made into the product Viokase. "I feel this is a little more natural and so has a few more helpful nutrients in it." He obtains the raw tissue from the manufacturers of Viokase.*

Vitamin C will be added to the program for pancreatitis. Dr. Kearns and Dr. Ralston will add sesame oil, which is helpful in producing T-cells. These T-cells help strengthen the immune system, which in turn helps naturally to fight off infection, which is usually an accompaniment of pancreatitis.

More frequent but smaller feedings can be very helpful. These will give the pancreas an evenly balanced daily workload, which is preferable to the organ's having to work extremely hard for an hour or so to digest large amounts, then take it easy for hours before it is hit again with another heavy workload. As Dr. Kearns puts it: "These small, frequent feedings keep all body systems working along at an even pace without undue stress." Smaller, more frequent feedings were recommended in Chapter 2.

(The same principle applies to human beings, too. And you might find that eating smaller, more frequent meals can be helpful for weight loss: since the metabolism never has a chance to get sluggish, there is less of a tendency to store unused calories as fat.)

---

*Veterinarians: Please see, "Of Interest Mainly to Veterinarians," Note 3, at the end of the chapter.

A BASIC DIET FOR DIABETES AND
CHRONIC PANCREATITIS

The following diet is recommended by the doctors Goldstein. They make changes in this diet according to the individual pet's needs.

- 50% complex carbohydrates, such as brown rice, millet, buckwheat, rye. Organic and flaked for easy digestion and preparation.
- 25% finely chopped green vegetables, carrots, and sprouts.
- 25% protein, such as fertile egg yolks, organic beef, steamed fish, organic chicken, raw milk, cheese, yogurt.

How foods are combined in each meal is extremely important for pancreatic problems. Acceptable combinations are:

- Grains and vegetables
- Grains and fruits
- Protein and vegetables

FELINE UROLOGICAL SYNDROME
(CYSTITIS, BLADDER STONES, URINARY BLOCKAGE)*

It is depressing to consider bladder problems in cats from the point of view of orthodox veterinary medicine. They are expensive to treat, painful, recurring. And, not the least depressing fact: these highly dangerous, expensive-to-treat, recurring problems are among the most common health problems in cats. Indeed, some veterinarians state they are *the* most common.

But much of this suffering is actually unnecessary. These problems are not so overwhelming as orthodox veterinary medicine presently finds them. The suffering continues because of the general lack of knowledge of nutritional veterinary medicine.

Nutritional veterinarians tell me they rarely see a case of feline urological syndrome (FUS) in cats raised basically according to the suggestions for a natural diet and supplements in Chapters 1 to 3 of this book. (Dr. Ralston says: "I think I may have seen one case, once.") They say that cats who are fed processed food—who *do* develop FUS—can be helped often without surgery or drugs and without great expense. And there are seldom the almost "inevitable" relapses.

Symptoms of FUS

Your cat may run to the litter box a lot more frequently than usual; he may strain, trying hard to pass urine—and yet on many of these trips he may

---

*Dog owners will find much information of value in this section even though it is written basically for the cat.

pass little or none. The reason for this behavior is that the itching and burning of the urethra make the cat think he has to urinate extremely often, when in reality he doesn't.

If the cystitis is left untreated, the urethra will plug up; and your pet won't be able to urinate even when he has to. Or your cat (or dog) may forget all his manners about where he is supposed to urinate and start urinating anyplace he happens to be at the time.* There may be blood in the urine. Dr. Ralston emphasizes, ". . . these last . . . symptoms may be an emergency, and the pet should be rushed immediately to a veterinarian."

Male cats, because of body structure, may exhibit the earlier signs of FUS for only a day or two before they advance to the emergency state of urinary blockage. Thus, if you own a male cat, try to keep an eye out for the symptoms mentioned two paragraphs before this.

Basic Diet for FUS

J. Keith Benedict, D.V.M., recommends a low-ash, low-phosphorus diet. "The food should have no more than a .5 content of phosphorus. An ash content of 1.5 is ideal," he states. "Many commercial pet foods have phosphorus or ash in higher proportions than this."

Veterinarians such as Carvel G. Tiekert, D.V.M., and Elinor A. Brandt, V.M.D., add that recent research has indicated that high levels of magnesium may also be critically important in causing FUS.

Dr. Benedict notes: "An all-natural diet is extremely helpful in treating FUS problems and preventing recurrence." (See Chapter 2).

Cystitis

As a case history, here is the story of Agnes, my literary agent's cat. It is particularly gratifying to me that Agnes has been helped by this book, since—at least in a small way—Agnes's existence was responsible for its publication. About two years ago I sent an outline for the book to Denise, my agent. The subject especially interested her because of Agnes. Denise found it comforting to know that if someday her orthodox veterinarian ran out of answers for a health problem her cat might develop, there would be "a compilation of information about alternative veterinary medicine that might help Agnes."

Agnes's orthodox veterinarian "ran out of answers" for her cystitis soon afterwards. Denise called to say that Agnes was on her third bout of cystitis.

---

*If you have a pet with this symptom, please realize that several of this book's veterinarians state that indiscriminate urination often can be misdiagnosed as psychological in origin; for instance, an attempt to "get back at you" for introducing a new pet or new baby to the household to impinge on his "territory." While emotional problems *can* be the cause of indiscriminate urination, please have your veterinarian check the urine for physical problems before the doctor and you pursue the psychological possibility.

"I did what the veterinarian prescribed," she told me. "I gave her the antibiotic once a day for a month, and the acidifier twice a day for two months. As soon as I stopped the acidifier, she just got the cystitis symptoms all over again. Now the veterinarian says she may have to stay on the two drugs indefinitely. Do any of the nutritional veterinarians you're writing about have any solution?"

It so happens I had come across something at that early point in my work on this book; and I mentioned that the simplest natural treatment for cystitis was vitamin C. I suggested that Denise ask her veterinarian to consider using it.

Denise called again the next day. "As I suspected," she said drily, "he doesn't *know* anything about vitamin C and cystitis, and so he doesn't believe in it, and so he won't try it."

I suggested she call the health line at the Veterinary Nutritional Association (VNA).* That simple phone call resulted in Agnes's relief from cystitis. On the VNA's advice, Denise gave Agnes 500 milligrams of vitamin C (ascorbic acid) every four hours around the clock, crushing the tablets up in her pet's food, until the symptoms disappeared. Now she gives her, as maintenance, 500 milligrams only twice a day. (Denise also now feeds Agnes on Cornucopia pet food, one of the few prepared pet foods this book recommends as being poison-free and truly balanced for your pet's needs. See the Appendix.)

Agnes still remains free of the "often-recurring" cystitis (which had attacked her body three times before the simple vitamin C treatment). Denise says, "I still can't get over how quickly those vitamin C tablets worked and how much cheaper they are than the drug therapy." When Denise and I counted up what she paid for both therapies, we found that the cost of the drug therapy—which didn't work—was more than *ten times* that of the natural therapy—which did work.

Dr. Brandt explains how vitamin C helps cystitis: "Ascorbic acid (vitamin C) fights the virus causing the disorder.** The vitamin also helps prevent a secondary bacterial infection."

A word of warning: Although Agnes's treatment sounds simple, do not give your cat vitamin C for cystitis until your veterinarian has established that your pet has cystitis and cystitis only. See the section on urinary blockage for the dangers involved. Remember that Denise not only had a clear diagnosis but also consulted with a nutritional veterinarian.

Dr. Ralston adds here the reminder repeated throughout this book: Once an acute attack is over, don't forget the importance of *continuing* a maintenance therapy. (Again, Agnes is being maintained on 1,000 milligrams a day

---

*The VNA is headed by R. Geoffrey Broderick, D.V.M See List of Nutritonally Oriented Veterinarians for the phone number.

**See the chapter on infectious diseases for a discussion of vitamin C and viruses and bacteria.

of vitamin C.) Warns Dr. Ralston: "An owner can become too confident that everything is all right, discontinue maintenance—and end up with a dead animal."

Other nutritional veterinarians, such as Dr. Benedict, recommend adding 100 to 300 IU of vitamin E a day for cystitis, to prevent and heal scarring of the bladder. "I use the water-soluble form of E," Dr. Benedict states. "This form is more easily absorbed than is the fat-soluble form, and so you can get superior results."

Dr. Benedict will also put the cat on a liquid diet, with gruel, "to allow the system to clean itself out." He uses B-complex, 15 milligrams twice a day; and the herb stinging nettle.* "This herb makes the cat feel warm," Dr. Benedict says. (If you're a woman who has ever had cystitis, you may know that a feeling of "freezing to death" can be one of the most annoying, and frightening, symptoms.) "The herb also gives the cat a feeling of well-being; and it helps tame the bladder spasms." Dr. Benedict gives 1 small tablet of the herb every 2 hours for 4 treatments; then 1 tablet every six hours for 4 treatments; 1 every 8 hours for 4 treatments; then 1 tablet daily, continued for a few weeks.

"This therapy usually controls cystitis in a week," Dr. Benedict tells me. "However, if the animals have been treated with drugs before they see me, it takes longer to control, maybe two or three weeks." Dr. Ralston echoes this experience.

Some veterinary books for the public seem to indicate that you don't have to worry about cystitis if you have a female cat. Others will tell you female cats get cystitis, too (which makes sense, considering that cystitis is very common among human females. Remember also our case history of Agnes). Dr. Benedict, a nutritional veterinarian who has a special interest in treating cystitis, confirms that both female and male cats are subject to cystitis. And he adds a point not mentioned in some veterinary books for the lay public: "Dogs get cystitis, too. As a matter of fact, it is a common problem and is discussed extensively in the technical veterinary literature."

Bladder Stones

"Bladder stones (and kidney stones) are completely a nutritional problem," says Dr. Kearns. "And once I've got the animal onto a natural diet, I've never seen a recurrence. Never." (See Chapter 2 for information on a natural diet.)

Dr. Kearns states that small bladder and kidney stones can often be dissolved by the following natural regimen. Larger stones, however, may have to be removed surgically. But the usually frequent recurrence of the stones can be prevented with the following suggestions.

---

*Dr. Tiekert uses some homeopathy in his practice. He will use the herb mentioned here in the homeopathic 3x preparation for treatment of both acute and chronic cystitis.

"What I stress, besides the natural diet," Dr. Kearns states, "is an extra-high vitamin C (ascorbic acid) content. Vitamin C helps keep the urine acid. And an acid urine can dissolve stones." The doctors Goldstein add that a urine that is *kept* acid (with a small maintenance dose of vitamin C) will help prevent the formation of further stones.

Dr. Kearns points out that there are some types of bladder stones, in Dalmations and other breeds, that *do* form in an acid urine; and "for those, you might have to use an allopurinol drug, which does the opposite from ascorbic acid: it makes the urine more alkaline, rather than more acid.

"But for the most part, stones are alkaline; and you can prevent them, and dissolve them, by keeping the urine acid with vitamin C in the form of ascorbic acid."

Dr. Kearns adds that he routinely uses vitamin E (400 IU a day) and pancreatic enzymes to help treat stones.

Urinary Blockage

Complete urinary blockage is an emergency situation. The retention of urine, and its waste products, causes poisoning throughout the body that results in death within forty-eight hours *or less*.* This is why I say you must have the diagnosis of cystitis before you try the simple vitamin C treatment for cystitis; if what you are really dealing with is urinary blockage, you will have a dead cat within two days.

Dr. Benedict uses the same therapy as he does for cystitis—and with the same successful results. However, for this problem the first step must be to flush out the bladder. This removes the "sand" collected in the urethra (the canal that carries the urine out of the body) and allows the urine to flow again. This release of the urine also relieves pressure on the kidneys, which is a problem with urinary blockage. The "sand," by the way, is caused by bits of bladder stones passing out of the bladder.

Dr. Benedict states that the common recurrences of urinary blockage (as well as cystitis) do not happen if the animal is maintained on a natural homemade diet. (See Chapter 2 for recommendations.) The use of distilled water is advised by a large number of this book's veterinarians, including Drs. Tiekert, Michael Kreisberg, D.V.M., and H. H. Robertson, D.V.M.** Distilled water is helpful because it can leach out of the body the harmful debris that may be clogging up the bladder.*** As Drs. Tiekert and

---

*The bladder can be so swollen with trapped urine that it is as hard as a stone—and as large as a big orange. As Nino Aloro notes, "A badly swollen bladder can rupture!"

**Dr. Robertson adds that distilled water should be used "in any kidney or urinary problem."

***The doctors Goldstein put in a warning here. While they also use distilled water for urinary blockages, they warn that "In the early treatment of a highly toxic animal, the leaching effect of distilled water may bring on stone formation as the body rids itself of toxic wastes." Dr. Kearns adds that this will not happen if

Kearns point out, distilled water is also free of tap water's impurities, which can cause even further harm to the sick animal.

Dr. Kreisberg's dietary recommendations include fresh raw beef liver, kidney, or heart several times a week. Also cooked chicken, cottage cheese, raw egg yolks (no whites), whole grain cereals. No dry food, no milk, no food containing fish. "Especially no tuna fish," stresses Dr. Kreisberg.

CHRONIC INTERSTITIAL NEPHRITIS

Chronic interstitial nephritis, a serious kidney inflammation, is a common problem in older dogs and cats. It is so common that some veterinarians believe that laboratory testing for kidney function should be run routinely on the older animal.

The most common symptom is that the pet drinks increasingly more water and excretes increasingly more pale or colorless urine. As the disease progresses, the animal may have bouts of vomiting, constipation or diarrhea. When these latter signs appear, your pet may be struggling to get along with only thirty percent kidney function!

Dr. Kearns and Drs. Robert and Marty Goldstein will seldom use drugs unless the animal has been allowed to deteriorate so long that he comes into these doctors' offices with uremia. Uremia is poisoning of the entire body caused by accumulation in the bloodstream of waste products that are normally helped out of the body by healthy kidneys.

Dr. Kearns gives details of the natural therapy he uses: "You must give the animal food that is going to take the strain off the kidney. You have to help the body produce as little waste as possible, so that the kidney is asked to do the minimum of work to remove that waste.

"This means," Dr. Kearns says, "you must give very little protein. However, what protein the animal does get must be of very high quality." (Many commercial pet foods have very low quality protein.) "You must also give a very low-residual diet; give such foods as rice, chicken and turkey, squash, well-ground grains, and greens.

"I also use a lot of pancreatic enzymes to help the digestion. And of course vitamins A, C, and E. Then I add sesame seed oil, because it stimulates the immune system, which is always weakened in any kind of stress.

"When all these things are combined," Dr. Kearns concludes, "the animals do very well in one hundred percent of the cases. We can make the animal comfortable and happy and keep him alive longer than could be expected with orthodox therapy."

For animals who already have the often fatal uremia, the doctors Goldstein will use—in addition to orthodox therapy—kidney extract, a form of

enough vitamin C is included in the therapy. Examples like this are my reason for reiterating that a knowledgeable veterinarian should oversee therapy.

glandular therapy. "When a diuretic is necessary, we will use an herbal one.*

INTESTINAL WORMS

Intestinal worms sap your pet's strength by "gobbling up" his food and thereby robbing his body of nutrients. They also feed on the blood and can damage intestinal tissue. A heavily infested pet can die.

A dog or cat can become infected through the mouth or through the skin. He may swallow a worm egg, or he may eat a "transport host," such as a mouse, that is carrying worms. Worms can enter the skin by way of blood-sucking insects such as mosquitoes or ticks. A puppy or a kitten can be born with worms passed on by his mother, or he may become infected by her while he is nursing.

Prevention

You might want to try garlic for prevention of worms. As a matter of fact, a number of nutritional authorities recommend raw clove garlic daily in the diet, for human beings as well as pets. It has a number of helpful properties, besides being a threat to worms.

Wendell O. Belfield, D.V.M., tells of Raymond and Margaret Hickely, who raise champion Cardigan Welsh corgis. From the time the puppies are four weeks of age, they get a daily garlic and parsley tablet. (The parsley neutralizes the smell of garlic.) "We have never had to worm dogs for roundworms since we started using garlic some thirteen years ago," they report. They add: "We don't have a problem with fleas either.[4]" As we have seen in the chapter on skin and hair problems, garlic can be helpful in preventing fleas.

Dr. Kearns makes some important comments regarding the prevention of worms in kittens and puppies. "These worms can be prevented," he says, "simply by giving a natural diet and whole clove garlic to the mother at the start of her pregnancy." (See Chapters 2 and 3.)

How is worrying about the mother's diet going to help to keep her babies worm-free? "Puppies and kittens are either born with worms," Dr. Kearns explains, "or they pick them up from the mother's milk while nursing. The mother may even test out negative for worms, yet she may have round-worms enclosed in a sort of sac (encysted) in her muscle tissue. Pregnancy causes a hormonal change in her system which releases these encysted larvae into her bloodstream. Now that they are in the bloodstream, they can attack the growing fetus. They can also get into the mother's milk, so that the nursing pup or kitten picks up the eggs of the worms while he is nursing."

---

*Veterinarians, please see "Of Interest Mainly to Veterinarians," Note 4, at the end of the chapter.

Symptoms

It is important that you have your veterinarian make regular fecal checks, since the most serious worms cannot be seen by the eye. However, you can also take a look at the feces every several days. If you see squiggly things moving around, or if you see what looks like grains of rice, those are roundworms or tapeworms. You will not be able to see hookworms or whipworms in the stool. The latter two types are the most serious. Dr. Ralston warns that hookworms can kill very quickly. *So if you see any of the following symptoms—and do not see signs of worms in the feces—*take a sample of the feces to your veterinarian for microscopic testing.

In puppies, a common symptom of worms is a skeletonlike little body accompanied, peculiarly enough, by a potbelly sticking out of the skeleton. The dog is a skeleton because the worms have been "gobbling up" his nutrients. The potbelly comes from the damage the worms do physically, which causes weak muscles, gas, and fluid buildup.

A puppy or adult dog with worms may also suffer from convulsions and diarrhea. There may be loss of appetite, or there may be a huge increase in appetite.

A pet with worms may drag his "behind" along the carpet, trying to get rid of the worms around his anus.* Or he may try to achieve the same result by licking constantly at the anal area.

What You Should NOT Do for Your Pet

We will cover here ways in which orthomolecular veterinarians rid dogs and cats of worms without using harmful chemicals. Before we do, please let me give you a bottom-line warning: If, ever, your pet is given a chemical dewormer, it *must* be by prescription of a veterinarian, and it must be administered under his or her supervision.

What about those dewormers you can buy so inexpensively in the supermarkets? What's wrong with using them? They are poisons; and as poisons, they can kill not only your pet's worms, but your pet. Dr. Ralston adds even a further warning here:

"Even if the veterinarian prescribes the dewormer, please be sure you inform the doctor if you have been giving your pet any medication whatsoever—for worms or for any other problem. Because what your veterinarian might give your pet for worms, in combination with whatever drug you may have been giving him, can kill your pet."

As Dr. Belfield states, with worm infestation there may be malfunction of organs. He tells of the frantic woman who called him one Sunday morning about her puppy, saying, "It's just lying there." The puppy had worms, she

---

*Dr. Tiekert points out that dragging the anal area is much more often the result of an anal sac problem than the result of worms.

went on. "I went to the supermarket and bought a preparation and used it according to the directions. Now the dog is dying."

The dog was beyond help. "On autopsy," says Dr. Belfield, "I found a swollen liver. Apparently the liver was unable to cope with the chemical dewormer. The product had killed the worms that were infesting the small intestine. The damaged liver was unable to detoxify the chemical, however, and it circulated through the system and caused the death of the animal."[5]

Dr. Ralston adds: "I have seen many similar tragic cases."

Another case: A wild mother cat once chose my friend Nick as an adoptive parent for her children, whom she apparently had no intention of "settling down" long enough to raise. While pregnant, she was, it seems, casing Nick for his suitability to raise her prospective kittens; she was often seen loitering at safe distances from the house while he ministered to the numerous pets he already had.

Then, one midnight, a wild clamoring was struck up in Nick's basement. When Nick ran down, he saw the cat hanging tenaciously onto a screen door. Using her entire body with all her might, she was swinging the door back and forth to make a loud banging.

Having in this unique manner caught Nick's attention, the wild mother leaped off the door and disappeared—never to be seen again. She had left, at the foot of the door where Nick would be sure not to miss them, her six newborn kittens.

No adoptive parent ever took better care of his charges. One kitten seemed dead shortly after birth; Nick resuscitated it and eventually nursed it to a healthy adulthood.

But another kitten developed worms. Nick did what all of us have been led to believe, through advertising, is the proper thing to do. He got a dewormer at the supermarket.

That was years ago. Still Nick will periodically agonize: "She died right in my hand. You know, I did exactly what the instructions said. But she died right in my hand."

Until now, we have been talking about your using chemical dewormers yourself. Are the chemical dewormers used by orthodox veterinarians also dangerous? Yes. They are poisons, too. And any poison strong enough to kill a lot of strong worms is powerful enough to kill a weakened dog or cat, too. (However, your veterinarian's more individualized prescription and follow-up should help decrease the risks of your doing it on your own.)

You can help your pet's body detoxify itself of the poisons in the standard dewormers by giving him large amounts of vitamin C before, during, and for two or more weeks after the deworming, according to Dr. Ralston and other nutritional veterinarians. Dr. Kearns adds that pancreatic enzymes are very important here, too.

Now let's see how orthomolecular veterinarians get rid of worms without poisoning them—and therefore without risking the poisoning of your dog or cat.

Therapy

Dr. Robertson uses an organic wormer called Fossil Flour, which, he reports, is one hundred percent effective in treating essentially all internal parasites if properly administered. There are no side effects, and no other therapy is required." Fossil Flour is made from fresh water algae (types of plants). Dr. Robertson recommends one tablespoon daily on the food for large dogs and one teaspoon for small dogs and for cats. "I would use caution in giving Fossil Flour to a pregnant animal."*

Another nontoxic therapy for roundworms and hookworms is given by the doctors Goldstein. They use an herbal dewormer put out by Herbal Animals in Oakland, California. "We simply have owners follow the directions on the package," the doctors tell me: "a twenty-four-hour fast and three days on the herbs.

"We also use high doses of garlic," the doctors continue. "The brand we recommend is a freeze-dried one called Kyolic. [The process of freeze-drying helps keep nutrients intact.] For a twenty-five- to thirty-pound dog, we recommend one capsule three times a day; for a cat, one capsule twice a day. The liquid Kyolic put into capsule form is the most effective." The doctors add: "After one month, the stools should be reevaluated by a veterinarian to test for worms."

If you're reading this section closely, you may wonder, "Well, if the garlic kills the worms, how come it can't kill the animal, too, in the same way the chemicals that kill worms can harm the animal?"

"Garlic doesn't kill the worms," the doctors Goldstein state. "As a matter of fact, it doesn't even *hurt* them. What it does is to remove the physical environment they need to live in; so they have to get out of the pet's body fast, or perish." Specifically, intestinal worms thrive in large amounts of mucus. A dog or cat who has worms has an abnormal amount of mucus in his intestines. (Again, a pet on a natural diet, as detailed in Chapters 2 and 3, does not tend toward too much mucus, and thus does not tend to have worms.) "Garlic helps remove the excess mucus from the intestines. Once the excess mucus is out, the worms will follow, because they cannot thrive, or breed, without a lot of mucus."

The Goldsteins also recommend a high-fiber diet, which helps accomplish the same purpose of removing excess mucus.

For pets who are extremely overloaded with mucus by the time the doctors Goldstein see them, "we will use Sonne #7, or other products containing comfrey leaf [a natural herb], or a product called Glauber's salt (sodium sulfate), a salt laxative that is very similar to epsom salts."

Please remember, as I stated earlier, that the preceding therapy is for roundworms and hookworms. It is not for tapeworms and whipworms.

---

*Veterinarians: Please see "Of Interest Mainly to Veterinarians," Note 5, at the end of the chapter.

Dr. Kearns finds a product containing proteolytic enzymes very useful for removing the mucus that worms need to thrive on: specifically, a product called Zymex-II which other nutritional veterinarians, such as Dr. Ralston, also use. It is made from a fig extract and "will rid the body of roundworms, the most common intestinal worms," says Dr. Kearns.

Dr. Kearns adds that this product also rids the body of harmful bacteria that may be present in the intestine. In this way, it not only can be helpful in ridding your pet of worms, it can be helpful also if your pet has become poisoned from eating spoiled food.*

Orthomolecular veterinarians often work with pets presented to them in the last throes of disease. "In such cases," the doctors Goldstein tell me, "we will have to resort to traditional medications. In these cases, of course, we will back up the medications with nutritional supports to help the body detoxify the poisons of the medications. Then, when the crisis is past, we will prevent the recurrence of worms with the proper diet and with garlic."

---

*"As a matter of fact," Dr. Kearns tells me, "a lot of M.D.'s with a special interest in nutrition recommend that humans take Zymex-II when they go traveling. It will ward off poisonous effects from food and water that are fine for the natives of the country but are toxic for foreigners. I myself pack up Zymex-II whenever I travel. And you find that you can eat and drink almost anything without any problems." (See the Appendix for how to obtain Zymex-II.)

OF INTEREST MAINLY TO VETERINARIANS

NOTE 1. Carvel Tiekert, D.V.M., regarding the rationale for the use of pancreatic enzymes in diabetes: "Pancreatic enzymes—i.e., N.F. 3x in 5x porcine pancreas concentrate—help supply enzymes often lacking due to pancreatic exocrine deficiency. It is thought that they play a role in the absorption of zinc, an important mineral in insulin synthesis. Zinc requires picolinic acid for proper absorption, and pancreatic enzymes are a high source of picolinic acid."

NOTE 2. The doctors Goldstein state: "For a 30-pound animal, we give one capsule goldenseal (530 mg of the herb) once or twice a day, depending on the animal's needs. We have a number of animals on use of the herb for well over a year with no side effects. If an animal does have side effects, the following might be tried: 6 days on, 1 day off; or 3 weeks on, 1 week off."

NOTE 3. Pancrelipase USP (25 USP lipase units/mg)
Viobin Corporation
Monticello, IL 61856

NOTE 4. Herbal Diuretic NutriDyn Co.
5705 W. Howard St.
Niles, IL 600648

NOTE 5. Fossil Flour
Agri-Tech
4722 Broadway
Kansas City, MO 64112

REFERENCES

1. Margaret Reister, *Cat Fancy*, December 1981, p. 45.
2. Cited by Herbert Bailey, in *Vitamin E*, (New York: Arc Books, Inc.), 1970, p. 84. Bailey lists some eighteen sources for Dr. Ugo Butturini's work, including *Ann. N.Y. Acad. Science*, 52:397, 1949; and *Proc. 3rd Internat. Cong. Vit. E.*, Venice, Italy, September 1955, p. 46.
3. Bailey, *op. cit.*, p. 86.
4. Wendell O. Belfield, D.V.M., and Martin Zucker, *How to Have a Healthier Dog* (Garden City, New York: Doubleday and Co., Inc.), 1981, p. 123.
5. Belfield, *op. cit.*, pp. 122, 123.

CHAPTER NINE

Heart Problems and Hypertension

RICHARD J. KEARNS, D.V.M.:
"We can get most of our animals with heart problems off drugs, when people go along with me in using natural foods and natural supplements."

MICHAEL W. LEMMON, D.V.M.:
"I've had cases of heart disease that were absolutely given up on by other veterinarians, because the cardiograms indicated there was no hope. Nutritional therapy improved the animals' health greatly and has given them years more of life."

S. ALLEN PRICE, D.V.M.:
"Almost all—if not, indeed, all—cases of hypertension can be traced, I believe, to the commercial foods.
"I virtually never have to use digitalis or digitoxin anymore."

HEART PROBLEMS

Duchess was only three years old when she was given her "death sentence" by an orthodox university veterinary center on June 29, 1977. The German shepherd mix was vomiting blood. She was retaining fluids, so much so that her stomach had to be drained every week. (This problem is called dropsy.) She was extremely anemic.

The university center hospitalized Duchess for three days and gave their diagnosis: a leaking heart valve and an abnormally slow heartbeat. Their prognosis: Duchess might live another six weeks. She might last as long as six months.

That was five years ago. Today, Duchess is alive. She is a "completely normal, healthy dog with no symptoms of dropsy or any other heart condition," according to S. Allen Price, D.V.M. It was Dr. Price who worked the "miracle" of Duchess's recovery, the miracle consisting of chelated magnesium and potassium, H/D food, and Geritol.*

Introduction

It is estimated that today's dog has a *fifty to eighty percent chance of developing a heart problem by the time he is seven years old*. While some books written for the public state that cats generally don't have heart problems, Jan Bellows, D.V.M., who has made heart disorders one of his special interests, says: "Cats have heart problems all right, although they're not generally the same type of problems dogs have. Cats often have cardiomyopathy, or a thickening of the muscles of the heart. They're usually born with it; and it keeps getting worse and worse. This congenital problem," Dr. Bellows continues, "can develop into a congestive type of heart failure, where fluids are retained in the body. Or the heart muscles can become dilated—which is a *very* serious condition."

Processed foods will enhance the possibility of heart disease in your pet, even if the animal has no predisposition to such a problem. At the beginning of this book, it was stated that human beings rarely died of today's major killers until we started falsifying our food. Similarly, our pets rarely died from these killers until we started mucking around with their food.

Sugar, for instance, is just one of the many unnatural substances that are pumped into your pet's (and our) processed foods. Studies have shown that

---

*Dr. Price adds that although he very often uses vitamin E for heart problems, as do the other veterinarians mentioned in this chapter, it wasn't used in the case of Duchess.

a person eating four ounces of sugar a day has more than *five times* the chance of having heart disease than a person has who eats two ounces.[1] This is just one of the many reasons that prompted R. Geoffrey Broderick, D.V.M., to refer to sugar as "the assassin." And sugar isn't the only villain. The milling out of vitamin E and the addition of salt, among other processes, also contribute to heart disease.

Symptoms

Even if your dog or cat seems healthy, he should have periodic examinations; heart problems can't always be properly diagnosed without X rays and cardiograms. But trouble can develop between examinations. So that you will know when you should report any possible problems to your veterinarian, this section discusses some symptoms you can watch out for.

Dr. Bellows describes the progressive stages of congestive heart failure vividly:

- Coughing and a slight decrease in exercise tolerance;
- The gums start to become blue; exercise tolerance becomes even less;
- "The dog comes into the office puffing; if he takes more than several steps, he coughs hoarsely;
- "In the last stage of congestive heart failure, the dog or cat can't walk into the office at all; he is carried in on his side.

"In this last stage of congestive heart failure," Dr. Bellows says, "the animal is literally drowning in the excess fluids accumulated in his lungs. Even at this stage we can save a few animals, but they have to be put on oxygen and given . . . drugs." (At this point, vitamins A, E, C, and B-complex, and other nutrients can be used only as supportive therapy, to help increase the pet's chances of surviving.)

If your pet has a heart problem, he also may show swelling in the legs. This swelling will result from an accumulation of fluids.

Here are a few suggestions on how to listen to your pet's heart for signs of possible trouble. (Again, this is *not* to be used as a substitute for periodic examinations by your pet's doctor.) Just put your head on your cat's or dog's chest and listen. Or make yourself a sort of stethoscope by putting a drinking glass over the heart area and listening through the open end. If your dog or cat's heart skips a bit around the fifth or sixth beat, don't panic. Dogs and cats are naturally prone to have an irregular rhythm. As a matter of fact, if your pet's heart rhythm is quite regular, you should bring this to your veterinarian's attention. At the same time, if the heart seems to be skipping an entire beat, this should be brought to the doctor's attention.

Is the heartbeat confined to the immediate heart area? Good. (Sounds that can be heard all over the chest may mean an enlarged heart.) Do you feel a buzzing or vibration over the heart? This may be due to a narrowed valve or a hole in the heart. Do you hear a hissing sound? This may be due to a leaky valve. Does the heartbeat sound muffled? This also should be brought to your veterinarian's attention.

Basics of Treatment

These are the basics of the therapy shared in common by the orthomolecular veterinarians who have participated in this section.

- Vitamin A. Depending on the severity, Richard J. Kearns, D.V.M., will use up to 400,000 IU a day of the water-soluble form of the vitamin.
- Vitamin C. As you may know, drugs called diuretics are routinely used in the orthodox treatment of heart problems, both for people and for pets, to rid the body of excess fluids accumulated. Vitamin C is a natural diuretic, with no side effects when used properly. (Dr. Kearns will use up to 20 to 25 grams a day.)
- Vitamin E. (Dr. Kearns will use up to 4,000-6,000 IU a day of the water-soluble form.) This is another natural diuretic. It also enhances circulation; a damaged heart has trouble fulfilling its major function, circulating the blood through the body. Vitamin E also has been well proven to strengthen all the muscles of the body—and the heart is a muscle. (Dr. Robert Goldstein, V.M.D., and Dr. Marty Goldstein, D.V.M., stress that while vitamin E is quite safe for less serious heart problems, it can be "very dangerous" if used indiscriminately on a very weak heart. The doctors recommend that a serious heart problem be stabilized first before adding vitamin E, and that the vitamin be prescribed for a pet with a very weak heart only by orthomolecular veterinarians.)
- The elimination of salt (or sodium)
- Moderate exercise
- Weight reduction in the overweight animal
- And, as always, a natural diet as detailed in Chapter 2

To this basic regimen some of our nutritional veterinarians sometimes add other natural substances. We'll cover those additional aids after a closer look at the how's and why's of some of the nutrients our veterinarians use in the basic therapy.

Vitamin C. We have previously said in this book that most nutritional veterinarians routinely use the sodium ascorbate form of vitamin C rather than the more widely known ascorbic acid form, which can sometimes cause minor problems when taken in large doses. However, for heart problems, veterinarians such as Dr. Bellows use ascorbic acid; they don't use sodium ascorbate because it contains sodium, which is salt.* As we cover in this chapter, the elimination of salt is very important in treating heart disease.

---

* Veterinarians: Please see "Of Interest Mainly to Veterinarians," Note 1, at the end of the chapter.

Vitamin E. As we've already said, vitamin E can strengthen a weakened heart and can function as a diuretic, helping the body to remove dangerous excess fluid. (Let me reemphasize that the doctors Goldstein stress that in congestive heart failure and in animals with very weak hearts, vitamin E must be used only under the supervision of a nutritional veterinarian.) This vitamin also reduces the body's need for oxygen. Oxygen starvation is a major problem in heart disorders.

Studies have shown that undersupplying animals with vitamin E produced abnormal electrocardiograms and heart degeneration.[2] Studies with human patients who have already had heart attacks show improved electrocardiograms and more regular pulses than before they took vitamin E.[3]

In 1945, Dr. N. H. Lambert began using vitamin E in over 1,200 dogs and cats with heart problems. He had good results with everything from angina to valvular murmur to congestive heart failure. Dr. Lambert's very first case was a nine-year-old dog who was dying; previous treatment had not helped her. With vitamin E, the "dying" dog lived for another six years, to the ripe old age of fifteen.[4]

Dr. Kearns sums up the usefulness of vitamin E this way: "E will cure many heart problems without using the drug digitalis at all. When the dog is in really bad shape, you may have to use a little digitalis." Even in these very advanced cases, however, "if you use enough vitamin E, you can cut the drug down to about ten percent of what you'd have to use normally."

The Question of Exercise. Sporting breeds are particularly prone to heart trouble, and their recovery is often more hindered than it is in other breeds. This is no mere fluke of nature. These dogs are often asked to lie around inactive, sometimes for months; and then, when the sporting season starts, suddenly they're asked—indeed, ordered—to run around pell-mell for hours on end every day. You can see how harmful this can be if you remember that the heart is a muscle. Then imagine you had been lying around in bed for a month, and suddenly sprang up and did an hour's strenuous arm pushups. You'd strain your arm muscles, of course.

While vigorous, *regular* exercise is a good preventive for heart trouble, once the heart is damaged, you must take a middle-of-the-road approach to your pet's exercise. As Dr. Bellows advises: "If you just sit the dog in the apartment, he's going to get worse. If you go out and jog him, constantly, five miles a day, he's going to get worse, too. The pet should be given limited, regular walks."

Low-salt diet. The low-salt diet is so important to the treatment of heart disease that some veterinarians, such as Dr. Bellows, report that in the early stages of a heart problem, simply cutting out salt alone can sometimes dramatically help the dog or cat. Dr. Bellows offers the following for a sample of a well-balanced low-salt diet:

- ¼ pound lean beef*
- 1 cup cooked long-grain white rice. (You may have read that *brown* rice has more nutrients. That is correct; but it also has more salt.)
- 1 cup corn kernels (not canned)
- 1 tablespoon corn oil**
- 2 tablespoons dicalcium phosphate.***

Under 50 milligrams of sodium per 100 grams of dry weight food is recommended for the animal with heart problems; these recommended foods yield a total of 42 milligrams.

Dr. Bellows lists some other low-salt foods; corn grits or farina, oatmeal, lima beans, squash, dried beans, sweet potato, black-eyed peas, egg yolks (not whites). The doctor reports sadly that many well-meaning owners keep their pets on a special low-salt diet, then add "treats" of beef jerky or bologna, both saturated with salt. "Such foods," Dr. Bellows says, "totally defeat everything." Some other *not*-permitted foods are cornflakes, wheat flakes, cheese, margarine, cottage cheese, frankfurters, canned stew, bacon. "Foods like these," Dr. Bellow says emphatically, "can get the pet into BIG trouble."

We do not have the space here to list all the permitted and not-permitted foods on a low-salt diet. So please check with your veterinarian before adding a food he or she has not already recommended. What you don't know can kill your pet. Many packaged and canned foods, for instance, are loaded with salt; and even tuna, which we've previously okayed as a once-in-a-while food for your healthy pet, weighs in at a stupendous 700 milligrams of sodium (salt) per 3 ounces! So you see, even the addition of an apparently "safe" food could kill your pet. Again, check with your veterinarian.

Additional Aids
Magnesium and enzymes. H. H. Robertson, D.V.M., believes that "one major cause of heart problems—in dogs and cats—is improper breakdown of proteins. The proteins don't get broken down by the body into amino acids; therefore, it is complex proteins that are circulating in the system. And of course the body cannot utilize complex proteins.

"When these complex proteins reach too high a level in the circulatory system, the heart rate is increased. Eventually, the heart wears itself out."

With heart problems, therefore, Dr. Robertson always does a urine analysis to determine whether proteins are being broken down correctly. If

---

*Dr. Kearns adds that chicken, turkey, or lamb may be substituted here.
**Dr. Kearns prefers sesame oil.
***John B. Limehouse, D.V.M., does not use this substance. He uses herbs such as alfalfa and lobelia.

the test indicates that the proteins are indeed *not* being broken down, Dr. Robertson will give magnesium to the animal. "Magnesium will cause the desired release of the nonprotein nitrogen in the body." Or, in other words, it will help the body to get rid of the undigested protein.

Dr. Kearns adds that he will use pancreatic enzymes to help improve tne breakdown of protein. Dr. Robertson adds: "Pepsin and trypsin are particularly important."

Lecithin. This is a natural substance (occurring in high amounts in soybeans and eggs, for instance) that many nutritional D.V.M.'s and M.D.'s alike add to their therapy for heart problems. Why? Well, lecithin's pet name among doctors is "The Great Emulsifier," because it emulsifies—that is, cuts through—fats. As Dr. Kearns states, by emulsifying the plaques of fats adhering to the walls of blood vessels, lecithin also helps improve an animal's circulation.*

Vitamin B$_{15}$. Orthomolecular veterinarians such as Dr. Kearns and Michael W. Lemmon, D.V.M., include B$_{15}$ in the therapy for heart problems.** This vitamin has been shown in many double-blind studies in Russia to be "extremely effective" in treating heart disease—as well as circulatory disorders, emphysema, liver diseases, and premature aging.[6]

Vasculin and Cardio-Plus. Drs. Lemmon and Kearns report that they get even better results than they get with vitamin E by using the natural products Vasculin and Cardio-Plus. Vasculin contains vitamin E plus

---

*I'd like to use the story of lecithin as another example of how medical knowledge can get buried in the medical literature for years, where not only the public, but also most doctors, don't learn about it. I make this point for one reason: to dispel the myth held by many of the public that "if my doctor doesn't know about it, it can't be true."

Dr. L. A. Simmons and colleagues in Australia were recently working with a number of people with high blood cholesterol levels. Suddenly—for no apparent reason—the cholesterol of several of the patients dropped sharply; and these were people for whom all known drug therapy and diet management had already failed. Dr. Simmons was stumped. He questioned the patients: Did *they* have any clue as to why their blood cholesterol should suddenly have dropped so mysteriously? Well, it turned out that they had all started taking lecithin a little while before—on their own.

Dr. Simmons thereupon ran a scientific analysis which has become one of the definitive studies on lecithin and cholesterol regarding human beings.

The irony lies not only in the fact that this study was begun because a few "hopeless" patients tried something out on their own—but in the fact that a similar study had been published in a widely circulated medical publication, read only by doctors and other medical professionals, some *two decades* previously.[5]

**Veterinarians: Please see "Of Interest Mainly to Veterinarians," Note 2, at the end of the chapter.

thiamine (a B-vitamin) and beef heart extract. The nutrients in this product are unsynthesized—that is, truly natural. Cardio-Plus contains vitamin E, riboflavin and niacin—both B-vitamins—and beef heart extract. Again, all ingredients are unsynthesized.

"I've had cases that were absolutely given up on by other veterinarians," Dr. Lemmon tells me, "because the cardiograms indicated there was no hope. These two products, though, improved the animals greatly and are giving them years more of life."

Homeopathic remedies. Some of our orthomolecular veterinarians use the field of homeopathy along with more strictly nutritional medicine. Homeopathy is a branch of medicine founded in 1796; it is based on the theory that disorders can be helped by giving patients very small amounts of substances that can produce similar symptoms in healthy individuals. Homeopathy was, until the 1920s, a major medical specialty in this country. It is still held in high esteem in Europe. Indeed, the official physician to the Queen of England is a homeopathic physician.[7]

Dr. Kearns sometimes uses homeopathic diuretics. Diuretics are employed to rid the body of the dangerous excess fluid that tends to accumulate when there are heart problems. The diuretics used in orthodox medicine can have dangerous side effects. In particular, they tend to rob the body of many necessary minerals—most specifically, potassium. (This is ironic, because potassium is absolutely necessary for the strength of every muscle in the body, and the heart is a muscle.) As Dr. Kearns says, "Homeopathic diuretics don't rob the body of potassium. They're substances that only help the body do what it would do naturally, if it weren't sick—and the body doesn't naturally rob itself of potassium."

Cell Salts. Sometimes Dr. Kearns will also use certain of Dr. Schuessler's cell salts; these are formulations of salts that are found naturally in healthy cells but are often missing in the unhealthy body. These cell salts are not to be confused with the villainous salt we've been talking about elsewhere in this chapter, sodium chloride.

Herbs. Like many of our orthomolecular veterinarians, John B. Limehouse, D.V.M., draws from the entire spectrum of orthomolecular veterinary medicine (and orthodox medicine), according to what seems best for the particular animal in the particular stage of the particular disease. For instance, Dr. Limehouse will sometimes use the commercial diuretic Lasix when an animal is in need of a fast-acting diuretic. When the crisis is over, he shifts to a natural diuretic, such as the herbs parsley or juniper berry. Dr. Kearns adds that other effective herbal diuretics include hawthorn berries and bearberry.

For dogs and cats with heart problems that are not terribly severe, Dr.

Limehouse does not use digitalis or digitoxin drugs. Instead, he uses the herb capsicum or cayenne (more commonly known as red pepper).

Raw honey? No! I have seen several published recommendations for raw honey as a natural heart stimulant for the animal with heart problems. This puzzled me, because honey is sugar. Indeed, nutritional authorities often refer to honey as "the same thing as table sugar, with a few more nutrients."

As we have seen previously, sugar can be very harmful to the heart, so I took the matter up with Dr. Bellows. He said, "Honey will give the animal's body more sugar, and so will give him an immediate boost of energy and make him feel a bit better for a short time. However, it will also cause more fluid to be retained; and the last thing an animal or a human with heart problems needs is to retain more fluid. Honey will not help the pet with heart problems; it will quite definitely harm him."

The doctors Goldstein agree with Dr. Bellows. So please do not feed honey to your pet (or to yourself) when a heart problem exists, even if you do read somewhere else that honey is a good addition to natural therapy.

HEARTWORMS

Heartworms are worms that congregate in the heart. If not removed, they can damage not only the heart but also the lungs, kidneys, and liver, and can eventually cause death.

Since heartworms are transmitted by mosquitoes, to prevent heartworms you must protect your pet from these insects. For natural ways to do this, please see the section on fleas in the chapter on skin and hair problems. The brewer's yeast and garlic recommended to help repel fleas will also help repel mosquitoes.

Therapy

I was unable to locate any nutritional veterinarians who had a successful natural way to cure heartworms. This seems to be, then, one of those disorders for which orthodox veterinary medicine presently has the best answer.

I have previously said that the ideal veterinarian will, as Carvel G. Tiekert, D.V.M., put it, "use the best of both worlds"—orthodox and orthomolecular—in his or her practice. That is precisely what the nutritional veterinarians I talked with about heartworms do for this problem. They recommend orthodox drug therapy, and then add supportive natural therapy. As all drugs do, the drugs for heartworms stress the body and can cause harmful side effects. To prevent these problems, Michael Kreisberg, D.V.M., and Drs. Robert and Marty Goldstein recommend that you give your pet a good diet supplemented with the B-complex and vitamins C, A, and E.

Heart problems can often cause hypertension, so please read the next section.

HYPERTENSION

I have on hand some twenty-five veterinary books written for the lay public. These books either do not mention hypertension at all, or indicate that the disorder is really not a problem in the dog or cat. It would appear, then, that we pet owners don't have to worry about hypertension.

This seemed strange to me, because I know that one of the major causes of high blood pressure (hypertension) in human beings is an excess of salt in the diet, and I know that many of the processed foods our pets eat are highly laced with salt.

I took this perplexity up with our nutritional veterinarians.

"High blood pressure is really an everyday occurrence in a veterinary practice," said S. Allen Price, D.V.M., who has made hypertension a special interest in his work. "It's often overlooked, because most veterinarians concentrate on the heart problems that hypertension causes. I find quite a lot of hypertension in my practice because I look for it.

"External symptoms that I look for," Dr. Price noted, "include extreme nervousness—often to the point where the dog or cat has ceased to be a good pet." Indeed the hypertensive pet can sometimes be so nervous that he makes his owner a nervous wreck. "Also, animals with high blood pressure have about two or three times the amount of skin problems that other pets do. If the animal has a painful condition, the pain is three times worse than it would be for another pet." Dr. Price summed up: "In short, nothing seems to go right for the poor animal with hypertension."

For a number of years now Dr. Price has been using hair analyses to help test for hypertension and finds that "most of these dogs have an extremely high level of sodium." As we have established, sodium (salt) is a primary cause of high blood pressure.

We have also stated before in this book that hypertension is a "new, improved" epidemic we have helped devise for our pets (and ourselves) with our "new, improved" foods. As Dr. Price tells me: "Almost all—if not, indeed, all—cases of hypertension can be traced, I believe, to the processed foods, most particularly those 'meaty-looking' products. . . . Sometimes you can even see a courageous little dog who has heart and/or circulatory problems, but whose body is managing to compensate for the problems so that the animal has no symptoms. Then the owner puts him on one of those fake meat products—and in three weeks' time the little fellow has dropsy."

Dr. Kearns adds that the same fate can befall a cat who is put on the semimoist products.

Therapy

Dr. Price's treatment for hypertension is fairly simple, and "—except in very far advanced cases—it works extremely well."

First, if you haven't already guessed, is a nonsalt diet. Dr. Price will recommend meat, eggs, and raw vegetables supplemented with nonprocessed dry food. (See Chapter 2 for how to shop for such a food.) If the owner feels this is too complicated, the doctor will recommend a preformulated food that's salt-free: H/D,* to which he will often add supplements.

"For the really bad cases," Dr. Price tells me, "I'll resort to the drug aminophylline, which is a bronchial dilator, and maybe a mild diuretic. But even when I do have to use a drug or two, I find I don't have to use them very long; I can delete them once the more natural approach has had a little time to take effect. I virtually never have to use digitalis or digitoxin anymore.

"I also use the minerals magnesium and potassium in the chelated form.** These two natural substances I *do* use for a long time," Dr. Price says. "Magnesium is a very mild natural tranquilizer and helps the nervous hypertensive calm down naturally, without the side effects of drug tranquilizers. Magnesium also is an excellent support for producing enzymes that digest blood clots." (Any of you unlucky enough to have high blood pressure know that the possibility of blood clots is one of the major dangers of this disorder.)

"I use potassium," Dr. Price goes on, "to balance the high sodium level present in the hypertensives." Sodium and potassium work together in a certain balance in the body. Many of today's people and pets who are fed processed food take in so much more sodium than potassium that the

---

*Other of this book's veterinarians will use H/D, particularly when owners feel that chopping up some vegetables and putting a hunk of meat in their pet's bowl is "too much trouble." H/D stands for "Heart Diet" and has no salt. Other products put out by this company are nutritionally formulated for other health problems.

You should be aware, however, of the objections some nutritional veterinarians have to these products. For instance, the doctors Goldstein state: "These products have preservatives." (See Chapter 1 for the harm preservatives can cause.) "The minerals are inorganic. We feel that inorganic minerals are a major contributing cause to all diseases."

Dr. Kearns agrees: "These products are a poor alternative to proper diet. The owner who cares for his pet really should take a few extra minutes a day to feed more natural foods."

**Dr. Robertson adds a further detail here: "While potassium is always used in hypertension, magnesium should be used only if the nonprotein nitrogen in the blood tests out to be too high."

Dr. Robertson also uses calcium in the hypertensive dog or cat. He always tests the pet first to see whether the particular animal's body is overly acidic or overly alkaline, before he decides whether to use an acidic or an alkaline form of calcium. As he points out, "If the dog is already too alkaline, you certainly don't want to be giving him an alkaline form of calcium."

healthful balance is seriously upset. Too much sodium tends, in turn, to rob the body of what potassium it does take in. So perhaps you can see why Dr. Price bothers not only to subtract the sodium (salt) from the hypertensive's diet, but to add potassium.

Those of you who are concerned about hypertension have surely heard about "the salt connection," but "the potassium connection" may be new to you. This, again, is not a new notion made up by Dr. Price or any of our other nutritional veterinarians. Studies going back some three decades have shown that high blood pressure can be caused in animals and in human beings not only by giving them too much salt, but just as easily by giving them too little potassium.[8]

Animals in the wild, of course, don't know about the decades of research on the body's need for a balance between potassium and salt. However, as Adelle Davis points out, when an animal in the wild "overdoses" on eating leaves and grass—which contain high amounts of potassium and no salt— he'll walk hundreds of miles, if he has to, to find the nearest salt lick.[9] This is an instance of what we said early in the book: that an animal in the wild instinctively eats what is best for his body. And of course he never eats the fake foods we have decided in the past decades are "best" for our pets.

OF INTEREST MAINLY TO VETERINARIANS

NOTE 1. As Dr. Robertson states: "When vitamin C is used I.V., it must always be used in the sodium ascorbate form."

NOTE 2. Drs. Kearns and Lemmon use Aangamik-15. This product is the original B₁₅ formula used successfully in Russia for over twenty years. It is available from L & H Vitamins, Inc., 38–01 35th Avenue, Long Island City, NY 11101.

NOTE 3. These two products are available from L & H Vitamins, address above.

REFERENCES

1. Studies by Dr. John Yudkin, professor of nutrition and dietetics at the University of London, and his colleagues, cited by Richard A. Passwater, Ph.D., in *Supernutrition* (New York: The Dial Press), 1975, p. 114.
2. K. E. Mason et al., *Anat. Rec.*, 92, 33, 1945; F. R. Bacigalupo et al., *Am. J. Vet. Res.*, 14, 214, 1953; R. H. Follis, *Am. J. Clin. Nut.*, 4, 107, 1956. Cited by Adelle Davis, *Let's Get Well* (New York: Harcourt, Brace & World, Inc.), 1965, p. 68.
3. E. V. Shute et al., *Nature*, 159, 772, 1946; E. V. Shute, *Med. Rec.*, 160, 279, 1947. Cited by Davis, *op. cit.*, p. 69.
4. N. H. Lambert, "Clinical Experiences with Vitamin E in Dogs and Cats," *Proceedings of the Third International Congress on Vitamin E*, September 1955, pp. 611–617. Cited by Wendell O. Belfield, D.V.M., and Martin Zucker, *How to Have a Healthier Dog* (Garden City, New York: Doubleday & Company, Inc.), 1981, pp. 186, 187.
5. Pat Lazarus, "Lecithin: Key to a Hardier Heart (Part One)," *Let's LIVE*, November 1979.
6. Passwater, *op. cit.*, p. 34.

7. Robert Thomson, *The Grosset Encyclopedia of Natural Medicine* (New York: Grosset and Dunlap), 1980, p. 104.
8. W. H. Blahd et al., *Metabolism*, 2, 218, 1953; P. Fourman, *Clin. Sci.*, 13, 93, 1954; and several other studies cited by Davis, *op. cit.*, p. 265.
9. Davis, *op. cit.*, p. 265.

CHAPTER TEN

Cancer Need Not Be a Death Sentence for Your Pet

H. H. ROBERTSON, D.V.M.:
"What you have to do is bring the body chemistry back to normal. Once you've done that, you can just get rid of the tumors without any problem. I don't cure the cancer; all I do is put the animal's body into shape so it can do the job."

MICHAEL W. LEMMON, D.V.M.:
"When my clients cooperate, thirty to forty percent of pets in the 'terminal' stage of cancer can be successfully treated. With early cancer, the success rate rises above ninety percent."

S. ALLEN PRICE, D.V.M.:
"I've been dealing with feline leukemia for years; and I get disgusted with most veterinarians, who advocate Test and Slaughter—that is, if the cat tests positive, it's best to kill it. We've had cats who have been able to climb trees and look normal in less than ten weeks. And I'm talking about cats who were brought in to us when they were too weak even to stand up."

Your veterinarian examines your pet. The doctor looks up at you and pronounces the last word you ever wanted to hear: cancer. The veterinarian explains to you the enormous cost of surgery, chemotherapy, radiation. The risks. The terrible side effects. And the strong possibility that all of this will not even help your pet's cancer.

You never thought you'd hear yourself say such a thing, but there you are, saying, "Yes. Put him to sleep, right now, before he suffers more." You try not to look in your pet's eyes as the veterinarian administers the fatal dose of anesthesia.

Please don't put your pet—and yourself—through this excruciating scenario without giving the field of orthomolecular veterinary medicine a chance.

Can nutritional veterinarians successfully treat cancer? Yes, they can. Can they do this without any surgery or drugs? Often, yes. Can they control cancer in animals that are "terminal"—that is, "sure" to die? Yes, surprisingly often. (I asked five of our nutritional veterinarians to estimate their success rate. For terminal patients, the doctors estimated their respective successful treatment rate as being five percent, ten percent, ten to twenty percent, twenty-five percent [H. H. Robertson, D.V.M.], and thirty to forty percent [Michael W. Lemmon, D.V.M.]. For early cancer, Dr. Lemmon gives a success rate of "ninety percent plus" and Dr. Robertson estimates ninety-five percent success.)

Am I telling you that veterinarians in this new field are "miracle" workers? No, I'm not. As I've said previously, a miracle is something that is worked by means we cannot understand. There is absolutely no secret involved when a pet under the care of an orthomolecular veterinarian experiences tumor disappearance and is saved from the "certain death" pronouncements of traditional medical care.

You see, an orthomolecular veterinarian will simply use a battery of natural substances that together restore the pet's body—most importantly, the pet's immune system—to its natural balance. When this can be accomplished, the pet's own immune system fights off the cancer—just as a strong immune system fights off cancer that invades all our bodies every day of our lives. And just as an animal's body fights off cancer every day in the wild. There is no "miracle" in that; there is, instead, sublime medical common sense—more common sense than in having your animal's body pumped full of poisons (drugs) and hoping those drugs will kill only the cancer, not the animal.

As a matter of fact, time after time orthomolecular veterinarians have repeated to me, as has Dr. Robertson, "*I* don't cure the cancer. As a matter of fact, *I* don't cure anything. All I do is run tests to see where the animal's body chemistry is—and then bring the chemistry back to where it should be. It's the animal's body that actually does the healing."

You probably won't ever need the information in this chapter if you are starting off with a brand-new puppy or kitten and raising him as orthomolecular veterinarians have detailed for you in Chapters 2 and 3. The cancer rampage did not exist among our pet's ancestors, as it did not exist among our own ancestors, when we all ate nonpoisonous foods. Indeed, cancer is still virtually unknown in the wild. Dr. Robertson, who has a rural practice and treats animals roaming free, tells me: "You hardly ever see a case of cancer in the wild. I have seen benign [noncancerous] tumors in deer, in coyotes, and in foxes—but even these are rare. This points, of course, to the fact that unnatural diet is a major problem in causing cancer."

The initial diagnosis of cancer is very often a much more definitive death sentence for animals than it is for humans. Why? Well, traditional therapy—surgery, drugs, radiation—is horribly expensive. Just one week's treatment and hospitalization for a pet can amount to $1,000 to $2,000. While orthomolecular medicine is not exactly free, you can compare that $1,000 to $2,000 for a week of orthodox therapy to the following estimates from Robert Goldstein, V.M.D., and Marty Goldstein, D.V.M., for nutritional therapy; $125 to $150 for nutritional analysis of blood, hair, and urine; supplements can run $15 to $25 a month." Richard J. Kearns D.V.M., stressed to me that nutritional therapy for cancer is expensive. When I asked him to compare the cost of orthodox therapy with the cost of nutritional therapy for cancer, he stated: "Hundreds of dollars versus dollars."

Not only is traditional therapy expensive, it can be extremely painful and traumatic for the pet. And it often doesn't work. Add to all this the fact that the pet's natural life-span is short. If you *do* spend your life savings, if you *do* put your pet through the traumatic treatment, and if it *does* work, your animal may have gained only a year or two of life.

As John E. Craige, V.M.D., points out, all of this usually results in owners opting, sorrowfully, for putting the animal to sleep once the word "cancer" is pronounced by the doctor. "The orthodox approach to cancer therapy is seldom even used in veterinary medicine." Dr. Craige also points out that this situation should lead the compassionate owner to give the less expensive orthomolecular approach to cancer at least a try. He adds: "The fact that orthodox cancer treatment is often not even tried by owners should give veterinarians more of a rationale for trying alternative therapy than many M.D.'s may feel they have."*

---

*Veterinarians: Please see "Of Interest Mainly to Veterinarians," Note 1 at the end of the chapter.

BASIC PROBLEM IN TREATING THE CANCER:
OWNER SKEPTICISM

Orthomolecular veterinarians report to me that they have two basic problems in successfully treating cancer. Neither one of these two basic problems lies in the cancer itself; the problems lie mostly with the owner. Problem number one, as Dr. Kearns expresses it: "We almost always get the animals after they've been through everything else—the surgery, the radiation, the chemotherapy." (All of which, by the way, destroy the important immune system, rather than build it up.) "When everything else has failed, when the cancer has had time to spread, when the animal is terminal, then we get a chance to help it." As we have seen, nutritional veterinary medicine can have an impressive success rate even with these cases deemed "totally hopeless" by orthodox medicine.

Problem number two is expressed by S. Allen Price, D.V.M. (who, by the way, echoes that he seldom gets to use natural therapy on a pet "until the owners realize it's either try natural therapy, or the pet will surely die"). Dr. Price states: "Even once they've agreed to try natural therapy, all they have to do is read somewhere in a newspaper that no natural therapy can possibly work for cancer; and they're on the phone saying, 'Absolutely. I see it here, right here in the newspaper: only drugs and surgery can help cancer.' And the totally frustrating thing is that so often these are people whose pets were given up to die because the drugs and surgery couldn't work; and they can see that their pets are doing well on the natural therapy. But they read a paragraph in a newspaper . . ."

Dr. Price goes on: "For instance, I've got two people right now who are driving me wild over a couple of dogs with tumors of the cranial cavity. The only thing orthodox veterinary medicine offered them was to try to cauterize the tumors. Not only is this type of operation dangerous, but it certainly would never have corrected the tumor; the most it would have done would be to reduce its size, not eliminate it. With the more natural treatment, the dogs are functioning well and are not even showing any problems at all. The only problems the dogs are having now is that their owners keep reading things in newspapers, and keep thinking they should take the dogs off the therapy that's keeping them alive and functioning."

Dr. Price summarizes: "The disease of cancer worries me to death—not because of the cancer itself, but because so often you can't fight the owner's skepticism so you can save the animal."

Basics of the Nutritional Therapy for Cancer
First, let me add a paragraph or two for those of you who have read orthodox medicine's warnings that human patients who try alternative cancer therapies are depriving themselves of orthodox therapy. For one thing, as we've said, orthodox cancer therapy is often not even tried on animals, for

the reasons we've mentioned. Also, every nutritional veterinarian with whom I talked about cancer said that he or she would not rule out surgery and/or drugs in certain cases. First, if the tumor is pressing on a vital part of the animal's body, or is in any other way impeding the functioning of the body, a nutritional veterinarian will remove it surgically. In this way, functioning can be returned while the more natural, metabolic approach to treating cancer can have time to rebuild the animal's total health. In the same way, there are some cases for which nutritional veterinarians will use a drug along with the metabolic approach. However, the drug, if used, will be used as an adjunct to the therapy, not as the total therapy. Also, nutritional veterinarians report to me that as they use more and more vitamins, minerals, and enzymes, they are able to use less and less of a drug to achieve the same effect, thereby cutting down the drug's dangerous side effects.

(Note that an orthomolecular veterinarian is not averse to a minimum of surgery and drugs in some cases. As I said in the Introduction: 1. An orthomolecular veterinarian was trained just as thoroughly in orthodox veterinary medicine as your traditional veterinarian. In fact, orthomolecular veterinarians and orthodox veterinarians were trained at the same medical schools, took all the same courses, and got the same medical degree. 2. The orthomolecular veterinarian simply has branched out to make nutritional medicine his or her special interest. 3. Orthomolecular veterinarians are sincerely involved in trying to save your pet's life; they are not involved in saying that their special-interest field has all the answers for all problems.)

The basic therapy shared by most of the nutritional veterinarians I talked with includes:

- Vitamin A. This is used because it helps greatly in rebuilding the immune system and in detoxifying the body of poisons.
- A full complex of the B-vitamins. As Dr. Kearns states: "The B-vitamins enhance appetite, increase the feeling of well-being, detoxify the liver, protect the nervous system, *plus*."
- Large amounts of vitamin C. This vitamin is used for the same reasons as vitamin A.
- Large amounts of vitamin E. Used for the same reasons as vitamins A and C.
- Pancreatic enzymes. These help break down the hard protective coating that shelters most cancers, and in this way allow the other nutrients to attack the tumor. These enzymes also help cleanse the intestines and increase their efficiency. In turn, this increased health of the intestines allows the body to utilize nutrients more fully.
- A return to as natural a diet as possible. (See Chapters 1 through 3.) After all, it is counterproductive for you, your pet, and your pet's doctor to try to control cancer in an animal that is still having its body assaulted by the same poisons that probably helped cause the cancer in the first place.

A number of our veterinarians referred me to the work of Harold Manner, Ph.D., Chairman of the Department of Biology at Loyola University in Chicago, stating that many of the basics of their therapy are derived from the doctor's protocol.*

There are various additional nutrients sometimes used by orthomolecular veterinarians that I'll detail a bit later.

You may have preferred that I tell you there was one magic substance which you could buy at your corner store for a pittance; that you could slip a spoonful of this substance into your pet's bowl; and that in twenty-four hours the cancer would have vanished. You may have preferred that, but would you have believed it? As I have said previously, this is not a book about magic; it is a book about medicine. Medicine is a serious business, and cancer is a most serious disease. Nutritional veterinarians know they can't rebuild the shattered health of an animal with one nutrient.

For skeptics, I would like to stress that numerous scientific studies have shown the relationship between cancer and diet and various nutrients.[1] Nutritional veterinarians have attempted to combine these studies into an all-out therapy for cancer.

ADDITIONAL INFORMATION ON DESTROYING CANCER

Dr. Robertson stresses that he does extensive testing of the body chemistry of the animal to discover in exactly which ways the individual's chemistry is "off base." Then he uses whatever nutrients are needed to restore that particular body to a normal balance. Agreeing with other orthomolecular veterinarians, he points out that "if the animal's body chemistry were in normal balance, of course, it would be dissolving the tumors by itself. So as long as the doctor can find out in what way the chemistry is unbalanced and can restore the balance, the tumors just remove themselves without any problems."

Dr. Robertson, Dr. Kearns, the doctors Goldstein and other veterinarians believe that very often in long-standing tumors the body is too alkaline, and they work to bring the body back to the neutral acid-alkaline base. Massive doses of vitamin C in the form of ascorbic acid are helpful in decreasing alkalinity and increasing the acidity of the body chemistry.

With long-standing tumors, Dr. Robertson will initially use a natural enzyme, bromelain, along with other natural therapy. This enzyme (derived from pineapple) helps dissolve the fibrous coating that forms around a tumor that has been "alive" for a long time. This fibrous coating acts as a shield for the tumor so that the immune system, as it gains health, cannot

---

*You can read more directly of Dr. Manner's work in his book, *The Death of Cancer*, published by Cancer Books (Advanced Century Publishing Corporation, 4908 N. Lincoln, Chicago, IL 60625). You can obtain this book by sending $10.95 (California residents add 6% sales tax) to Eden Ranch Book House, P.O. Box 370, Topanga, CA 90290.

penetrate the tumor to dissolve it. "Once you've rebuilt the immune system—and have got rid of that fibrous coating that protects the tumor from assault—the body itself will take care of most tumors," says Dr. Robertson.*

The doctor also makes sure the animal has adequate essential fatty acids. His preference is for oil of evening primrose because, as he says, it not only acts to increase the production of health-producing hormones, but also helps to decrease the production of harmful hormones.

Many orthomolecular M.D.'s stress a low animal-protein diet for human cancer patients. This won't surprise you if you remember what I reported in Chapter 1 about our not being natural carnivores; that is, our bodies are not equipped to handle animal protein adequately. So it shouldn't surprise you, either, that Dr. Craige reverses the low-protein recommendation for people and recommends a high-protein diet for dogs, who *are* actually carnivorous.

Such nutritional veterinarians as Dr. Lemmon and Dr. Kearns, among others, use raw glandular extracts corresponding to the organ system that's affected with the cancer. (This is in accordance with Dr. Manner's protocol, which, as we have previously mentioned, is followed, basically, by many orthomolecular veterinarians.) Obviously, if a glandular system is hit with cancer, it is weakened; and the raw extracts of that particular system can help to strengthen it.

Dr. Lemmon is one of our veterinarians who incorporate the use of herbs in their practice. Herbs are highly concentrated natural sources of various nutrients. For cancer, Dr. Lemmon will often use a red clover combination formulated by Dr. Christopher.**

Dr. Price tries to make sure that all salt is cut out of the diet. (There is very little salt in the natural diet recommended in Chapters 2 and 3.) A salt-free diet can help alleviate pain, as Dr. Price explains, because "excessive sodium [salt] attaches with water around the cell, forming sodium hydroxide, a very irritating substance." Dr. Price also uses digestive enzymes, particularly Viokase.

Dr. Price stresses that the powdered form of supplements should be used rather than tablets. If obtaining the powdered form is inconvenient, the tablets should be crushed (thereby making them, of course, into a powder). "The whole tablet sometimes goes through the dog's or cat's short digestive system so fast that it comes out still a whole tablet," Dr. Price warns. In other words, the nutrients in the tablet are not being utilized by the body—and this is the same as not giving your pet any therapy at all.

Raw thymus is an extract of the thymus gland, and it is used as part of the cancer regimen by such veterinarians as Dr. Lemmon, Dr. Kearns, and

---

*Veterinarians: Please see "Of Interest Mainly to Veterinarians," Note 2, at the end of the chapter.

**Veterinarians: Please see "Of Interest Mainly to Veterinarians," Note 3, at the end of the chapter.

Carvel G. Tiekert, D.V.M. If using a glandular extract to help treat cancer sounds a bit strange to you, please realize that the thymus gland is a crucial part of the immune system, which is the body's major line of attack against all diseases. There have been so many medical studies showing that raw thymus extract can help diseases related to poor immunity, that the major drug companies are hoping to put out a whole new class of thymic drugs within the next few years.[2]

Laetrile

Laetrile is also known as, vitamin B17 and amygdalin. Many orthomolecular veterinarians with whom I talked recommend the use of laetrile as a *part* of the cancer therapy; they do not believe it is a magic substance that in and of itself cures cancer. However, laetrile is a nutrient that was present in the dog's and cat's natural diet in the wild (in such foods as grains and nuts); and it is a nutrient, therefore, that their bodies need for health.*

I know you have read the headlines of the medical establishment's tests that seem to have proven laetrile worthless. Actually, many M.D.'s and veterinarians believe strongly that most of these studies have been conducted incorrectly. Indeed, sometimes members of the testing institutions themselves have come out in public and denounced the methods used. A number of recent books discuss details of how laetrile studies are thought to have been conducted improperly. See, for instance, Dr. Richard A. Passwater's *Cancer and Its Nutritional Therapies* (Keats Publishing Inc., New Canaan, Connecticut, 1978).

The results of a study that many of our nutritional veterinarians believe *was* conducted properly are very interesting. The study was done by Dr. Manner, the doctor whose recommendation many of our orthomolecular veterinarians follow. Dr. Manner found that tumors in ninety percent of the mice disappeared—and the other ten percent showed improvement.[3]

How did Dr. Manner's study differ from many of the studies reporting that laetrile is ineffective? First, he did not use laetrile alone, just as doctors who report success with laetrile in human patients do not use it alone. He also used large amounts of vitamin A and enzymes. Second, he used mice that had developed cancer spontaneously, just as human beings do, through a breakdown in the health of the body. The usual way to run similar cancer studies is to deliberately inject cancer cells into the animal. Dr. Manner points out that this is not analogous to the development of human cancer. "When a person is healthy, he does not enter the doctor's office and ask for a shot of cancer cells."[4]

Basically, there are three different reasons why orthomolecular veterinarians use laetrile. First, as Dr. Robertson mentions, laetrile increases the

---

*Veterinarians: Please see "Of Interest Mainly to Veterinarians," Note 4, at the end of the chapter.

level of vitamin C in the cells. As was said earlier, C is all-important in strengthening the immune system, which is so vital in destroying cancer. Second, laetrile has been widely shown to alleviate pain in human cancer patients. Third, it is believed that, through a rather complicated biochemical reaction, laetrile can destroy cancerous cells while leaving healthy cells alone, a feat not achieved by chemotherapy and radiation.

I'll try to explain this biochemical reaction to you as clearly as possible in plain English. One of the substances in laetrile is the poison cyanide. This poison is kept inactive (and nondangerous) when it is taken into the body. That is, it is kept inactive unless it meets with a particular enzyme (beta-glucosidase) which acts as a sort of "key" to the cyanide and unlocks it from its laetrile "house."

Cancer cells have large quantities of this "key"; noncancerous cells do not. Therefore, in the body, the poisonous cyanide is drawn to the cancer cells and basically bypasses the healthy cells. What little cyanide does get to the healthy cells can be inactivated by a particular enzyme (rhodanese) that is present in healthy cells but not in cancer cells.

As a medical reporter, I am privy to some "underground" information that seldom reaches the public. For a decade now I have been aware of a number of M.D.'s across the country who refuse to prescribe laetrile for their patients for fear of raising the wrath of the establishment, but who have used it with success as part of a regimen to treat their own (often terminal) cases of cancer. As I compiled information for this book, several veterinarians mentioned that they knew of additional M.D.'s who quietly used laetrile to help treat their own cancers. Dr. Price, for instance, told me of an M.D. who had cancer of the colon and liver (once cancer hits the liver, it is considered very grave in orthodox medicine). "He's still the picture of health," Dr. Price tells me, "nine years after starting to take laetrile." Five years without cancer is generally considered a cure.

To sum up, if you take your pet with cancer to an orthomolecular veterinarian and he or she wants to use laetrile as part of the treatment, I hope you won't call the doctor a quack because you have read in the newspaper somewhere that it "doesn't work."

A warning about laetrile: Dr. Craige, who uses laetrile both for prevention and therapy of cancer, warns that once pits containing laetrile (such as apricot, apple, and peach pits) have been ground up, they should be refrigerated. Also, the pits should not be allowed to soak in water for any length of time, nor should they be put in water at all after they are ground. This might cause the laetrile compound to break down and unlock the poisonous cyanide radical. Dr. Craige, while pointing out that at recommended dosages laetrile is not toxic, adds that "overdosage can also cause breakdown of the compound in the intestine," setting the cyanide free.

FELINE LEUKEMIA

It saddens me every time I read in a pet magazine that this disease is hopeless; or when I turn to veterinary books now in the bookstores and read such statements as, "At the present time, for humanitarian reasons, we recommend euthanasia for the afflicted pets."[5] It saddens me because I know that pets around the country are being put to sleep because of this belief in leukemia's hopelessness—and because I know that to veterinarians working in the new field of orthomolecular medicine, feline leukemia is no longer hopeless. And I'm not talking just about those cats who test out positive but who have no symptoms; I'm talking also, in many cases, of cats so riddled with symptoms that they can't even stand up.

As with all disorders, you can go a long way toward preventing leukemia in your pet by feeding a natural diet. As discussed earlier, the processed commercial foods can very well be causing chronic lead toxicity in your pet. Wendell O. Belfield, D.V.M., states strongly: "The entire predisposition to feline leukemia virus can very likely be charged to chronic lead poisoning."[6] He points to a study that indicates that lead may suppress the very important immune response.[7] As we'll see, vitamin C is of prime importance in treating leukemia; studies in both animals and humans show that C can help reverse lead poisoning.

Drs. Robert and Marty Goldstein add that other causes of leukemia include preservatives and other additives in foods, poor nutrition, drug therapy, and radiation. "We practice seven miles from a nuclear reactor," the doctors write me, "and we see so many leukemic cats and dogs that it is becoming an epidemic."

Dr. Price reports an interesting observation to me, which can be used to help prevent leukemia. "The only leukemic dogs that I've seen," he says, "have been dogs who have a habit of lying near the television." (Television emits a lot of radiation.) Dr. Price also points out that many cats not only often lie near the TV, but even on it. Of course, Dr. Price is not saying that curling near the TV is the only cause of leukemia; but you will be cutting down on the chances of the disease hitting your household if you keep your dog and your cat—and, by the way, yourself—more than six feet away. Dr. Kearns comments: "Many children are damaged by TV radiation, although the blame is placed elsewhere."

Also, if you must use chemical pesticides, please be aware that studies show that many such pesticides can cause leukemia not only in animals but also in human beings.[8] Therefore, before you spray poisons around to clear your house of insects, clear your house of animals and people. And take every possible precaution for yourself.

I came upon my first clue that "something new was up" to help feline leukemia back in August 1980, when I read a letter to the editor of an animal newsletter. The letter was from a cat owner who hoped her letter might help a previous writer whose cat was dying of leukemia. "I hope it is not too late for her to get help as I have for my cat affected with the same disease. I wrote to Orthomolecular Specialties for . . . Mega [C] Plus. It did wonders for my cat, and he has now recovered and looks splendidly healthy."[9] Ironically, this letter was printed right under another letter from a reader who had just lost her beloved cat to leukemia. "I brought my cat for all his shots and always brought him to the vet if I thought he was sick. It was a terrible shock to me how he could be well one week and be dead the next!"[10]

The lifesaving Mega C Plus the first writer referred to is a mixture of the generally recommended daily allowance of vitamins and minerals, plus a very high amount of vitamin C in the form of sodium ascorbate. The formula is distributed by Dr. Belfield, mentioned many times in this book as one of the major pioneers in orthomolecular veterinary medicine.

One dedicated animal worker having good success using the Mega C Plus is Pat Widmer, founder and president of Pet Clinicare in New York City. She reports that cats testing positive for leukemia but having no symptoms can be turned from positive to negative "by feeding one teaspoon of the powder in food daily over six weeks to six months. . . . It is necessary to continue the maintenance dose of the powder thereafter." (Ms. Widmer tells me personally that the maintenance she refers to is one-fourth to one-half teaspoon daily.)

For the cat who is very sick with leukemia, Ms. Widmer uses "1 teaspoon Mega C Plus powder in his daily food and ½ cc Mega C drops 6 to 8 times a day for 6 weeks." Eventually, the pet not only should be symptom-free, but should also test negative for leukemia. Then you can start gradually reducing the dosage to the maintenance level.[11] Dr. Kearns reports similar positive results using Mega C Plus. (For how to obtain Mega C Plus, see page 177.)

Ms. Widmer writes me that she has seen "many hundreds" of symptomatic cats recover with the use of this product. What percentage of nonsymptomatic cats testing positive for leukemia eventually test negative with the use of Mega C Plus, according to her experience? "One hundred percent," she states.

Let me add something important here: the value of loving nursing care. The importance of such care was emphasized to me by several people, in the course of writing this book; but nowhere was its potential value brought home so dramatically as it was when I was trying to find the answer to a puzzle regarding feline leukemia and Mega C Plus. The puzzle: Pat Widmer was stating in print fine results with Mega C Plus in the symptomatic leukemic cat; at the same time, Dr. Belfield—who formulated Mega C Plus—was reporting little or no success with symptomatic cats, although excellent results in turning nonsymptomatic positive cats to negative cats.

It has been my goal in this book to report to you the most successful therapies my research could dig up. As you may know, the success of therapy (either drug or nutritional) can sometimes stand or fall on such factors as how much of a particular substance is used, how long the therapy is pursued, etc. Therefore, I asked Pat Widmer: Was she using more of the Mega C Plus than Dr. Belfield? Was she sticking with the therapy longer? Was she combining the Mega C Plus with any other therapy? The answer I got back from Ms. Widmer had nothing to do with medicine; it had to do with nursing, or—if you will—with love. "Dr. Belfield and I discussed this discrepancy recently," she told me. "The truth is that the *owners* of Dr. Belfield's patients get very good results with Mega C Plus and their symptomatic cats."

Owners getting better results than a doctor? Was I onto a new secret of medicine? No, I was onto an old secret of medicine. "A veterinarian, of course," as Pat pointed out, "deals with many, many animals. He or she can't spend all day—and all night—ministering to any one animal. However, owners who love their pets will get up every hour or two all night, if need be, to administer treatment. They will also hold the cat in their lap, stroke it, groom, it, give it love. All this helps eliminate stress." Stress is generally recognized nowadays as a very strong negative influence in disease.

Dr. Price also emphasizes vitamin C for some fine results he has obtained with leukemia, although he doesn't use Dr. Belfield's particular combination of nutrients. Besides vitamin C, Dr. Price uses vitamin A, 100 milligrams of laetrile, and Viokase, a digestive enzyme. "And . . . except for the really far advanced cats . . . most of them recover." Sometimes Dr. Price will also use chlorophyll from fresh green plants, or iron, liver, and vitamin B_{12} to help increase the red blood count. Dr. Price sums up that with his regimen, "We've had cats who came in to us without even enough strength left in them to stand up. And in less than ten weeks they've been scampering around, climbing trees, totally normal."

Of course, by the time a cat doesn't have enough life left in him even to stand up—especially from a disorder that is generally considered hopeless even in the early stages—you wouldn't expect he would have any chance of being alive ten weeks later, let alone climbing trees. I asked Dr. Price what percentages of these "hopeless" cats completely recover. "About a third," he tells me.

Dr. Price told me the case history of Rupert, one of several cats belonging to a well-known author. The cat became ill with leukemia early in 1981. "Nutritional therapy included," Dr. Price tells me, "100 milligrams of laetrile daily, vitamins and minerals mixed with liquid vitamin C, and Viokase," When Dr. Price saw Rupert again later in the year, the cat was free of symptoms. At last report—one and a half years after Rupert's bout with the "hopeless" leukemia—he is still free of symptoms. Not only that, he now has "more energy than all the other cats living with him."

Dr. Kearns, like Dr. Price, also uses laetrile as part of the therapy for symptomatic ("hopeless") cats with leukemia. "You get cats in with high fevers, 105–106–108 degrees. There is literally nothing you can give them that will bring down that high a fever—except laetrile. Laetrile brings it down in a day." Dr. Kearns uses 50 milligrams of laetrile orally two or three times a day until the leukemia is under control. (For critical cases, Dr. Kearns *injects* laetrile—along with vitamin C and amino acids.) His maintenance regimen includes pancreatic enzymes, vitamins A, B, C, and E, plus thymus.

SOME REPRESENTATIVE CASE HISTORIES OF CANCER AND BENIGN TUMORS

I have selected representative case histories sent to me from the files of some of the veterinarians participating in this book. I've tried to pick those that represent somewhat differing regimens.

The first case history shows what can sometimes be done in "terminal" cancer using exclusively an orthomolecular approach. Rush was a male German shepherd, eight and a half years old; he weighed 110 pounds. One day Rush's owner noticed a raised nodule on her pet's head; within the next few days, four more such nodules had developed on both the head and the forelimbs. Whatever it was, it was spreading rapidly. An operation removed the lumps, and a biopsy revealed malignant histiocytoma, a rare type of cancer in dogs. Even though the tumors had been removed, several more new ones developed *within only a week after the operation*. As you might guess, at this point a prestigious university veterinary medical school said that nothing could be done; no further treatment should even be tried.

Robin M. Woodley, D.V.M., ended up treating this doomed animal nutritionally. Now, Dr. Woodley is not, as are most of the veterinarians participating in this book, a veterinarian working primarily in orthomolecular medicine; she describes herself to me as an orthodox veterinarian who incorporates nutrition and vitamin therapy into her practice—and it is my hope that this book will help to increase the number of such veterinarians across the country.

Obviously, in Rush's case, if something was to be done, it couldn't be the orthodox approach; that had already been tried and had not worked. Indeed, orthodox veterinary medicine had decided it was useless to try to help Rush.

"Every 'specialist' I contacted had only his condolences to offer as 'help' for Rush," Dr. Woodley comments.

Doctors offering their condolences to another doctor with a hopeless patient? Dr. Woodley explains, "Rush was my own dog."

Dr. Woodley proceeded to administer to Rush 10 grams of vitamin C daily, given orally and divided into two doses. In only two weeks, all the lumps—which had previously been spreading so fast—had disappeared.

Rush was maintained on 10 grams a day of vitamin C, plus 5,000 IU vitamin A, 400 IU vitamin D, 800 IU vitamin E, and the B-complex vitamins. Ten months later (or the equivalent of about six years of human lifetime), Rush was still in excellent health; and there was no sign of cancer.

At around that time Rush, unfortunately, died of something quite unrelated to cancer: complications resulting from a myelogram, a rather risky diagnostic test involving the spinal cord. But Rush had gained months of healthy life, and Dr. Woodley had saved her pet from a slow, painful cancer death.* Perhaps Dr. Woodley's determination will result in other owners and other veterinarians considering similar treatment for doomed pets.

Our second case history is another one given me by Dr. Woodley. It represents a successful combination of traditional drug therapy and orthomolecular therapy. Duke is a male Shetland sheepdog, ten years old; he had developed granulocytic leukemia, which in turn had spread to the liver. Dogs are not, as widely thought, immune to leukemia. As we discussed earlier in this book, leukemia in a pet is generally considered hopeless, and involvement of the liver in any type of cancer is also considered extremely grave.

Dr. Woodley's combined orthodox-orthomolecular therapy has consisted partly of the drugs Cytoxan and prednisolone. (By the way, several orthomolecular veterinarians, such as Dr. Kearns, have told me that when they feel they must use a drug for cancer, they prefer prednisolone.**) To the two drugs, Dr. Woodley has added high amounts of crystalline vitamin C (in the form of sodium ascorbate), 2 tablespoons a day of brewer's yeast (which contains the B-complex vitamins), vitamin E, and ½ teaspoon cod liver oil every day.

Duke has been on this combined orthodox-orthomolecular therapy for eleven months now (about six and one-half years in human lifetime). Dr. Woodley tells me: "The dog is alert, active, and playful." However, Dr. Woodley gives more scientific proof of Duke's improvement: eleven months ago, at the beginning of therapy, the Sheltie's white blood count was an abnormally high 197,000 (a high white blood count is one of the major physical parameters of the type of cancer Duke has). As of this writing, his white blood count has dropped slowly but steadily to 32,000.

Dr. Woodley sums up this combined-therapy approach: "I believe the vitamin therapy has made a tremendous difference in his feeling and attitude, and has protected him from serious side effects from the immunosuppressive drugs." Dr. Woodley has also found, as I've previously said most orthomolecular veterinarians find, that with the vitamin therapy she has been able to use lower dosages of the potentially harmful drugs. Dr. Wood-

---

*Veterinarians: Please see "Of Interest Mainly to Veterinarians," Note 5, at the end of the chapter.
**Veterinarians: Please see "Of Interest Mainly to Veterinarians," Note 6, at the end of the chapter.

ley's latest words to me: "I am slowly starting to eliminate the two drugs altogether."*

The next case, treated by Dr. Lemmon, seems to me to point out how laetrile can help when used in conjunction with other natural substances. This was a case of a noncancerous tumor; but noncancerous tumors can be fatal, too, if they happen to attack a vital organ and keep it from functioning. Dustin is a male cat who, at the age of five, developed a one-centimeter tumor on the back of his neck. Pancreatic enzymes were given for two and a half months, but at the end of that time the tumor had doubled in size. It was removed surgically; but the biopsy report was ominous. It was a neurofibroma, and there was almost a one hundred percent chance that it would come back all over again—and probably within six months, according to the report of the veterinary pathologists.

Dr. Lemmon put the cat back on the pancreatic enzymes, and added a mere one-half level teaspoon of ground apricot or apple seeds a day (apricot and apple seeds, as we have said previously, contain a lot of laetrile). Whereas in two and a half months the pancreatic enzymes had not prevented the tumor from doubling in size, the simple addition of the laetrile prevented the "almost certain recurrence within six months" for a period of four years (about twenty-eight years in human lifetime), at which time the cat died of other causes.

Although, as we've said, most orthomolecular veterinarians do not use laetrile by itself for cancer, the following is a case history where laetrile alone was used for experimental purposes.

Cindy was a female mongrel who was about ten and a half years old when it was discovered she had a form of cancer (squamous cell carcinoma) that is quite prone to spreading to distant parts of the body. Surgery did no good. A prestigious university veterinary clinic evaluated the case and decided that neither radiation therapy nor more surgery would do any good. The owners decided to let Cindy live until the pain became too much for her and then to have her put to sleep.

Then they found a glimmer of hope: an experimental treatment with laetrile. They agreed to let George Browne, Jr., D.V.M., and James D. Mortimer, D.V.M., conduct this experiment with their dog. After all, what did they—or their beloved pet—have to lose?

In a little over ten months, the doctors report, "the lesion appeared to be completely healed." When they last examined the pet, the cancer was still nonexistent—and this was over three years after the dog's death sentence had been pronounced.[12] I asked Dr. Browne what ultimately happened to Cindy. He tells me that when Cindy eventually died, an autopsy found no evidence of cancer. The doctor took the trouble to mail me the autopsy

---

*Veterinarians: Please see "Of Interest Mainly to Veterinarians," Note 7, at the end of the chapter.

report—not conducted by him—to confirm the fact that Cindy did not have cancer when she died.*

The following is another case history involving a tumor that had not been helped by strictly orthodox means but was helped dramatically by strictly orthomolecular means. This case history also points out how the proper dosage of nutrients, and the proper combination of them, can make the difference between success and failure.

Eldridge is a male semi-Labrador. He was thirteen years old and had a noncancerous tumor around the anus that was almost two inches in diameter. An orthodox veterinarian had given stilbestrol shots, but they had no effect. Then the owner, a believer in natural medicine, decided to take matters into his own hands and devised a therapy of his own. Actually the therapy he devised happened to be a fairly good one, as far as educated guessing goes, but the owner was not an orthomolecular veterinarian; and his particular combination of sodium ascorbate, vitamin E, PABA, pantothenic acid and herbal combination had no effect in the one month he used it.

Finally, he did what I hope all of you will do to start with: he consulted an orthomolecular veterinarian; in this case, Dr. Lemmon. Among other changes to the owner's self-devised regimen, Dr. Lemmon approximately quadrupled the amount of sodium ascorbate. The doctor also added a lot of pancreatic and other enzymes. Did this have an effect on the large tumor that had not responded to orthodox veterinary treatment and had not responded to the owner-devised natural treatment? The tumor disappeared within a month.**

Dr. Craige tells of a dog with cancer of the jaw that cleared up completely and allowed him to die a natural death several years later. Dr. Price tells me of two dogs with osteosarcoma (cancer) of the lower jaw. "The cancers cleared up completely in about four and a half months. They didn't even leave a blemish. No, that's an exaggeration; one dog lost a tooth."***

While I have given you just a small sampling of the successful case histories in orthomolecular medicine, I must also stress again that there are failures. As we have said previously, these failures are often due to the fact that the nutritional veterinarian usually does not get to see the animal until orthodox medicine has given up on him, or to the fact that the owner fails to keep up the prescribed natural therapy. Dr. Craige also believes the age of the animal plays an important role in the success or failure of nutritional therapy: "I think you'll find most of the failures are in the very old dog or

*Veterinarians: Please see "Of Interest Mainly to Veterinarians," Note 8, at the end of the chapter.
**Veterinarians: Please see "Of Interest Mainly to Veterinarians," Note 9, at the end of the chapter.
***Veterinarians: Please see "Of Interest Mainly to Veterinarians," Note 10, at the end of the chapter.

cat, because it can be extremely difficult to rebuild the immune processes in an ancient animal."

The purpose of this chapter has been to show that the diagnosis of cancer need not be an automatic death sentence for your pet. Indeed, even the pronouncement "terminal" need not be an automatic death sentence.

OF INTEREST MAINLY TO VETERINARIANS

NOTE 1. Dr. Craige makes the following statement: "I have consistently pointed out to those who conduct animal studies that there is an opportunity to study laetrile and similar reputed cancer therapies on the animals that are put to sleep because of cancer every year. I feel that it is unconscionable that such studies have not been done."

NOTE 2. Dr. Robertson believes that most bromelains on the market have poor results. He recommends Anavit-F3, obtainable from Chemical Consultants International, P.O. Box 88041, Honolulu, Hawaii 96815; and a product called Pineappa, obtainable from the Key Co., P.O. Box 3307, St. Louis, MO 63122 (phone 314-965-6499).

NOTE 3. Available from L & H Vitamins, Inc., 38-01 35 Ave., Long Island City, NY 11105.

NOTE 4. Two veterinarians participating in this book, Drs. Robert and Marty Goldstein, have found that laetrile in heavily toxic patients can cause "depression, vomiting, and a downhill course." They feel these effects may be due to "too rapid breakdown of tumor cells, further overloading the body with toxins." They stress that in treating cancer, a doctor should not become involved solely in watching tumors shrink, but should keep a close check on what changes may be occurring in overall body chemistry. ("It is possible to have a shrunken tumor and a dead animal.") Conversely, the doctors point out that "it is very common initially in treatment for the tumor to increase in size due to an accumulation of toxins from the detoxifying process."

NOTE 5. You will have noted that no laetrile was used in this case. Dr. Woodley initially began with 10 g crystalline ascorbic acid. This was later changed to sodium ascorbate due to persistent diarrhea and excessive flatulence.

NOTE 6. Dr. Kearns, seeing his name mentioned in the same paragraph with Cytoxan, wrote me: "I do not use Cytoxan, as this and similar drugs affect all cells in the body. I feel laetrile, B_{17}, is the drug of choice, as it affects only diseased cells."

NOTE 7. Drug therapy: Cytoxan, 25 mg 4 days of 7 for 3 weeks, then no treatment for 3 weeks; now changed to no treatment for 6 weeks. Prednisolone 30 mg every other day, now reduced to 5 mg every other day.
- Crystalline sodium ascorbate, 6–8 g, b.i.d. in food.
- Vitamin E: 400 IU daily
- Brewer's yeast, 2 tablespoons daily
- Cod liver oil, ½ teaspoon daily
- Methionine, choline, inositol combination (Lipo-caps)
- "Liver-sparing" diet: cottage cheese, rice, preservative-free kibble.

NOTE 8. You might find of interest another case history of the use of amygdalin: G. Browne, Jr., *Veterinary Medicine/Small Animal Clinician*, February 1974, p. 189.

NOTE 9. Dr. Lemmon's therapy:
- 2 Seroyal Hi Pan 8 (from 8x Pancreatin), b.i.d., at least 2 hours away from meals

- 1 Bronson multiple enzyme with each of 2 meals
- 1 Nutri Dyn GSF (raw thymus, parotid, spleen and adrenal) A.M. and P.M.
- Vitamin E: 400 IU
- PABA: 100 mg
- Pantothenic acid: 250 mg
- 1 herbal tablet Dr. Christopher's Red Clover combination
- 4,000-8,000 mg. sodium ascorbate daily.

NOTE 10. One of the dogs (female, 2 years) presented with osteosarcoma "the size of an egg" on lower jaw. Treatment: 1 g laetrile orally daily, Viokase, and H/D dog food. After 4½ months, no visible signs of tumor. Owner stopped treatment; the tumor returned, larger and involving both sides of the mandible. Treatment was reinstated, with the addition of chaparral and red top clover. In 4½ months, no visible signs of tumor. Laetrile, 500 mg daily, and herbs have been continued many months with no visible recurrence.

REFERENCES

1. For a compilation of some of these studies, see Adelle Davis, *Let's Get Well* (New York: Harcourt, Brace and World, Inc.), 1965; Chapter 31; and Richard A. Passwater, Ph.D., *Cancer and Its Nutritional Therapies* (New Canaan, Connecticut: Keats Publishing, Inc.), 1978.
2. Jonathan Rothschild, "The Thymus: Master of Immunity," *Let's LIVE,* April 1982, pp. 43–47.
3. Harold W. Manner, Lecture at the National Health Federation Regional Meeting, Chicago, September 1977; *Choice,* 3:8, 16-19, 1977; *Nat. Health Fed. Bull.,* 23:10, 1-3, November 1977.
4. Harold W. Manner, Ph.D. et al., *The Death of Cancer* (Evanston, Illinois; Advanced Century Publishing Corp.), 1978.
5. Donal B. McKeown, D.V.M., and Earl O. Strimple, D.V.M., *Your Pet's Health from A to Z* (New York: Dell Publishing Co.), 1973, p. 119.
6. In a paper presented by Dr. Belfield at the Annual Orthomolecular Medical Society Meeting, March 15, 1980, at the Jack Tar Hotel, San Francisco, California.
7. Fox, Aldrich, Boylen, Jr. "Lead in Animal Foods," *J. of Toxicology and Environmental Health,* 1:461-467, 1976.
8. *The Lancet,* August 8, 1981, p. 300.
9. Mrs. John Sisco, in *Humane News,* August 1980, p. 17.
10. Rita Mulholland, *ibid.*
11. *Patricia P. Widmer's Cat Book* (New York: Charles Scribner's Sons), 1981.
12. George Browne, Jr., D.V.M., and James D. Mortimer, D.V.M., *Veterinary Medicine/Small Animal Clinician,* November 1976, 1561-1562.

Appendix

WHERE TO FIND PRODUCTS MENTIONED*

Green:
   Neo-Life Co.
   Hayward, Ca

Mega C Plus:
   Orthomolecular Specialties
   P.O. Box 32232
   San Jose, CA 95152

Lick Your Chops Yeast Tonic:
   Lick Your Chops
   RR #4
   Box 89B
   Elmwood Rd.
   South Salem, NY 10590

Petzymes:
   Lick Your Chops
   RR #4
   Box 89B
   Elmwood Rd.
   South Salem, NY 10590

Zymex-II:
   Standard Process Laboratories
   P.O. Box 652
   Milwaukee, WI 53201

Prepared foods:
   The following prepared foods have been recommended by some nutritional veterinarians as being acceptable:

Cornucopia
Veterinary Nutritional Associates Ltd.
229 Wall Street
Huntington, NY 11743

Solid Gold
9490 Loren Drive
La Mesa, CA 92041

Lick Your Chops
RR #4
Box 89B
Elmwood Rd.
South Salem, NY 10590

*Veterinarians: This is a list only of products the public may use. Information on obtaining a number of other products is given at the ends of chapters in the "Of Interest Mainly to Veterinarians" sections.

LIST OF NUTRITIONALLY ORIENTED VETERINARIANS

The following is a list of orthomolecular veterinarians who have agreed to be available for consultation. Each doctor will follow his or her usual policy regarding consultation fees. Stamped, self-addressed envelopes are suggested for mail queries.

These doctors are primarily nutritionally oriented unless otherwise noted. Doctors who also use acupuncture are so indicated. Inclusion in this list does not necessarily represent a personal recommendation by the author.

Nationwide

The American Veterinary Holistic Medical Association (AVHMA) has offered to refer readers to its members. As of this writing the AVHMA has 110 members and is growing continually. While the AVHMA has agreed to lead you to its members nearest you, for personal visits, these members have not individually agreed to be available for *consultation,* as have the veterinarians in the following list. For AVHMA members, write Carvel G. Tiekert, D.V.M., whose address is given in the following list under Maryland.

The International Veterinary Acupuncture Society (IVAS) can help you find veterinarians who use acupuncture. These veterinarians, however, have not individually agreed to be available for *consultation,* as have the veterinarians in the following list. The IVAS is at 203 Pembroke Place, Box 958, Thomasville, Ga. 31792.

Alabama

S. Allen Price, D.V.M.
Vestridge Animal Clinic
1444 Montgomery Highway
Birmingham, AL 35216
Phone: (205) 822-0210

E.E. Saffen, D.V.M.
Animal Clinic
2940 Highway 45
Eight Mile, AL 36612
Phone: (205) 457-1247
Uses acupuncture.

California

Sheldon Altman, D.V.M.
2723 W. Olive Ave.
Burbank, CA 91505
Phone: (213) 845-7246
Uses acupuncture extensively. Otherwise, basically an orthodox veterinarian.

Ihor John Basko, D.V.M.
Animal Care Services
948 El Rio Drive
San Jose, CA 95125
Phone: (408) 723-7024
Uses acupuncture. Equine and small animals.

Wendell O. Belfield, D.V.M.
3091 Monterey Hwy.
San Jose, CA 95111
Phone: (408) 227-8844

Stephen Reeve Blake, Jr., D.V.M.
Carmel Mountain Animal Hospital
9888 Carmel Mountain Road,
Suite F
Rancho Penasquitos, CA 92129
Phone: (714) 578-0314
Uses acupuncture.

Elinor A. Brandt, V.M.D.
8709 Sunland Blvd.
Sun Valley, CA 91352
Phone: (213) 767-7116

Robert Brantley, D.V.M.
4433 Highway 101 South
Eureka, CA 95501
Phone: (707) 442-4885

Bruce Cauble, D.V.M.
Encinitas Veterinary Clinic
222 N. Highway 101
Encinitas, CA 92024
Phone: (714) 753-1162
Basically an orthodox veterinarian.
Uses acupuncture.

John E. Craige, V.M.D.
Acupuncture Health Clinic, Veterinary Division
13509 Ventura Blvd.
Sherman Oaks, CA 91423
Phone: (213) 788-1300
Uses acupuncture.

Gloria Dodd, D.V.M.
2355 San Ramon Valley Blvd.
San Ramon, CA 94583
Phone: (415) 837-7759
Uses acupuncture.

Edgar R. Folkers, D.V.M.
25571 Marquerite Pkwy.
Mission Viejo, CA 92692
Phone: (714) 586-1220

Michael Kreisberg, D.V.M.
5226 Atoll Avenue
Van Nuys, CA 91401
Phone: (213) 846-7743

Jack Long, V.M.D.
Forestville Veterinary Hospital
5033 Gravenstein Highway North
Sebastopol, CA 95472
Phone: (707) 823-7312
Uses acupuncture.

Thomas A. Newland, D.V.M.
% Los Angeles SPCA
5026 W. Jefferson
Los Angeles, CA 90016
Phone: (213) 732-0113

Alfred Jay Plechner, D.V.M.
1736 S. Sepulveda Blvd.
Los Angeles, CA 90025
Phone: (213) 473-0960

Dana Waer, D.V.M., S.T., C.H., D.D.
Family Clinic for Pets
5831 Kenneth Ave.
Fair Oaks, CA 95628
Phone: (916) 961-6510
Uses acupuncture.

Robin M. Woodley, D.V.M.
Castro Valley Veterinary Hospital
2517 Castro Valley Blvd.
Castro Valley, CA 94546
Phone: (415) 582-3656
Basically an orthodox veterinarian.

Florida

Jan Bellows, D.V.M.
9111 Taft St.
Pembroke Pines, FL 33024
Phone: (305) 432-1111

John S. Eden, D.V.M.
329 N. Cocoa Blvd.
Cocoa, FL 32922
Phone: (305) 632-0445
Basically an orthodox veterinarian.

Mark W. Woodring, D.V.M.
Santa Rosa Veterinary Clinic
Rt. 6, Box 5
Stewart Street
Milton, FL 32570
Phone: (904) 623-2564
Uses acupuncture. Also deals with
birds and exotic animals.

Georgia

H. Grady Young, D.V.M.
203 Pembroke Place
Thomasville, GA 31792
Phone: (912) 226-6435
Uses acupuncture. Small and large
animals.

Indiana

Terry Durkes, D.V.M.
Western Avenue Animal Hospital
909 North Western Ave.
Marion, IN 46952
Phone: (317) 664-0734
Uses acupuncture.

Richard Katz, D.V.M.
Glen Park Animal Hospital
3150 W. Ridge Road
Gary, IN 46408
Phone: (219) 980-4944

Iowa

Terry K. Moore, D.V.M.
Animal Medical Center
4419 Mt. Vernon Rd. S.E.
Cedar Rapids, IA 52403
Phone: (319) 366-7567
Basically an orthodox veterinarian.

Maryland

Frank L. Earl, D.V.M.
2613 Hughes Rd.
Adelphio, MD 20783
Phone: (301) 434-1811/8480

Carvel G. Tiekert, D.V.M.
2214 Old Emmorton Rd.
Bel Air, MD 21014
Phone: (301) 838-7777
Uses acupuncture and chiropractic.

Massachusetts

J. Keith Benedict, D.V.M.
75 Davis Straits
Falmouth, MA 02540
Phone: (617) 540-4323

Richard J. Kearns, D.V.M.
124 Old Derby St.
Hingham, MA 02043
Phone: (617) 749-2800

Minnesota

John H. Wright, D.V.M.
6608 Flying Cloud Drive
P.O. Box 127
Eden Prairie, MN 55344
Phone: (612) 920-1393

Missouri

H. H. Robertson, D.V.M.
P.O. Box 628
1100 Main
Higginsville, MO 64037
Phone: (816) 584-3522

Montana

M. P. Doran, D.V.M.
P.O. Box 1665
3700 Second Ave. N.
Great Falls, MT 59403
Phone: (406) 453-1629

New Jersey

James G. Greene, D.V.M., M.S.
35 Heights Rd.
Clifton, NJ 07012
Phone: (201) 473-6196

New York

Kathy Berman (animal nutritionist)
Eubiotics, Ltd.
90 New York Ave.
West Hempstead, NY 11552
Phone: (516) 485-9252

R. Geoffrey Broderick, D.V.M.
Veterinary Nutritional Associates
229 Wall Street
Huntington, NY 11743
Phone: Health Line (USA): (516) 427-7479
Health Line (NYC): (212) 895-5175

Ronald J. Chaikin, D.V.M.
9518 Avenue L
Brooklyn, NY 11236
Phone: (212) 444-5151

Robert Goldstein, V.M.D.,
and Marty Goldstein, D.V.M.
RR #4, Box 89B
Elmwood Rd.
South Salem, NY 10590
Phone: (914) 533-6766
(914) 533-2500
Dr. Marty Goldstein uses acupuncture.

Ivan Szilvassy, D.V.M., P.C.
East Manhattan Veterinary Clinic
131 East 61st St.
New York, NY 10021
Phone: (212) 751-9416

Pat Widmer (animal nutritionist)
Pet Clinicare, Inc.
112 Chambers St.
New York, NY 10007
Phone: (212) 732-5560

Ohio

W. Davis, D.V.M.
Great Northern Veterinary Clinic
Great Northern Shopping Center
North Olmstead, OH 44070
Phone: (216) 777-4900

W. Wayne Kaufman, B. Sc., D.V.M.
Fairview Veterinary Hospital
3004 Bellefontaine Rd.
Lima, OH 45804
Phones: (419) 227-3408; (419) 225-9876
Treats horses as well as dogs and cats.

Oregon

John B. Limehouse, D.V.M.
650 S.W. Third St.
Corvallis, OR 97330
Phone: (503) 753-2223
Uses acupuncture.

Pennsylvania

Stephen Dubin, V.D.M.
269 Orchard Rd.
Springfield, PA 19064
Phone: (215) 544-7163 (7–7:30 A.M.)

Donald Ford, D.V.M.
Spruce Hill Veterinary Clinic
267 South 44th St.
Philadelphia, PA 19104
Phone: (215) EV 6-9100
Uses acupuncture.

Texas

Norman C. Ralston, D.V.M.
Grove Animal Clinic
426 S. Buckner Blvd.
Dallas, TX 75217
Phone: (214) 391-7186
Uses acupuncture.

William Hartnell, D.V.M.
1549 South Ohio Ave.
Mercedes, TX 78570
Phone: (512) 565-1410
Research, with limited large animal
management consultation.

Leon Slatko, D.V.M.
7327 Long Drive
Houston, TX 77087
Phone: (713) 643-0633
Uses chiropractic with canine cases;
is incorporating nutritional medicine
into his practice.

Virginia

Nino Aloro, D.V.M.
2212 Laskin Rd.
Virginia Beach, VA 23454
Phone: (804) 340-5040

Joseph Stuart, D.V.M.
4000 Burke Station Rd.
Fairfax, VA 22032
Phone: (703) 273-5110

Washington

Michael W. Lemmon, D.V.M.
Highlands Veterinary Hospital
Box 2085
Renton, WA 98056
Phone: (206) 226-8418
Uses acupuncture.

William H. Sudduth, D.V.M.
9505 35th, N.E.
Seattle, WA 98115
Phone: (206) 523-1900

George M. Thue, D.V.M.
7521 Greenwood Ave. N.
Seattle, WA 98103
Phone: (206) 784-9200

Wisconsin

Charles P. Maier, D.V.M.
1949 Highway 24
East Troy, WI 53120
Phone: (414) 642-5967
An orthodox veterinarian newly incorporating nutritional medicine
into his practice. Treats large and
small animals. Uses acupuncture.

Out of the United States:

Canada

James Stowe, D.V.M.
R.R. #5
Simcoe, Ontario
N3Y 4K4
Canada
Phone: (519) 426-2310

New Zealand

John J. Kelly, B.V.Sc.
Millbrook Veterinary Clinic
31 Papanui Road
Christchurch, New Zealand 8001
Phone: (011-64-3) 558-444

Index

Aangamik-15, 155*n*
Abdominal pain, 129
Abortions, 27, 37
Academy of Orthomolecular Psychiatry, 8*n*
Acidifier, 133
Acidity, cancer and, 163
Acupressure, 75, 76
Acupuncture, 67-68, 90, 101
  for crippling disorders, 74-78
  for distemper, 111-12
Addiction, 15, 31
Addison's disease, 97
Additives, 3-7, 31, 167
Advanced Nutritional Formula, 67
Age, cancer and, 173-74
Aging
  oxidation process and, 52
  premature, 150
Alabama, nutritionally oriented veterinarians in, 179
Alfalfa, 149*n*
Alkalinity, cancer and, 163
Allergic dermatitis, 61, 100-01
Allergy, 95, 96
  flea-bite, 100-01
  to foods, 35, 38-39
Aloro, Nino, D.V.M., 11, 29, 48, 50*n* 54, 57, 123, 135*n*
  address, 183
  on diet, 22, 31, 35-36, 50
Altman, Sheldon, D.V.M., 76, 77-78
  address, 179
Amatraze, 102
American Biologics, 88, 90*n*
American College of Veterinary Ophthalmology, 89*n*
American Veterinary Holistic Medical Association (AVHMA), 179
Amino acids, 114

  taurine, 9, 89
Aminophylline, 154
Amygdalin. *See* Laetrile
Anavit-F3, 175*n*
Anemia, 27, 56, 65
Animal Medical Center, New York City, 75, 115
Antibiotics, 87, 103, 105, 108
  for pancreatitis, 130
  for parvovirus, 116
  respiratory diseases and, 118
Antigen, flea, 101, 104*n*
Antistress diet, 86
Appetite, 138
  stimulants, 15
Apple cider vinegar, 63, 101
Apricot pits, 19, 35
  See also Laetrile
Arthritis, 6, 7, 27, 29, 37, 61-65, 78
  rheumatoid, 25, 65
  therapy, 63-65
Artificial coloring, 3
Artificial flavorings, 4
Artificial preservatives, 41
Ascorbic acid. *See* Vitamin C

Ash, 132
Aspirin, 63, 75
Ataxia, 77
Atony, uterine, 48
Atrophy, progressive retinal, 9, 89-90
Avocado, 43

Bacteria, 105
Bald spots, 100
Basko, Ihor John, D.V.M., 63*n*
  on acupuncture, 76, 78*n*
  address, 179
Baylor University, 74
Bearberry, 152
Beef heart extract, 151
Belfield, Wendell O., D.V.M., 1, 3, 17*n*, 59, 67, 137
  on feline leukemia, 167, 168, 169
  on older dogs, 53
  on parvovirus, 115
  on posterior paralysis, 71-74
  on pregnancy, 49
  on ruptured discs, 74

188